THE IDEA
OF THE CHURCH

B. C. BUTLER

Abbot of Downside

HELICON PRESS

BALTIMORE

HELICON PRESS INC.
1120 N. Calvert Street
Baltimore 2, Maryland

Printed in Great Britain at the University Press, Aberdeen. Nihil obstat: A. M. Young, O.S.B. Imprimatur: H. K. Byrne, O.S.B., Ab.Pres., May 31st, 1961. Nihil obstat: Joannes M. T. Barton, S.T.D., L.S.S., Censor deputatus. Imprimatur: E. Morrogh Bernard, Vic. Gen., Westmonasterii, die 3a Mai, 1962. The Nihil obstat and imprimatur are a declaration that a book or pamphlet is considered to be free from doctrinal or moral error. It is not implied that those who have grauted the Nihil obstat and Imprimatur agree with the contents, opinions or statements expressed.

The first step is to learn to speak to one another without embarrassment.

ARCHBISHOP LORD FISHER

The crucial problem of all theology is the link between the past fact of revelation and its actualisation here and now.

P. EVDOKIMOV

Some hypothesis, this or that, all controversial-ists, all historians must adopt, if they would treat of Christianity at all. . . . The question is, which of these theories is the simplest, the most natural, the most persuasive.

NEWMAN

CONTENTS

Chapter 4. THE EARLY COUNCILS (1)

Chapter 5. THE EARLY COUNCILS (2)

Chapter 6. CYPRIAN AND THE CHURCH

Chapter 13. ESCHATOLOGY AND INCARNATION

Chapter 14. CONCLUSION

ACKNOWLEDGEMENT

We are indebted to Macmillan & Co. Ltd. for an extract from *The First Epistle of St Peter* by E. G. Selwyn, and to S.P.C.K. and The Seabury Press for material from *The Lambeth Conference 1958*.

PREFACE

THE aspirations and movements towards a visible union of Christian believers have become a powerful and important factor in the religious situation of the present day. Our divisions are an inheritance from history. Often enough, many of the causes that promoted their origin have lost their actuality for us. Often enough, when these causes still seem to have significance, we are driven to wonder whether schism was the only way of doing justice to them. Meanwhile, the divided Christian bodies have, in some cases, grown away from one another in various ways which were not contemplated at the date of the original separation. And often, again, these consequential differences hardly seem to us of such importance as to justify our continuing divisions.

The progress of the Ecumenical Movement is leading the divided bodies to an examination of their consciences; and this is helping them to discriminate between those elements in their respective traditions which, however venerable and dear, are not strictly essential, and those which appear to them to belong to the very substance of their Christian faith.

Sooner or later, to the extent that the Movement looks forward to a future Church which shall be visibly one, interest is bound to become focused on the very idea of the Church. What do we mean by the word Church, when we use it in that sense in which it is incapable of having a plural? What do we mean when we profess that we believe 'one holy catholic and apostolic Church' or 'the holy catholic Church'? Most of us would agree with the statement of a Committee of the Lambeth Conference of 1958, that *this* Church 'takes its origin in the will of our Lord Jesus Christ'. What is the Church in the mind and will of our Redeemer? What sort of a thing is it?

The following pages attempt to offer an answer to this question. It should be noted that their subject is the Church as 'militant here on earth'. Whenever they employ the word 'Church' they mean it in that sense, unless the contrary is clearly indicated by the context. At the present day, we speak not only of the Church militant, but of the Church 'triumphant' and the Church 'suffering' or 'in waiting'. These, however, are extensions of the original meaning of the word. The name 'Church' (*ecclesia*) was given to the original historical community of believers gathered before God around the Twelve. It marked this community off from the unconverted Gentiles, and also from those Jews who had not accepted Jesus as the Christ. The word still retains this primary reference to the sphere of Christian probation. Cyprian never uses it with any other meaning, though he once looked forward to the day when the Church, now militant on earth, would have its warfare crowned with final victory and would reign in triumph with Christ after his Second Coming. It was a natural, if subsequent, development to speak of the faithful departed as still members of the Church, and so to proceed to the ideas of a Church *already* triumphant in heaven, and a Church whose members were in the 'intermediate' state, past the gate of death but still awaiting their entry into glory. But there is no justification for adding together the members of these three 'Churches', treating them on the same level, and excogitating an ecclesiology which will make sense of this procedure. Or, if there is any justification for so doing, at least it remains legitimate and convenient, with due warning, to use the word 'Church', as in these pages, to refer to the Church militant exclusively, and to ask whether, when so restricted in its application, it relates to any coherent object and can express a consistent idea.

Some may question whether the time is ripe for such an investigation, and whether its pursuit may not rather retard than subserve the movement towards Christian unity. However, the intellectual scandal of our actual divisions, over against the admitted oneness of the mystical Body of Christ, was already evident at the Evanston Conference. An intellectual problem which is persistently evaded, despite the fact that it lies at the heart of a great human endeavour, is a dangerous and potentially explosive thing. I hope that what I have written in the following chapters is charitable in its intention and courteous in expression; if it can be received in the same spirit in which it has been written, it may, with God's blessing, do more good than harm.

I am most grateful to those who have helped me with their advice and criticisms in my self-imposed task. One of them regretted that I had chosen to fashion my argument round the notion of the Church as a 'society', instead of developing the significance of the Scriptural designation of her as 'the body of Christ'. In reply, I would submit two considerations. (1) The exegesis of the biblical passages in which the 'body of Christ' description occurs is a very delicate matter. A full-length study of the underlying doctrine could not evade the problems raised by these passages. But a thorough examination of them would have taken me beyond the limits required for my present purpose, and in any case might have led to only disputable conclusions. (2) I wished to present my meaning in terms which could not be misunderstood; and I suspect that those who talk about the Church as the Body of Christ may often, in fact, be speaking at cross-purposes. The 'Body of Christ' is sometimes taken as designating a unity made up, as described above, simultaneously of the saints already in heaven, the faithful departed in the 'intermediate state', and baptised persons on earth. A term that carries, for some theologians, this implication would have been liable to conceal, rather than to clarify, my meaning.

But I realise that the word 'society' also has its disadvantages. It suggests to many a preoccupation with matters of government, jurisdiction, and law which they find extremely distasteful. I have not shrunk from stating clearly that, if the Church is such as I believe it to be, it must have *some* government, *some* system of jurisdiction, *some* rules and regulations. But having admitted so much, and having used the word 'society' to show beyond the possibility of mistake what sort of a thing I conceive the Church to be, I have been ready, especially in the later pages of this book, to fall back on the more thoroughly Christian term 'communion', which has the great merit of presenting the Church in her true colours as a fraternity of charity, and of suggesting that the real heart of her unity is in the sacrament of Holy Communion.[1] And, while 'communion', in its full meaning, means 'sharing *together*', the word may also remind us how much, even while our divisions continue, we 'share' of the grace-gifts flowing from the Act by which we were redeemed.

[1] For this emphasis on 'communion' I express my debt to an as yet unpublished book by Fr Adrian Hastings, whose criticisms of previous studies of mine have helped me greatly.

This essay is conceived as a contribution to a dialogue between Christian believers. Should it fall into the hands of an unbeliever, he may wonder what all the fuss is about. May I suggest to such perplexed persons that the answer to their question may be found in the twentieth chapter (*Special Transcendent Knowledge*) of Bernard Lonergan's *Insight*?

Downside, 1961

Chapter 1

THEOLOGICAL SIGNIFICANCE OF
THE CHURCH

THE purpose of this book is a narrowly restricted one. It is
to pose clearly, and to suggest an answer to, a particular
question about the Church: What sort of a real thing is the
Church in its historical existence in this world?

An analogous question can be asked, and has been asked,
about Christ. Granted that he is the world's Redeemer, come
from the divine sphere to save us, what sort of a real thing was
he in his historical existence in this world? The answer to that
question is not in doubt today. But erroneous answers have been
given in the past. The Docetists held that he had but a phantom
body on earth. The Apollinarians maintained that, while his
body was real, he had no human soul; why should he have, since
his divine nature could supply the rational principle for his life
on earth? The Monothelites suggested that, though he had a
human soul, yet he possessed only one will, the divine will which
was his as the second person of the Holy Trinity. The general
Christian tradition has rejected these Christological errors, and
none of us finds any difficulty in believing—it never really
occurs to us to doubt—that the incarnate Lord was (as he remains) fully human; that he had a complete human nature
consubstantial with our own. There is a mystery of Christ. But
the mystery does not concern his human nature as such, but
only his divine nature and person and the relation between his
human and divine natures.

For fifteen hundred years there was hardly more doubt about
the nature of the Church in her historical existence than there
is today about the human nature of Christ. The Church is indeed a mystery of faith, a mystery closely related to the mystery
of Christ. But in those days it was scarcely questioned that she
was also a historical reality. There might be doubt about where
to find her in the world, but there was little doubt as to what

sort of thing you would find in finding her. Perhaps this is why she rarely became an object of particular theological debate; the earliest full-length treatise 'on the Church' comes from the later Middle Ages.

At the present day, Christians are deeply divided in thought about the answer to be given to our question. There can be little dispute that the diversity of their views on the subject is a product of the Reformation, although I shall argue that the Reformation was not itself caused by such diversity. I am convinced that, sooner or later, the Ecumenical Movement will have to examine the question of the nature of the Church with full seriousness, at least if it takes the unity of all believers in a single communion as its ultimate goal.

There is, however, a great deal that can be said about the Church while this particular problem remains without an agreed solution; just as there was much that could be said about Christ before the full truth about his human nature was defined. There is a wide area of theological thinking about the Church where Roman Catholics, Eastern Orthodox, and many Protestants and Anglicans, can meet in common. It may be valuable to consider some aspects of the theological significance of the Church before embarking upon the question which will occupy the remainder of this book.

Perhaps there are few thoughtful Christians who would deny that the Church is an important element in the Christian totality. Most Christian communions accept either the Nicene or the Apostles' Creed, in which we affirm our belief in 'one, holy, catholic, apostolic Church' or 'the holy catholic Church'. The Church seems to have found its place in Christian creeds since the second century A.D. And indeed the word 'church' (*ecclesia*) is frequent in the New Testament, and the idea behind the word is frequently present even when the word itself is not used. Modern scholarship tends to emphasise the fact that the New Testament books are themselves a creation of the Church; and it is being increasingly realised that our saving knowledge of Christ, whether through the pages of the New Testament or otherwise, is mediated to us by the Church. It is abundantly clear that, for the Christians of New Testament times, the Church was the legitimate heir to the status of the Old Testament People of God.

The importance of the truth about the Church appears when we see how closely this truth is related to the truth about Christ himself. In the 'new creation' sprung from the death and resurrection of Jesus, the Church seems to hold the central place. Those later writers were not so far from the mind of the New Testament, who said that, just as Eve was formed from the side of Adam, so the Church was born from the pierced side of the second Adam.

A modern Anglican writer has said: 'We cannot understand the Church if we have misunderstood the Christ. Conversely, we may make bold to say that an understanding of Christ necessarily entails an understanding of the Church. For the Church is the Body of Christ.'[1] An earlier, and a very great, Anglican thinker tells how 'there rose up before me the idea of a Church Universal, not built upon human inventions or human faith, but upon the very nature of God himself, and upon the union which he has formed with his creatures'.[2] This union is, of course, above all the union of a human and the divine nature in the person of Christ. The present Archbishop of Canterbury, himself a follower of Maurice, finds the truth about the Church to be 'included within the Christian's knowledge of Christ crucified'.[3]

A contemporary Roman Catholic states—and many outside his own communion would agree with him—that 'if Christ is the sacrament of God, the Church is for us the sacrament of Christ; she represents him, in the full and ancient meaning of the term, she really makes him present'.[4]

The New Testament has more than one astounding metaphor to express the closeness of the relation of the Church to Christ. She is his 'body'; or she is that body of which he is the Head. A man's body lives with that man's life, so that St Paul is fond of saying that the member of the Church is 'in Christ'. And since the life of the body inheres in all the body's parts, he can also say that Christ is 'in us'. The incarnate Christ was not only the Son of God. He was also the Messiah in whom dwelt the Holy Ghost in the fullness of his seven-fold gifts. The Holy Ghost triumphed in him in his resurrection, and the Spirit of

[1] D. L. MacKinnon, *The Church of God*, p. 11.
[2] F. D. Maurice, *The Kingdom of Christ*, vol. 2, p. 363, S.C.M. Press, 1958.
[3] A. M. Ramsey, *The Gospel and the Catholic Church*, 2nd edn., p. vi.
[4] H. de Lubac, *Catholicism*, p. 29.

the Father can equally be called the Spirit of Christ. So, as the Church is the body of Christ, she is indwelt by the Spirit of Christ; her supernatural life flows from him as from its creative source. Her life is the fullness of life of the risen Christ, sprung from the fullness of the Spirit which glorified his humanity in his resurrection and now vivifies the Church.

From another point of view, taking up an Old Testament description of the People of God as the 'spouse' of the Lord, the New Testament speaks of the Church as the 'bride' of Christ, and applies to her in this relation to him the mysterious fullness of the saying 'the twain shall be one flesh'. It was for her sake that he 'gave himself up' to death, to make her immaculate and worthy of her bridal dignity.

It was natural to apply to the Church the Old Testament designations of the People of God, for the Christians of the apostolic age identified her with that 'holy community'. And as the holy community, for the Jews, was represented by Jerusalem and the Temple, so the Church is the heavenly Jerusalem, the spiritual Temple of the new dispensation, built on Christ as its foundation-stone, or culminating in Christ as its chief corner stone.

None of these metaphors and descriptions exhausts the content of the New Testament idea of the Church, and sometimes we find a fusion of metaphors. The body of Christ, with which the Church is identified, is that Temple which he himself would 'raise up in three days'. The Temple of the Lord is 'growing'— like a body; and on the other hand the body of Christ is being 'built up'—like a Temple. Or again: 'Come with me', he said, 'and I will show you that bride, whose bridegroom is the Lamb. And he carried me off in a trance to a great mountain, high up, and there he showed me the holy city, Jerusalem, as it came down, sent by God, from heaven, clothed in God's glory,'[5] Such combinations of metaphors bring home to us the fact that the Church is one of those mysteries within the total Christian mystery that are for ever greater and richer than the ideas and images by which we seek to acclimatise them in our human thought and experience.

[5] Apoc. xxi. 9-11. The Jerusalem which 'comes down from heaven' at the post-historic finale of 'the consummation of the age' is identical with the Church in her earthly warfare, just as the Christ of the final Parousia or Advent is identical with the Christ of Calvary.

If we turn from the New Testament to the patristic literature, we find it, of course, full of the Church. Of Irenaeus a Methodist scholar writes:

> The Church to Irenaeus was the New Israel, and the true Israel, the prophetic and priestly People of God. . . . It would be a mistake . . . to suppose that the doctrine of the Church in Irenaeus is superficial only. . . . It is a profound part of his religious faith, and a valuable element in his constructive work.

And again:

> Irenaeus was a Catholic Christian indeed. He was no individualist. He knew nothing of a faith which is purely interior and secret, or of a solitary walk of the soul with God. The institutionalism which is the inescapable concomitant of the life of an actual human community was accepted by him as a matter of course, being the natural background for personal piety. Indeed, he glorified in this institutionalism. Yet he did not love it for its own sake, but because the life of the Church set forth the Gospel by which the believer lives.[6]

A quotation will show how, for Irenaeus, the Holy Spirit of truth is linked with the Church:

> Where the Church is, there is the Spirit of God; and where the Spirit of God is, there is the Church and all grace. Now the Spirit is truth. Wherefore they who have no share in that Spirit are neither nourished from the breasts of their Mother unto life, nor do they receive of that clear stream that flows from the body of Christ. . . . For they are not founded on the one Rock, but on the sand and all its pebbles.[7]

Clement of Alexandria, speaking of 'the true, the really ancient Church, into which those that are righteous according to the divine purpose are enrolled', says:

> God being one and the Lord being one, that also which is supremely honoured is the object of praise, because it stands alone, being a copy of the one First Principle: at any rate the one Church . . . is bound up with the principle of Unity. We say then that the ancient and Catholic Church stands alone in essence and idea and principle and pre-eminence, gathering together, by the will of the one God through the one Lord, into the unity of the one faith, built upon the fitting covenants (or rather the one covenant given at different times) all those who

[6] John Lawson, *The Biblical Theology of St Irenaeus*, pp. 252, 255.
[7] Irenaeus, *Adversus Haereses*, iii. 38, 1-2.

are already enlisted in it, whom God fore-ordained, having known before the foundation of the world that they would be righteous.[8]

De Lubac, in his sympathetic study of Origen, writes as follows of Origen's views on the relation of the Incarnation to the Church:

> For a body Christ has not only that individual flesh which John bears witness that he saw and touched. The whole Church also is his body. His taking of the individual flesh has of course a unique importance, as being the point of insertion of God into our humanity. But it was not an end in itself. Its purpose is to make possible his taking to himself the Church. Hence this body which is the Church . . . must, in Origen's way of speaking, be 'truer' than the body of the individual flesh, because it constitutes a more perfect, a 'fuller', realisation of the divine plan. It is the end; the body of the flesh was the means. It is the reality, of which the flesh, even in its reality, is the 'type', the symbol. The historic life of the Saviour symbolises a vaster life, that of his 'true and perfect body'. 'The body of Jesus,' says Origen, 'seems to me to be a figure of the Church'.[9]

It would perhaps be difficult, while remaining within the limits of Biblical orthodoxy, to give the Church a higher status than that of the antitype of which the 'body born of Mary' was the type. We may compare the New Testament teaching that Christ himself and the Gospel are the antitype of which all that was valid in the Old Dispensation was typical.

To prolong this examination of the ancient Fathers would be superfluous for the purposes of this book. And for the Middle Ages we may restrict ourselves to the witness of Thomas Aquinas, conveniently summarised by Congar,[10] whom I shall closely follow. Congar emphasises that much the same ecclesiology could be derived from an examination of any of the great scholastics of Thomas's time. We can therefore accept the following summary as representing the ideas on the Church

---

[8] Clement, *Stromateis VII*, chapter xvii; the translation is from the edition of Hort and Mayor. I have omitted one clause, identifying (by implication) the one Church with the communion to which Clement himself belongs. The passage echoes the Epistle to the Ephesians: 'One Lord, one faith, . . . one God and Father of all.' Note, in the insistence on 'one covenant', the implication of a unity of purpose expressed in the two 'dispensations'.

[9] *Histoire et Esprit*, p. 360. The text from Origen is from the Commentary on St John, 10, 35; the word translated 'figure' is *tupos*, 'type'.

[10] *The Idea of the Church in St Thomas Aquinas*, in *The Mystery of the Church*, pp. 97-117.

held in the Christian West before the first rumblings of the Reformation storm were heard.

The Church, for Thomas, is a living body (the body of Christ), composed of many members. Her soul is the Holy Ghost. From the Holy Ghost there spring, in these members, the virtues of faith, hope, and charity. These virtues all tend to the same object, namely God self-revealed, and Congar points out that in combination they too, like the Holy Ghost whose effect they are, may be considered as the soul or vivifying principle of the Church. The soul of a body is its unifying principle, and so the unity of the Church, as seen in her members, is a social unity of personalities; we are not depersonalised by absorption into a super-personal entity. The substance of the Church is made of the new life which men receive by the three virtues of faith, hope and love, a life impelled Godwards, having God for its end and the objects of divine life as its determining principles.

But if the Church is unified in and by the Holy Ghost, if, that is to say, it is Spirit-centred, it is also true that, from another point of view, it is unified in Christ and is Christo-centric. Christ incarnate is the head of all creation. In his human soul there was the fullness of grace. All grace for men flows from Christ the Head, and is a participation of his grace. He is thus the Head of the Church. 'Christ plus the Church', says Congar, 'do not make more than Christ alone, in the same way as God plus the world . . . do not make more than God alone.'[11] The Church receives from Christ, but adds nothing to him. The degrees of our assimilation to God are degrees of our assimilation to Christ.[12]

[11] This is a most important consideration when applied to the doctrine of the Eucharistic sacrifice. Calvary plus the Eucharist do not make more than Calvary alone. Yet Calvary does not make the Eucharistic sacrifice superfluous, any more than Christ makes the Church superfluous.

[12] The two aspects of the Church, centred in the Holy Ghost and centred also in Christ, may be synthesised if we bear in mind that the Holy Ghost was bestowed in limitless fullness on the humanity of the Messiah. The fullness of grace with which he was endowed flowed from this indwelling of the Holy Ghost in the human soul of Christ. All our participation in the Holy Ghost and in grace flows from the fullness that was in Christ. Such participation was rendered possible through the sacrificial death and resurrection of Christ, before which 'the Holy Ghost was not yet given, because Jesus was not yet glorified'. As we have seen, the New Testament calls the Holy Ghost not only the Spirit of God the Father, but the Spirit of Christ; and though this may have implications for Trinitarian theology and doctrine, the primary reference in the New Testament is not to the procession of the Holy Ghost but to his 'mission', flowing from the 'mission' of the Son of God in his incarnation.

The Christocentric aspect of the Church is perhaps nowhere more impressively stated by Aquinas than when, in full harmony with the tradition which he had received, he described 'the unity of the mystical body' as the *res* of the Eucharistic sacrament. According to this terminology we can distinguish in the Eucharist 'the sacrament pure and simple' (*sacramentum tantum*), 'the sacrament-and-the-reality' (*res et sacramentum*) and 'the reality pure and simple' (*res tantum*). The first is the outward sign of the sacrament, the second is that outward sign as making Christ himself present in the outward sign. The third is the inward reality of grace produced by the Eucharist in the faithful. It is this inward reality of grace which is identified by Aquinas with 'the unity of the mystical body', in which, for him, it is itself manifested in an outward, visible, unity of the members. It has to be remembered that, for Aquinas, Holy Communion may only be received lawfully within the unity of the Christian fellowship. And since, for him, the unity and the reality of a thing are inseparable, the unity of the mystical body is only conceptually different from the Church herself. Thus the Church is not only created by Christ; she is maintained in being by him through the communion of her members with him in the sacramental rite which he himself instituted, a real communion in his body and blood, a communion whereby he is 'with us till the consummation of the age'. As Origen had said that the 'flesh' of Christ incarnate was a type of his body the Church, so Aquinas says in effect that the sacramental body of Christ is a type of the Church in her unity, a type that subserves and maintains its antitype.

It will be observed that what Aquinas is here saying in his own language is what St Paul appears to say in I Corinthians 10, 17: 'Because the (Eucharistic) Bread is one, we Christians, multitude though we are, are one body, since we all partake of the one Bread.' The unity of the Church as the body of Christ is the effect or the expression of the unity of the heavenly food on which her members are nourished and which, as the Fathers say, is not assimilated as natural food is assimilated, but rather assimilates the banqueters to itself. The unity of the Church is in the end a facet of the unity of Christ, the one Mediator.[13]

---

[13] St Paul may here seem to be at variance with the doctrine that baptism is the sacrament by which we are made members of the body of Christ. There is no

Our review of Biblical and traditional teaching about the Church has been brief and incomplete. But it may suffice to lead us on to the theme of this book. If the Church is the body and the bride of Christ; if her 'soul' is the Holy Ghost; if she is the 'pillar and ground of truth', may it not be a matter of no little moment to identify her so as to be sure that we adhere to her? And if the Eucharist is the sacramental cause of her conservation as a reality and a single organism, can we rest content with a situation in which there is a multitude of Christian 'communions'? Is it tolerable that holy communion, which is intended by God to unite all Christ's members, should in fact be an action in which, willy-nilly, we give outward expression to our separation from our brethren?

In the early Church the scandal of 'altar against altar' was regarded as a practical evidence of the heinousness of schism. Today there are those connected with the Ecumenical Movement, or attracted by it, who would like to short-circuit our problems by admitting 'inter-communion' between bodies still divided from each other in doctrine and jurisdiction. But the very mention of doctrine and jurisdiction reminds us that the sacramental life of the Church is set in a rich complex of intellectual, institutional and mystical elements and cannot be adequately treated apart from them. The Christian fact, already in the pages of the New Testament, already in the Synoptic Gospels, has the many-sidedness of a living organism. There is no escape from the question of the nature of the Church to which, according to tradition, the gospel and the means of grace have been entrusted. What sort of a thing is the mystical body of Christ in her historical mode of existence?

disharmony if we concede, as Aquinas taught, that all the other sacraments are directed towards the Eucharist as their end. Baptism, by making us members of Christ, habilitates us for Holy Communion, which is its *raison-d'-être*. Is there a deep significance in the fact that the word *communion*, in Christian tradition, refers both to the Eucharist and to the fellowship of Christians in a single society? If so, this linguistic fact brings us close to the real scandal of our visible divisions. How can participation in one sacramental body produce a multiplicity of communions? And if it does not produce them, can it justify them? Should we emend the Pauline text and say: Though we participate in one bread, we are nevertheless a multiplicity of bodies? Is Christ divided?

Chapter 2

IDEAS OF THE CHURCH: THE POST-REFORMATION ERA

THE question 'What is the Church?' is not the same question as the question 'Which is the Church?' To ask the latter question is to imply that we already know what we mean by the term 'Church'; that we know what sort of a thing we are looking for, in seeking to identify the Church. It is true that if we already knew the answer to the second question, if we had already *identified* the Church, we could examine her to discover what sort of a thing she essentially is. But it is only too obvious that modern Christians do not agree about the identification of the Church. Some identify her with their own particular communion, to the exclusion of all others. Some identify her as including the three communions of Canterbury, Rome and Constantinople. Others take a still wider view, and hold that all regularly constituted bodies of baptised Christians are parts of the Church.[1] Others, again, viewing the matter in a different light, insist not so much on the great organised bodies but rather on the local congregations, and maintain that the Church is found wherever a group of true believers is congregated for worship and Christian life. And there are some who think that the Church cannot be identified by men, since its membership depends wholly on certain interior qualifications recognisable only by God.

Hidden within this diversity of answers to the question 'Which' or 'Where' is the Church there lies a diversity of views upon the *nature* of the Church. Part of the reason, in other words, why men answer the question 'which' so diversely is that they consciously or unconsciously hold different convictions about the right answer to the question '*What* is the Church?'

[1] The phrase 'regularly constituted bodies' manifestly raises further questions here.

Our main concern in these pages is with this question. What sort of a thing, in its essence, was the Church that Christ established, the thing described in the Nicene Creed as 'the one, holy, catholic, apostolic Church?' It is the same kind of question, we have already suggested, as could be asked about Christ in the incarnation. The answer to the question 'Who was the Christ?' is that given by the primitive Church at Jerusalem: The Christ was Jesus of Nazareth. But the answer to the question 'What was Christ in his incarnation?' was the subject of the great Christological controversies of the early centuries, and was answered in substance by the Council of Chalcedon: in his incarnation the Christ was perfectly man; he had a human nature. So, in turn, we are asking: what is the nature of the Church in its historical existence on earth?

No-one can pretend that there is, at the present day, a clear and unanimous response, on the part of Christian thinkers or leaders, or in the minds of Christian people, to this question.

The modern Western confusion of thought on this subject is in the main a product of the vast religious upheaval in the Christian West to which history has given the name of the Reformation. And indeed it is among the heirs of the Reformation, and between them and the Roman Catholic Church, that there is this divergence of opinion on the nature of the Church.[2]

As for the Roman Catholic Church, it is well known that she teaches that the Church established by Christ is, both de facto and by the necessity of its nature, a single communion. The

---

[2] Eastern Orthodox writers of the modern age are not agreed as to the limits of the Church. The more common view, however, and probably the more official view, is that the Church is confined to those Christian bodies which acknowledge the Patriarch of Constantinople as the leading bishop, that is, to what we have called the Eastern Orthodox Communion (the title is somewhat misleading, as immediate communion has often been broken between some of these various bodies. However, indirect communion, as of A with B and of B with C—while A and C are not in direct communion with each other—may be held to satisfy the minimum demands of communion). And there are writers who include 'unity of communion' in their definitions of the Church. The question may be raised whether oneness of communion is, in official Eastern Orthodox doctrine, held to be of the essence of the Church. On this, it may be said that at least the Eastern Orthodox Communion has never repudiated the ancient doctrine of the Church; that, as we shall see later, the ancient view of the Church was that it was essentially a single communion; and that the frequent designation of the Church, by representative Eastern Orthodox writers, as a 'society' only receives a satisfactory meaning if taken as implying unity of communion. On all this, cf. M. Jugie, Theologia Dogmatica Christianorum Orientalium ab Ecclesia Catholica Dissidentium, vol. iv, pp. 274-88, 299-316, 532-39, 578-80. See also the Additional Note at the end of this chapter.

Reformation has in no way shaken her on this point of doctrine. Indeed, it is possible that, in reaction against the Reformation, her theologians have been tempted to give an even excessive rigidity to their presentation of it. At least it is true that post-Reformation treatises on the Church have tended to concentrate on the external aspect of the Church and to pay too little attention to her interior life. However, there are not lacking at the present time Roman Catholic theologians who are concerned, not indeed to question the doctrine, but to repudiate some of its supposed consequences or corollaries. There is, for instance, a strong emphasis on the difference between deliberately sinful heresy or schism and sincere and inculpable loyalty to error. And there is also an encouraging insistence on the illimitable possibilities of grace and its fruits outside the visible limits of the Church.

The new views about the Church, which have found explicit or implied support in Western Reformed circles, were, it may be suggested, less the cause than the consequence of the Reformation. The great upheaval supervened upon a deplorable decay in late mediaeval Catholicism, and the period of the Anti-Popes and the Conciliar Movement had gravely shaken its institutional foundations. But the positive cause of the upheaval is to be sought rather in the profound religious intuitions of a great and turbulent genius, Martin Luther himself. Luther's controlling vision was of nothing so pedestrian as the historical nature of the Church militant. It was a vision of the supremacy of grace and the uniqueness of the divine initiative throughout the sphere of grace and salvation. Basically, Bouyer has argued, it was an intuition of a great traditional truth never denied by the Roman Catholic Church.[3] But it was expressed in forms which the contemporary Roman Catholic authorities were not prepared to tolerate, and Luther, on his side, was not willing to tolerate authority's control. It is no part of my present purpose to apportion blame between the parties.

The result, however, was schism. And this result, since on traditional grounds it put Luther into an untenable position, had, I suggest, to be rationalised. If the Church was identical

---

[3] A Methodist theologian has told me how he had heard the Thomist doctrine of justification expounded in terms acceptable to a Protestant. I have myself heard a Lutheran exposition of the Lutheran doctrine with which, as a Roman Catholic, I could find little fault.

with the Roman Catholic communion, a schismatical religious leader had of course no *locus standi*. And if the view were retained, that the Church is essentially a single visible society —which was the traditional view—then it would in the end be very difficult for a Western Christian to evade the inference that she is to be identified with the Roman Catholic Communion. Luther's connection with that communion had come to an end. It would seem necessary either to banish the word Church from the vocabulary of Reformed Christianity, or to adumbrate a new ecclesiology.

To discard the word Church altogether would have been a violent breach with a long and powerful Christian tradition, going back far behind the mediaeval period and already represented in both the Nicene and the Apostles' Creed. Luther was radical enough to reject the doctrine of the sacrifice of the Mass, for all its traditional backing. But the word 'Church' was not only traditional in the broad sense; it had the most manifest support of the New Testament documents. It was therefore taken over into the vocabulary of the Reformers. It was accepted by them not only that there were local congregations of believers, but that there was a catholic, that is to say a universal, Church, founded by Christ.

The Reformers' problem was, therefore, to provide the word Church with a content of theological meaning, consistent with the minimal notion which it implied, the notion, namely, of sociality, yet other than the meaning upheld by their Roman Catholic opponents. Various possibilities were explored.

(1) Could it be maintained that the Church is a purely invisible reality, as invisible as the pure essence of justifying faith or sanctifying grace? This idea appealed to Luther in some moods. It may have been suggested to him by the writings of John Huss.[4] If it could be established, it would be the most radical answer to the claims of the Roman Catholic Church. Can it be held that the Church is, indeed, a 'society' or a 'communion', but of a sort completely hidden from the eyes of men? After all, the Apostles' Creed speaks of 'the communion of the saints'. Are not the 'saints' those justified by faith? But faith is, in itself, a purely interior quality or act. Where faith is, then, there is the Church. But the Church, thus understood, will be

[4] Cf. *Dictionnaire de Théologie Catholique*, s.v. *Luther*, vol. 9.1, col. 1296.

no more visible than the faith which makes one a member of it.

There can be no doubt that such radicalism was congenial to one side of Luther's very complex temperament, and as late as 1539 he could still maintain that if, alongside the interior Church of Jesus Christ, there is also an 'exterior' Church, the latter is the Church of the devil. But hard experience led him, in other moods, to recoil from so extreme a position. It was, however, revived by modern liberal Protestantism, and is still, it would appear, a powerful tendency in Reformed circles: 'It is no secret that there are not a few in the World Council' of Churches 'who believe that unity is purely spiritual, and needs no organisational expression'.[5]

(2) Luther's more considered view appears to have been that the Church, though primarily and even essentially invisible, is nevertheless involved in history and thus acquires a contingent and variable visibility. If in one aspect, and at the deepest theological level, she is the 'communion'—in a purely and exclusively spiritual and unverifiable sense—of the 'saints', it is also true that she is present wherever the word of God is preached and believed;[6] and preaching is an external event. In performing her function of teaching, therefore, the Church maintains an existence in history. This is an externalised existence. The result of preaching and faith is that people come together to hear the word of God and for worship, and where there is common worship there must be organisation. Church organisation is therefore inevitable. But there is no one divine ordering of the Church thus outwardly manifested. Church order results from the contingent and variable decisions of those who belong to the local communities of the faithful.

Thus, on what may be taken as Luther's considered view, the one Church has an external manifestation in a diversity of—not necessarily intercommunicating—local congregations. On this view, the visible unity of the members of the universal Church is not an originally given property of the Church which she cannot lose without ceasing to be herself. If such visible unity

---

[5] *The Times*, August 4th, 1960. If the unity here in question is the unity of the Church, then the implication suggests itself that the Church is 'purely spiritual', i.e. invisible. At least it is difficult to conceive of a thing which is a body-and-soul affair, but which, while possessing a single soul has *no* bodily unity.

[6] Torrance, *Kingdom and Church*, p. 55.

were ever achieved, it would be, at best, the contingent result of human, grace-guided, decisions. External unity of the universal Church may be an ideal; it is not an actual and primordial characteristic. The Church is potentially a visible unity; it is not, by its own essential nature, a necessary and actual visible unity.

(3) Luther was not so much a systematic theologian as a religious volcano in continuous eruption. Calvin, a younger contemporary and a Frenchman, while deeply indebted to Luther, was a keen and logical thinker. The great Anglican theologian, Richard Hooker, by no means an undiscriminating disciple, thought him 'incomparably the wisest man that ever the French Church did enjoy'.[7] For Calvin it was indubitable that the doctrine of the divine election of those predestinated to salvation (as basic for him as the doctrine of justification by faith for Luther) involved belief in the visible Church as among the articles of faith.[8] Whereas Luther was inclined to speak of the real Church as wholly concealed beneath the 'mask' (larva) of the visible Church, Calvin could affirm that the 'true features' (vera facies) of the kingdom of Christ and the Church were 'visible in history'.[9] As a social fact, visible in history, the Church requires an organisation or order; and a 'right order' (rectus ordo) for the Church has indeed been established by God himself. It might seem that we are back in Catholicism again. But the rectus ordo was not the Catholic order but one which Calvin had deduced from Scripture, an order, it would seem, to be learned from Calvin himself.

The doctrine of the Church and her right order is not at all the heart of Calvinism, which has spread its influence into Christian bodies that have chosen quite different forms of organisation. It may be asked how far Calvin was really serious about it. The following quotation will show that, at times at least, he was prepared to go far:

> It is dreadful to read what Isaias (and other prophets) write about the disorder in the Church of Jerusalem. . . . For all that, the prophets did not invent a new Church for themselves, nor set up new altars for separatist sacrifices. Whatever the personal

[7] Quoted by R. Bayne, *Hooker*, in *Encyclopaedia of Religion and Ethics*, vol. 6, p. 775.
[8] Torrance, *op. cit.* p. 148.
[9] I am following Torrance closely.

qualities of the men in whom, they held, God had placed his word, they themselves, from amongst the wicked, lifted up pure hands to God and worshipped him with a pure heart. What led them to stay in the Church among the wicked was their wish to preserve unity. If, then, the holy prophets thought it wrong to separate themselves from the Church because of the great sins found in her (not the sins of a single man but those of virtually the whole people), how reckless is it in us that we should dare to separate ourselves from the Church's communion because someone's life does not satisfy our judgment. . . . Let us be sure that he who of his own will abandons the external communion of a Church in which the word of God is preached and his sacraments are administered is without excuse. . . . A good conscience is not affected by the unworthiness of others, no, not by that of the pastor himself.[10]

Despite the fact that Calvin's version of the 'right order' which God has established for his Church differs in some respect from the Roman Catholic version, this quotation would seem to imply that his mature view of the *nature* of the Church is closer to the traditional view than Luther's was. Where Calvin differed from the Roman Catholics was that he identified the Church visible in history not with the Roman Catholic communion but with, it would appear, his own, and those similarly ordered.

(4) What view of the Church is implied by the English religious settlement of the sixteenth and seventeenth centuries, from which present-day Anglicanism derives?

To this question it is not easy to give a clear and certain answer. The Elizabethan settlement of religion was a practical compromise rather than the expression of a single governing theological insight in a coherent set of defined doctrines. It was carried through by the political government and was instinct with that political hankering after religious comprehension which has made itself felt so often in Christian history. In

---

[10] *Institutes of the Christian Religion*, iv. 1, nn. 18, 19; quoted in *Dictionnaire de Théologie Catholique*, s.v. *Calvinisme*, col. 1421. The first reaction of a Roman Catholic reader of this passage may be to regret that the young Calvin had not followed its principles himself and refrained from 'inventing a new Church' in preference to that in which he had been brought up. Doubtless, Calvin could reply that the word of God was not correctly preached, nor his sacraments duly administered, in the Roman Catholic communion. But this only emphasises the dependence on one's private judgment that is necessary if one is to become what the ancient Christians called a 'heresiarch'. The history of Protestantism itself suggests some doubts whether Calvin's way of understanding Christianity is the only one countenanced by Scripture.

turning to the Thirty-nine Articles of Religion for enlightenment on the view of the Church underlying the settlement, we
may bear in mind a recent criticism of these Articles:

> Though not ostensibly vague, they avoid unduly narrow defini-
> tion. Much variety of interpretation has been put upon many of
> them without improperly straining the text, and probably this
> licence was deliberately intended by their framers. . . . Among
> typical points it may be noticed that Article 28 excludes both
> Transubstantiation (in the sense there defined) and Zwinglian
> Eucharistic doctrine, but can be interpreted in terms either of a
> doctrine of the Real Presence or of Receptionism.[11]

Are the Articles any clearer on the Church than they are on
the Eucharist? The 19th Article is entitled 'Of the Church'. It
tells us that 'the visible Church of Christ is a congregation
of faithful men, in which the pure Word of God is preached,
and the Sacraments be duly ministered according to Christ's
ordinance in all those things that of necessity are requisite for the
same'. Does this mean that the test of purity of doctrine and due
administration of the sacraments is whether the doctrine and
administration in question are guaranteed or rejected by the
Church? If so, the statement is in the tradition of Catholicism,
and it would remain to ask what is meant by 'a congregation of
faithful men'; the phrase seems to echo the classical description
of the Church as the society of the faithful. But on the other
hand, the Article may be taken to mean that the test of the true
Church is whether or not a body claiming to be the Church (or
part of it) teaches pure doctrine and administers the sacraments
duly. The latter interpretation can point to the fact that, for the
Articles, the test of the purity of a doctrine is *not* whether it is
taught by the Church. Article xix goes on to say that 'as the
Church of Jerusalem, Alexandria and Antioch, have erred, so
also the Church of Rome hath erred . . . in matters of faith'.
Article xxi affirms that General Councils 'sometimes have erred,
even in things pertaining to God'. There seems no clear statement or definite implication in the Articles that any organ of
teaching in the Church is exempt from the possibility of error.
It is true that Article xx states that the Church has authority in
Controversies of Faith, but when it goes on to deny that some—

[11] *The Oxford Dictionary of the Christian Church*, ed. F. L. Cross, s.v. 'The
Thirty-nine Articles.'

apparently possible—ecclesiastical interpretations of Scripture are *lawful*, one cannot but wonder whether the Articles do not studiously avoid the assertion that the Church is ultimately incapable of error. One can therefore infer that the Articles leave room for the view that the Church is found wherever the true Gospel is preached and the Gospel sacraments are duly administered, and that the test of this truth and correctness is in a direct, unmediated appeal to Scripture. This would be a Protestant view of the Church, though whether its pedigree is Lutheran or rather Calvinist we may leave to the experts to dispute.

In any case, the Articles leave us in uncertainty about the meaning to be attached to the words 'congregation of faithful men' (*coetus fidelium*). One may question whether it was ever the intention of the framers of the Elizabethan settlement to claim the title of Christ's Church for their own communion exclusively. If they had no such intention, it would remain to ask what a congregation (*coetus*) is, if it is more than a local Church and yet something other than a single universal communion. That, however, is a question to which we shall have to return later on.

(5) The avoidance, by the Thirty-nine Articles, of 'unduly narrow definition' gave the Anglo-Catholics their opportunity. In his Anglican days, Newman had written his famous Tract XC to offer a particular interpretation of the Articles. Long afterwards, he wrote of this attempt: 'This Tract was written under the conviction that the . . . Articles . . . were, when taken in their letter, so loosely worded, so incomplete in statement, and so ambiguous in their meaning, as to need an authoritative interpretation.' But where is such an interpretation to be had? The Tractarian argument was that, in the absence of a clear necessity of taking the Reformers as the interpreting authority (and in fact the Reformers were often violently opposed to each other on points of doctrine), it was legitimate, and indeed obligatory, to have recourse to traditional Catholicism, of which the claims, as being in possession of the doctrinal and theological field at the time of the Reformation, must be obvious to an impartial judge.

Applying this argument to the Articles relating to the nature of the Church, it would seem to follow that the extreme view of the Church as a purely invisible entity, and also the mitigated

Lutheran view of her as visible indeed but not more than potentially a visible unity, must be discarded as anti-Catholic novelties. The traditional view must be accepted, that she is a divinely established and divinely guaranteed historical society of believers.

The Tractarians thought, and their successors among the Anglo-Catholics think, that they have in fact adopted this traditional view. Anglo-Catholics are accustomed to use language about the Church which is almost indistinguishable from the language of the Catholic tradition. Thus we read:

> The Church is just one historical phenomenon among many . . . a concrete, visible institution, its members individual, mortal human beings. . . . It is to the physical world that the Church belongs. . . . The Church is a society, possessing a visible structure.
>
> (The Church is an essential element in the Christian Gospel); disputes concerning . . . that society are at bottom disputes concerning . . . the Gospel, and the Gospel has its roots in history: 'the Word became flesh'. It is in and through a visible society that God had ordained that Christ should be manifested to the world. (The Church is) a visible fellowship. The antithesis . . . between spiritual and institutional religion is utterly without basis in the New Testament. (The functions of the apostolic ministry in apostolic times were) . . . (ii) to represent the one society, for only in the context of the one society can a local church grow into the fullness of Christ (*quoting Ramsey*). The historic episcopate is an organ of unity . . . linking the . . . local churches into one . . . (The bishops) are organs of a society. (In the midst of the whole world, threatened with catastrophe) the Church is set, a visible, separate society.[12]

These quotations are taken (*passim*) not from an official exposé of Anglo-Catholic beliefs, but from a book by a distinguished Anglican layman who is now a professor of philosophy at Cambridge, England. This book forms one of a series designed, as it would appear, to present Anglo-Catholic points of view on a variety of related topics. Professor MacKinnon's language about the Church could be paralleled from many other Anglo-Catholic publications.

The present Archbishop of Canterbury, though in the theological descent of F. D. Maurice rather than of the Tractarians,

[12] D. M. MacKinnon, *The Church of God.*

also speaks of the Church as 'a society which is one in its continuous life', 'one visible society', of which her outward order
tells; the one Church, of which the apostles were the original
officers, and on which every community of primitive Christians
depended; a 'new community' to which all the prerogatives and
claims of the Jewish people were transferred.[13]

In order to decide the question how far such language is to be
taken at its face value (for it is entirely consonant alike with the
pre-Reformation tradition and with modern Roman Catholic
teaching), it is altogether necessary to ask: With which society
of Christians do these writers identify the Church? The term
'a society' is their own, and as Christians they of course believe
that the Church exists somewhere in the world today. As they
are Anglicans, it might seem natural, *a priori*, to suppose that
for them the Church is that society known as the Anglican
Communion, just as for Roman Catholics the Church is the
Roman Catholic Communion, just as, it would seem, the
Christadelphians identify the People of God with their own
religious society.

In fact, however, this is not the Anglo-Catholic contention.
No more than any other body of responsible Anglican opinion
have the Anglo-Catholics ever maintained that the Church
founded by Christ survives in the world today exclusively as
the Anglican Communion.

The classical Anglo-Catholic teaching is that the society
which is the Church exists today in three divided fragments:
the Anglican Communion, the Eastern Orthodox Communion,
and the Roman Catholic Communion. These are the three
'branches' of the one Church. How is this view of the Church
reached? Its starting-point is a conviction, based on considerations which we need not here examine, that as members of the
Anglican communion the Anglo-Catholics (along, of course,
with all other Anglicans) are members of the Catholic Church.
But no one will wish to claim that the Anglican communion
is, by itself and exclusively, the whole Church. And on the other
hand, Anglo-Catholics proclaim, in unison with the ancient
tradition, that the Catholic Church is a society. Thus it can
only be that the Anglican communion is a *part* of that society,
a part separated from some other part or parts.

[13] *The Gospel and the Catholic Church*, 2nd edn, 1956.

At this stage of their reasoning, it becomes necessary for Anglo-Catholics to determine what other communion or communions are also parts of the Church. Their claim for their own communion involves the claim that it is continuous with the mediaeval *ecclesia Anglicana,* which itself was within the Roman Catholic Communion of those days; and since the Roman Catholic Communion itself continues to exist elsewhere, it was an obvious step to regard the modern Roman Catholic Communion as another 'branch' of the Catholic Church. The addition of the Eastern Orthodox Communion as a third branch was an invention of genius. The schism between Rome and Constantinople, dating (roughly) in its present form from A.D. 1054, had not been accompanied on either side by a rejection of dogmas already defined. And (at least in terms of Western theology) there was no doubt that both Communions had preserved a valid ministry. On the other hand, if it could be maintained that the schism had not de-Catholicised the Easterns, this would amount to a strong argument that the breach between Canterbury and Rome had not de-Catholicised Anglicanism; and at this point in the argument it was mose useful to be able to show that the Thirty-nine Articles were altogether too vague in their terminology to amount to an expression of positive heresy.[14]

The Branch Theory of the Church, as set forth by Anglo-Catholics, differs from some other theories of a divided Church by reason of its requirements of doctrinal orthodoxy and a valid episcopal succession. But, like so many other theories that have originated since the Reformation, it supposes the possibility of a visible historical society existing in separated parts. For this reason, it is profoundly different from the Roman Catholic view, despite the remarkable coincidences of language. The Branch theory implies a meaning for the word 'society' which is quite other than the Roman Catholic meaning of the word, and than the pre-Reformation meaning. The use of words must not be allowed to disguise the real issue. As regards the nature of the

[14] It is, however, worth noticing that formulae not positively heretical but capable of a heretical interpretation have, in antiquity, been reprobated by Catholicism. The Acacian schism of the late fifth century is a case in point; the East had accepted from the civil power a formulary which avoided explicit rejection of the Monophysite 'heresy'. The Holy See was intransigent, and the resulting schism was only terminated on terms subsequently imposed by the Pope.

Church, the Anglo-Catholics stand on the Reformed side of the great divide in Western Christendom.[15]

(6) The influence of the Tractarians and their Anglo-Catholic successors has been profound, and it has not been restricted to the Anglican Communion. But even within their own Communion, their views have not, so far at least, won general recognition as the single legitimate expression of her mind.

It is not easy to find an official statement of contemporary Anglican authority, laying down the essential beliefs of that communion. As we have seen, the Thirty-nine Articles are often susceptible of more than one interpretation. Moreover, while subscription of the Articles has never been demanded of the ordinary layman, the clergy, too, since 1865 'have been required only to affirm that the doctrine of the Church of England as set forth in the Book of Common Prayer and the Articles is agreeable to the Word of God, and to undertake not to teach in contradiction of them'.[16] Before that date, the clergy had had to give 'a more particular subscription' to the Articles (*ibid*); and it has been inferred that, widely as the Articles are framed, even they do not bind Anglicans in all particulars.[17]

In 1938 there appeared 'Doctrine in the Church of England', the report of a commission set up in 1922 by the Archbishops of Canterbury and York. But this report 'did not claim to be an authoritative epitome of the doctrine of the Church of England . . . but simply an examination of beliefs actually held'.[18]

---

[15] It is, of course, a misfortune for Anglo-Catholics that their claim that the Anglican Communion is a 'part' of the Catholic Church is repudiated by both the other supposed 'parts'; neither Roman Catholicism nor Eastern Orthodoxy regards the communion of Canterbury as being, as a communion, within the Catholic Church.

It is not necessary, here, to give separate consideration to those Anglo-papalists who identify the Catholic Church with the Roman Communion and repudiate the Branch Theory. If they regard the separateness of the Anglican Communion from Rome as objectively legitimate, they agree that the Church can be visibly divided, and therefore agree with the main body of Anglo-Catholicism. If they regard this separation as objectively illegitimate, their idea of the Church is identical with that of Roman Catholics, and we are not here concerned to examine their consciences on the subject of their actual separation from what on their own view, is the one fold of the Redeemer.

[16] *Oxford Dictionary of the Christian Church*, s.v. 'The Thirty-nine Articles.'

[17] The famous Gorham case revolved round the question whether Anglicans were required to believe in baptismal regeneration. The final decision was reached by the Privy Council, and it appears to imply that baptismal regeneration can be either affirmed or denied without disloyalty to the Established Church.

[18] *Oxford Dictionary of the Christian Church*, s.v.

Doctrinal statements do, however, sometimes emanate from the Lambeth Conferences in which the bishops of the Anglican Communion meet for periodical discussions of matters of current moment. The resolutions of these conferences, which are to be distinguished from the reports of their various committees, 'though not binding' either on the bishops or their flocks, 'are significant expressions of the opinions of the Anglican episcopate'.[19] It will therefore be of interest to study the record of the most recent of the Lambeth Conferences (1958) for the light it may throw on Anglican ideas about the nature of the Church.

The Resolutions of the Conference do not directly express any view of the Church's nature. But Resolution 13 states that 'the Conference welcomes and endorses the Statement on Christian Unity contained in the Report of the Committee on *Church Unity and the Church Universal*'. Bearing in mind, therefore, that 'endorses' is not necessarily a statement of unqualified acceptance, we turn to what the Committee had to say about Church unity:

> Conscious of the calling of the Church to be one family in Christ . . . we declare our ardent longing for the healing of our divisions, and for the recovery and manifestation to the world of that unity of the Body of Christ for which he prayed. . . . We desire to further negotiations with other Churches. . . . We believe in One, Holy, Catholic, and Apostolic Church, which takes its origin not in the will of man but in the will of our Lord Jesus Christ. All those who believe in our Lord Jesus Christ and have been baptised in the name of the Holy Trinity are incorporated into the Body of Christ and are members of the Church. Here is a unity already given. . . . The mission of the Church is . . . the gathering together of the whole human race. . . . (Hence) we must continually pray and work for the visible unity of all Christian believers . . . in a living Christian fellowship of faith and sacrament. . . . The recovery of unity, which we seek, is the unity of the whole Church of Christ. This means unity in living Christian fellowship. . . . We are working for unity with the nonepiscopal Churches. We . . . seek for such complete harmony of spirit and agreement in doctrine as would bring unity with the Eastern Orthodox Church and other ancient Churches. We must hope and pray for such eventual agreement in full faith and order as shall lead to the healing of the breach between ourselves and the

[19] *Oxford Dictionary of the Christian Church*, s.v.

Church of Rome. . . . We believe that the visible unity of the Church will be found to involve the whole-hearted acceptance of . . . a ministry acknowledged by every part of the Church as possessing not only the inward call of the Spirit, but also the commission of Christ and the authority of the whole body. (We are compelled to believe that) a ministry to be acknowledged by every part of the Church can only be attained through the historic episcopate. . . . This ministry we believe to have been given to the Church by Divine Providence from primitive Christian times with its traditional functions of . . . ordination . . . and . . . teaching. . . . The unity between Christian Churches ought to be a living unity in the love of Christ which is shown in full Christian fellowship and in mutual service, while also subject to sufficient agreement in faith and order, expressing itself in free interchange of ministers and fullness of sacramental communion . . . (We call upon our own people) to regard the recovery and manifestation of the unity of the whole Church of Christ as a matter of the greatest urgency.[20]

To these extracts from the Report may be added a phrase from the 54th Resolution of the whole Conference: 'The Conference . . . cannot recognise the Churches of . . . *episcopi vagantes* as properly constituted Churches'.

What idea of the Church is implied or expressed in these quotations? First, belief is affirmed in One, Holy, Catholic, and Apostolic Church; her origin is 'in the will' of Jesus Christ, a terminology which seems to avoid affirming that the Church was instituted by an outward act of Christ. The motive behind this reserved language may be to leave room for the traditional view that the Church pre-existed in the Old Testament People of God. Secondly, all who believe in Jesus Christ and have been (validly) baptised are members of the Church. The reference to baptism seems to imply that the Church is not merely a mystical, or purely invisible, union of believers, since baptism, a visible rite, presumably initiates its recipient into something which is itself visible. But thirdly, there is the fact of the 'divisions' which at present separate Christians into various communions, that is to say into corporate bodies which do not intercommunicate. Fourthly, these divisions run counter to Christ's prayer for the unity of his 'Body'. The divisions ought not to exist, and the Church is 'called' to be one family in Christ.

[20] *Church Unity and the Church Universal*, in *The Lambeth Conference, 1958*.

This presumably means that the Church ought to be one communion. Fifthly, this desiderated but at present not actual unity of communion is 'the unity of the whole Church of Christ'.[21] Sixthly, such unity will entail the universal acceptance of a ministry acknowledged by all to possess the commission of Christ. It is not stated whether this commission is to be derived by some sort of 'apostolic succession', or whether, rather, it is a commission derived immediately from the Church and only *mediately* from Christ as having instituted and endowed the Church. Is the ministry something instituted, with a given pattern of transmission, by the 'historical Jesus', or has the Church the power to determine the structure of its ministry, and to change that structure if circumstances change? Seventhly, however, there is a traditional form of ministry which includes the office of bishop. This ministry was 'given to the Church by Divine Providence' (we are not told that it was instituted by the historical Jesus, or indeed *when* it was given—perhaps not till after apostolic times?). The Committee holds that the ministry of the reunited Church will have to be of this special episcopal kind. To these seven points we may add an eighth, from the Conference's 54th Resolution, quoted above: there is such a thing as a 'proper constitution' of a particular (as distinct from the Universal) Church. But we are not told what such a proper constitution is, nor whether it is lacking in any of the great Christian communions.

What conclusions as to the nature of the Church can be drawn from these points? They imply, I think, that the Church is of its nature visible, since it is entered by the visible rite of baptism. It is a visible entity capable of becoming a single visible society or communion; indeed, it once *was* such, if we may press the phrase about 'recovering' unity. So long as the Church is not actually a single visible communion, she is failing to realise an ideal, not to say an obligation, laid upon her by Christ. In

[21] Here, then, we infer that the Church's unity is not actual but only potential and ideal. Is this the *same* unity as that professed when the Report states its belief in '*One*, Holy, Catholic, and Apostolic Church'? If the same unity is referred to in both these sentences, it follows immediately that the Church does not at present exist (and baptism cannot initiate us into what is non-existent). We must therefore conclude that the Report refers to two different sorts of unity. The Church is a single entity. It is also a visible entity. But it is not, essentially, a *visibly single entity*. The unity of the Church is essentially *invisible*. It can, and should, become visible.

short, the Church is, as a visible entity, a potential society; and she ought to be tending to become actually the single society that she potentially is. And, since structure, organisation, and government are essential to a society, the Church, if she ever becomes a single communion, will have such a structure, organisation, and government. We may expect this future government to be episcopal; but we are not told that this is *on principle* a *sine qua non.* The importance of all this, for our present purposes, is that if the Lambeth Conference can be taken as voicing the mind of the Anglican Communion, that Communion holds a view of the Church which is intermediate between the view that the Church is purely invisible and the view that the Church is essentially a single society or communion.

It may now be convenient to list the various opinions on the nature of the Church which our investigation has disclosed:

(*a*) The Church is a purely invisible entity. We have seen that this view was favoured by one tendency in the thought of Luther. It is the view held by the Society of Friends. It was reaffirmed by Liberal Protestantism, and it would seem that its influence is still felt fairly widely in the communions that sprang from the Reformation.

(*b*) The Church is *essentially* an invisible entity. But it has visible effects and expressions, all of which are purely contingent and can be varied without affecting her essence. On this view, the external unity of Christians in a single communion might be a good thing, but is not necessarily the one divinely intended ideal towards which Christians should be moving. This was perhaps Luther's mature position.

(*c*) The Church is essentially a visible entity, but not essentially a single visible society. It is potentially a single society, and if it is true to its divine calling it will be tending to become actually such a single society. This is the view of the Lambeth Conference. The Anglo-Catholic view is a special case of this 'potential society' view, inasmuch as it holds that an apostolic succession of bishops and orthodoxy of faith are so essential to the Church that a body lacking either of these is not even a 'part' of the divided—but potentially united—Church.

(*d*) The Church is essentially a single visible society.

These four views seem to exhaust the possibilities. If the Church is neither completely invisible nor yet a single visible society, it must be a visible entity that is not essentially a society. And if it is a visible entity, that is not essentially a society, it is either true or it is not true that it *ought* to be a single society. No further alternatives seem conceivable. The answer to our question: What is the nature of the Church? must be one or other of these; and while there may be a possibility of reconciling views (*b*) and (*c*), there is no possible reconciliation between views (*a*) and (*d*) or between either of these and either (*b*) or (*c*).

It may be well to observe once more that the living force of all these views, except (*d*), derives from the Reformation and the resulting divisions of Western Christendom. The Reformation was an upheaval which did not directly touch Eastern Orthodoxy and was, even in the West, eventually contained within certain broad geographical limits. At the present day the communions which, for purposes of convenience, we may call Reformation communions, are (for the most part) of north-western provenance and comprise about a quarter of the total of living Christians. It is within this not unimportant, but relatively small, sector of the Christian totality that opinions (*a*), (*b*), and (*c*) are actively canvassed.

Additional Note to Chapter 2
THE EASTERN ORTHODOX VIEW OF THE CHURCH

A recent book, *L'Orthodoxie*, by Paul Evdokimov (1959) is valuable alike for the information it gives on current Eastern Orthodox ideas about the Church and for its attitude to the Ecumenical Movement. The following quotations may be of interest:

> For Orthodoxy, the Church is objectively present where . . . the Bishop, by his apostolic power, celebrates the Eucharist, bears witness to its authenticity and integrates in himself those gathered together, in liturgical meeting, in the Body of Christ (p. 126).

> The visible Church is by no means simply the visible society of Christians, but also the Spirit of God and the grace of the sacraments living in this society (p. 127).

> (The Church) is the *theandric organism, the life of God in what is human . . . a sacramental community* (p. 127).

> The Eucharist . . . is the *Sacrament of sacraments* and . . . the most adequate expression of the Church. The Church is the eucharistic *koinonia* continued, perpetuated (p. 128).

Since Pentecost, the Church is there where the eucharistic *koinonia* is actualised (p. 129).

Every local Eucharist which is correct (i.e. that has the bishop at its head) possesses all the fullness of the Church of God in Christ (p. 130).

If the Churches communicate with one another, this is not so as to form by addition a fuller Church . . . but on the one hand to respond to the overflowing charity of the Body . . . (p. 131).

Horizontally, the scope of (the bishop's) jurisdictional power . . . is always localised. Thus the unity of the Church is constituted by means of the category of the communion of members of equal standing. . . . The *Una Sancta* is the unity of the different localities, in each of which it is equally manifested (p. 131).

Tradition recommends communion with the pentarchy of the five patriarchates. This bond shows that one is an equal member of the orthodox Communion (p. 131).

The Word of God is never addressed to isolated individuals, but to the chosen people, a collegial reality. . . . To be Christian consisted from the first, essentially, in belonging to the community of the brethren (p. 144).

(The modern term 'ecclesial') relates to the Church in the most interior sense of community and communion (p. 155).

The Church is basically one in dogma, the sacraments, the *koinonia* (p. 155).

In the Orthodox view, the dogma of the unity of the Church means that the Church is the Orthodox Church. Every Christian body outside the canonical limits belongs to Orthodoxy, in the measure in which it shares in the truth. . . . A heresy, a schism, is a phenomenon of the Church's life, its link with the centre-pleroma may be more or less loose; this determines its degree of orthodoxy. Thus, from every 'contingent' unity, we pass on to the essential ecclesial 'unity' which is seen to be of its nature 'unique': *the Church is one and she is unique* (p. 155 f.).

The acts of a bishop who is cut off from the eucharistic communion, from the Church, are void of all ecclesial content, of all spiritual power (p. 162).

The Church, by her nature, cannot be divided; on the other hand, Christianity is deeply fragmented (p. 335).

Respect for Canon Law[22] limits and draws the frontiers of the

---

[22] 'Respect for Canon Law' is an attempt to render 'la conscience canonique', for which, cf. *op. cit.* p. 186, where it appears to be described as 'a certain sense of orthodoxy', which tries to ascertain 'not the historic forms that come down from the age of the apostles, but the spirit which animated those forms and which will animate every form and every age with perfect self-identity'. It

visible body of our Church. . . . The 'branch theory . . . leads to a Christianity lacking the Church, (p. 336).

It is only when one is conscious of the 'absoluteness' of one's Church, only when one believes as catholic truth that she is the only true Church of God, that the scandal of division comes clearly to light and that the real question of unity is first really posed (p. 337).

Orthodoxy has the unshakeable awareness that she is *Una Sancta* (p. 378).

The non-Orthodox, considered from the point of view of their denominational allegiance, are no longer in the Orthodox Church; but for all their separation, the Church continues to be present and to act in presence of their faith and their correct intention of salvation. We know where the Church is; it is not for us to . . . say where the Church is not (p. 343).

These rather extensive quotations illustrate the danger of building too much on any one of them, and may serve as a touchstone of the ensuing attempt to state, in my own language, what I think to be the author's ecclesiology, so far as it concerns us here.

The visible Church is one and unique. It is a visible society and a sacramental fellowship. It is epitomised in the Eucharist, of which it may be considered the outward expression and effect. It is made actual wherever the Eucharist is duly celebrated by a bishop with the local flock around him. It is, in fact, the Eucharistic *koinonia* or fellowship. The bishop's own status is itself of the sacramental order, but it involves a jurisdiction, which is, however, restricted in local range. The Church, fully present at each such (correct) episcopal celebration of the Eucharist, is a unity of them all. Membership of this unity, whether for the individual or for the local Church, is expressed in the fact that one is in communion with one of the four (since 1054 A.D.) patriarchates. Thus the Church which Christ instituted is the Orthodox Church. A bishop, and therefore his flock, cut off from the communion of the Orthodox Church, is outside the unity which conditions the validity of ministerial acts and the validity of sacraments.[23] This is not tantamount to saying that, outside the

should be noted that 'the right to establish canons, to judge and if need be to apply sanctions' is derived from the Church's divine constitution (*ibid*. p. 185).

[23] Evdokimov does not mean that schismatical sacraments cannot be either valid or 'efficacious'—provided, of course, that the recipient is in 'good faith'; cf. *op. cit.* p. 343.

limits of the Orthodox Church, no grace is given. But it does mean that the Church of Christ, identical with the Orthodox Church, is present, in various diminished forms, wherever schismatics or heretics are in good faith. Objectively, then, everyone has an obligation to belong to the Orthodox Communion.

The upshot seems to be that, for our author—though he does not actually say it—the visible Church is essentially, of its very nature, a single communion. The strong insistence that this is a 'Eucharistic Communion' coincides with Thomas Aquinas's doctrine that the 'mystical body' is the *res* of the Eucharist.

It is right to add, that the author would be the first to distinguish between his own authority as a theologian, and the authority of the Church. It seems probable, however, that the views put forward by him on the nature of the Church are a fair specimen of modern Eastern Orthodox thinking on the subject. They differ in one respect from the view put forward in the following pages: Evdokimov seems to me to minimise the juridical aspect of the *Una Sancta*. He is aware that local jurisdiction is necessary, but is reluctant to extend the principle of jurisdiction beyond purely local limits. This difference does not affect the main issue, which is whether the Church is or is not essentially a single communion; Evdokimov's repudiation of the 'branch theory' may be significant in this regard. Of course, he also differs from Roman Catholics when it comes to *identifying* the *Una Sancta*. For him, she is the Orthodox Church; for Roman Catholics she is the Roman Catholic Church. But this does not affect our present concern, which is not 'where the Church is' but 'what sort of a thing' she is.

Chapter 3

THE IDEA OF A HISTORICAL SOCIETY

In the previous chapter we refused to identify the Anglo-Catholic notion of the Church with that maintained by Roman Catholics, although there is a remarkable similarity of language in the expressions used by both parties. If we can now justify this refusal, we shall have brought out into clear light what we mean if we affirm that the Church is essentially a single historical society, and why this affirmation carries with it the necessity of the visible unity of the Church as a single, indivisible, communion of baptised members. Once again, it may be well to remind the reader that we are not engaged on a proof of the 'Roman Catholic claims'. We are not proposing to *identify* the Church. Our purpose is to distinguish clearly two different notions of what the Church's nature is.

Although F. D. Maurice did not reckon himself a member of the Anglo-Catholic or any other party, his views and language about the Church approximated closely to those of the Anglican right wing. They may be studied in his celebrated work, *The Kingdom of Christ*.[1] The editor of a recent republication of this book quotes the Scottish Presbyterian, Principal David Cairns, as saying, 'There is' in Maurice 'more of the spiritual and eternal content of the Christian faith . . . than in any other of the theologians of England of the last century'. He also quotes the Roman Catholic Father Bouyer: 'If any Protestant had had a clear and deep intuition of the solution called for by Protestantism's chronic problem, it is, in my opinion, undoubtedly Maurice.' We can endorse the editor's own description of the book as 'outstanding among works of English divinity not only in the nineteenth century but in any century'.[2]

The Kingdom of Christ is described, in its sub-title, as *Hints*

[1] Second, revised, edition, 1842. My citations are from the New Edition, 1958, ed. Alec Vidler.
[2] Preface to the New Edition, p. 7.

to a Quaker Respecting the Principles, Constitution and Ordinances of the Catholic Church. We shall not here delay to examine the details of Maurice's case against the Quakers. They, like him, believed that Christ had come to establish a Kingdom, and our interest is in his positive account of that Kingdom.

Maurice contends not only against the Quakers but when dealing with the various forms of Continental Protestantism, with the English Noncomformist bodies, with Unitarianism, and with the 'parties' within the Church of England, that while the positive principles that gave rise to these various systems and groupings were true, important, and to be included in the total Christian fact, yet the 'notions' to which these principles had given rise were pernicious. Man does not fundamentally need a system of human thoughts expressed in a man-made religious institution. He needs, and God has provided for him, a Church which has God for its Founder and which is the expression of a divine, all-comprehending, purpose.[3]

Maurice identified the Church with the Kingdom of Christ; hence the title of his book.[4] The Church, he maintained, had certain characteristics or distinguishing marks, namely, the sacraments of baptism and the Eucharist, the Creeds, the liturgy and the Scriptures, and further a ministry 'grounded upon an episcopal order' and possessing a power of absolution.

It will be observed that all these characteristics, or (as Maurice calls them) *signs of the Kingdom,* have an outward and visible aspect. We should presume them (glossing, here, Maurice's teaching) to be the signs of a reality which, whatever its interior quality, has a definite external mode of self-manifestation, is in

---

[3] Cf. P. P Florensky, *Colonne et Affirmation de la Vérité,* p. 7, quoted by P. Evdokimov, *L'Orthodoxie,* p. 123: 'The idea of the Church does not exist, but the Church herself exists, and for every living member of the Church, her life (la vie ecclésiastique) is the most definite and palpable thing that he knows.' Von Hügel commented on the thinness of formulae as a basis for life.

[4] It is sometimes objected against Roman Catholics that they identify the Kingdom of God with the (institutional) Church. This is no part of Roman Catholic doctrine. It should be noted that Maurice, for his part, identifies the Church with the Kingdom of *Christ.* The kingdoms of God and of Christ are at least verbally distinguished, not only in St Matthew's Gospel but in St Paul. Remembering that the word here translated Kingdom would be better rendered Reign or Kingly Rule, it may perhaps be suggested that whereas God reigns from eternity to eternity, the reign of the Messiah is in process of extending its sway in history, and will only become conceptually identical with the Reign of God at the Second Coming. The Church may then be conceived as at once the sphere in which the Messiah's writ already runs and the instrument for the propagation of the Messianic kingdom.

fact a tangible historical reality, a *grandeur historique*. One finds it difficult to see how a purely invisible reality, or indeed a Church such as Luther's (invisible, but with a contingent variety of outward effects, with no structure given once and for all by Christ), could be 'signified' by a ministry grounded upon an episcopal order and possessing absolving power. If the Church is of its nature signified by these things, it must of its nature be a visible reality with a determinate structure. We are therefore not surprised to learn from Maurice that from the first the Church has been the generating principle of the modern nations and, since their constitution, has entered into a divinely intended alliance with each nation in its local setting.

If we now ask Maurice *what sort of a thing,* in its outward aspect, is the Church whose signs he has enumerated, his reply—so far as words go—is that she is a society. He tells us that it is equally impossible for man to be content with a spiritual society which is not universal, and with a universal society which is not spiritual. The word 'spiritual' here does not mean 'purely interior and invisible'. A constitution, for instance, is spiritual in Maurice's sense of the word, if it has the 'marks of a state which is designed for a voluntary creature; which is his, whether he approve of it or no; and against which he has a nature, or inclination to rebel'.[5] These marks of spirituality he finds in so tangible and historical a reality as the human family; and again, in a nation he finds 'some of the characteristics of a spiritual constitution.'[6] But in time a 'universal polity', the Roman Empire, superimposed itself upon the ancient families and nations, an Empire which 'answers exactly to the idea of a universal *world.* If there is to be anything different from this, if there is to be *a universal Church,* we ought to know of what elements it is to be composed' etc.[7] The Church, in fact, has conditions both human and divine, and 'the human conditions of it could no more be passed over than the divine; it was as needful to prove that the ladder had its foot upon earth, as that it had come down out of heaven'.[8]

'We have then a reasonable excuse for enquiring, whether there be on this earth a spiritual and universal kingdom . . . with which we of the nineteenth century may have fellowship.'

---

[5] Vol. i, p. 229.   [6] Ibid. p. 233.
[7] Ibid. p. 235.   [8] Ibid. pp. 252 ff.

If we turn to the New Testament, we find that it speaks of one who came to establish a kingdom that was to be at once an outward and universal kingdom or society and a spiritual kingdom of the heart. There is no contradiction between the inward and the outward aspects of Christ's kingdom. After all, the kingdom of David or Solomon was an outward kingdom, yet 'it stood upon the principle . . . that the visible king is the type of the invisible. . . . This principle . . . the Israelitish kingdom existed to enforce. . . . If this be so, what contradiction was there in affirming that the new kingdom' of Christ 'was the kingdom promised to David, the kingdom of his son'—and therefore a kingdom of exterior aspect—'and yet that it was in the highest sense . . . a kingdom within, a kingdom not of this world?'.[9]

The inference we drew from the visibility of the 'signs' of the Church is thus confirmed; the Church is an exterior reality, a palpable entity, and we note that it may be presumed, if it merits the name of 'kingdom', to be an organic unity. Maurice refers to the 'amazing' prayer which the New Testament puts on Christ's lips: 'That they all may be one, as thou, Father, art in me, and I in thee, that they may be one in us.' These words, he says, 'contain the essence and meaning' of the whole Gospel history; and that meaning must be embodied in *acts*.[10]

In harmony with this intrinsic requirement for an embodiment of the revealed truth not merely in ideas but in act, Maurice points out that we read, in the Gospels, of the Cross and resurrection of Christ, and then the risen Christ tells his apostles that they are to go out into the world and 'testify' of the achieved union between heaven and earth. They are 'not merely to testify of it, but to adopt men into a society grounded upon the accomplishment of it'. This society was the Church. If the Church's members find their places in locally distinct communities of Christians, still they are addressed by the apostles from Jerusalem as members of 'an entire community dispersed through different parts of the world'.

Maurice cannot wish to question the fact that this universal society, the Church, is a *concrete historical society*. He identifies it, as already stated, with the Kingdom of Christ, and he tells us that Christ came to reveal a kingdom 'which is founded upon

[9] Ibid. p. 248.   [10] Ibid. p. 251.

a union established in his person between man and God, between the visible and invisible world'.[11] Membership in the Church is bestowed by a concrete visible act (baptism), which is rightly administered to infants. The Eucharist, a visible sign, was to give to the Church 'permanency, coherency and vitality throughout all generations'.[12] The episcopate is part of the divine endowment of the Church, and bishops have, 'by the very nature of their office, held fellowship, and been obliged to hold fellowship with those who lived in other districts'. At Pentecost the Spirit of God declares that 'an organised body of men' has been provided for his habitation, and that through a portion of this body (namely, the bishops) 'his blessings are to be transmitted to the rest'.

Anyone who will read and reflect upon what Maurice has written, and with all possible emphasis, about the nature of the Church will surely conclude that here at last is an Anglican theologian who has completely and for ever discarded the notion, lurking in the Reformation from its very origin in Luther, that the Church is a purely interior and invisible unity of those who have been justified by faith. Here, surely, is one who has seen that the Church, by its very nature, represents the duality of the divine and the tangible-human in Christ himself, and that therefore she is essentially a concrete historical society. Moreover, like every Christian, Maurice must concede that if, as he holds, the Church is an essential element in what Christ came to give mankind, is in fact *the* essential element, since it is the very kingdom which he came to establish (in Maurice's view), then the Church must be contemporary with every age of humanity from the first Christian Pentecost till the Second Coming of Christ. The Church must be a 'kingdom' with which men of our own century 'may have fellowship'.

If, then, the Church established by Christ was in New Testament times a concrete historical society, which Maurice affirms, and if it was (and therefore remains) *essentially* a historical society, as his argument would seem to suggest, it is time to ask ourselves squarely what a society is. There is perhaps no more important question than this in the whole field of ecclesiology today.

[11] Ibid. p. 259.
[12] Cf. Thomas Aquinas on the 'mystical body' as the *res* of the Eucharist, and P. Evdokimov on the Church as fully present wherever the Eucharist is (duly) celebrated by the bishop.

We may begin by distinguishing *a* society from 'society'. Leaving aside voluntary and involuntary hermits, we are all members of 'society'. That is to say, we enter into manifold social relationships with our fellow-men. These relations are often of the most casual and variable kinds, involving us in commitments and obligations which are transitory and evanescent. Society, in this vague meaning of the term, is capable of various fluid concentrations. One of these had great significance in the culture of nineteenth-century England, when it mattered much whether a man, or (more particularly) a woman, belonged to 'Society'.

It is obvious that society, in this meaning of the term, is not *a* society, despite the confusing fact that, even in this vague sense, the word can occasionally carry the article, so that we can speak of 'the society of the human race'. If we use this term to describe mankind in its present predicament, we mean by it that a network of reciprocal relationships can, and to a large extent does, knit together all the members of our species at any given moment of the world's history. Manifestly, however, mankind does not at present constitute an actual society, but at best a potential one. The true society of mankind may be in the womb of history. Many of its constitutive elements are already present: the human race of whose members it might be composed, and a host of particular networks of relationships, some of them (such as those which bind the citizens of a nation into a single state) of more stability and permanence than others. It cannot be denied that some creative coup of emergent probability could fashion, out of these elements or with their help, an actual universal society of mankind. But in the interests of clear thinking and for the guidance of practical effort, it is essential to realise that such a society does not actually exist at the present time.

For examples of actual societies, we have to turn to humbler and more particular illustrations, such as a society for the prevention of cruelty to animals, a trade union, a cricket club, a debating society.

Let us suppose that one of us wants to start a debating society in our village. What does he do? He talks about his idea to others who, he thinks, might be attracted by it. A group of us get together. We consider the possibilities, rival claims upon the time and interest of the local inhabitants, the sort of subjects we should wish to debate and those we should wish to debar, frequency of meetings, financial implications. We find ourselves drawing up a provisional constitution and rules. Eventually, deciding to proceed with the idea which has now become a plan, we elect a chairman, a secretary, a treasurer and a committee. We issue some sort of manifesto and invite others to become members. They are admitted on the understanding that, as members, they will be bound by the rules of the society. Membership of our society, in other words, will imply some sort of contract between the society and each individual member. There will be mutual privileges and responsibilities.

Now the same process may have been going on in some neighbouring villages; or the influence of our initiative may lead to other such initiatives elsewhere at some future date. There may thus be several debating societies in a single area of our county. Indeed there might be a rival one in our own village. Each of these will be *a* society. There would be no sense in speaking of them as forming, in the aggregate, a single society. A society implies a constitution, a set of rules, a governing body, and a set of actual members who accept this constitution and these rules as binding on them so far as concerns the purposes of the society—and who consent to the decisions of the governing body. What the society *is*, however, is precisely the association of its members.[13]

Debating societies often have a short life. Let us now take the example of a more permanent society. A college in a university is a society; indeed the words 'college' and 'society' are almost synonymous. A university college is an association of human beings, possessing a constitution or articles of association, its standing rules or statutes, and its variable rules, together with a governing body. It may be noted that among the rules of the college there may be some that are unwritten, and that will remain unwritten unless persistent breach or neglect of them compels the society (or its governing body) to decide whether

---

[13] The word 'association' is ambiguous. It may mean an *act of associating*; but it may also mean the resultant of that act, the associated set of persons. It is in the latter sense that a society is an association. It should be added that, unlike some associations, a society has an at least relative permanence. Four people playing cards together have formed an association. We should hardly describe them as a society.

the rule in question is to lapse by desuetude, or on the other hand is to be reinforced by formulation. There is a certain tendency for common law to evolve into statute law.

A college, we have said, is an association of human beings. Let us, then, suppose that a group from among the fellows and scholars of our college ceases, for reasons good or bad, to recognise the legislation and government of the fellows as a whole. *Odium theologicum* has its counterpart in *odium academicum*; and each of them is schismatical in tendency. We may suppose that our dissident group has a millionaire patron behind it (probably a former alumnus of the college), and that it buys a new residence in the university city and there establishes itself, under the governance of the fellows who have led it into 'schism'. Powerful influence may secure for it a charter from the State or recognition from the university as a whole. It will draw up a constitution for itself (probably very similar to that of the body from which it has seceded). It can now admit new members, and in fact will behave in all respects as *sui juris*.

Is there any legitimate sense in which it can be said that the two establishments now existing, the new college and the old, are *one society*?[14] Can it be said that the corporate acts of the new establishment are corporate acts of the previously existing college? Can such acts bind even the members of the new establishment *in virtue of* their former association with the old college? Can it be argued that the scholars and fellows who did not join in the schismatical movement no longer, in default of the seceding members, constitute a whole society, and are no longer to function validly as what they were?

There is no question here of the moral rights and wrongs of the secession. The seceders may say—and it is not our task here

[14] It may be objected that they remain one society as being both members of the same university. That is quite true. But the university is not the *same* society as the individual college. The college is a society by having its own members associated under a common constitution and a common government. The university, for its part, has its own constitution and government. A fellow of Balliol is a member of Oxford University; and so, too, is a fellow of St John's. But a fellow of Balliol is not, by virtue of his membership either of Balliol or of the University, a member of St John's. As we shall see, it is a peculiarity of the Church, if it is a society, that it is not subordinate, in the sphere of religion, to any other society. It is autonomous in its own sphere. When an individual or a group dissociates himself from the Church, he does not and cannot become a member of a wider religious society of which the Church forms part; there is no such wider religious society—there is nothing corresponding to the University, of which the 'Churchman' and the 'schismatic' can both be members.

to contradict them—that their withdrawal from the old college was necessitated by corruptions, or stagnation, that created a morally intolerable situation. It may well be argued by the members of the new establishment that they themselves *are* the real college, the original college.[15] Such a claim will inevitably carry with it the affirmation that those from whom they have seceded are *not* the old society, but a rump that has lost its *raison-d'-être*. Such in fact was the contention of the original Christians *vis-à-vis* 'Israel according to the flesh'. But what neither they nor their former colleagues can maintain, nor will any onlooker wish to maintain, is that, once the schism has been established, the two groups, as groups, are one society, one college.

In the case of a purely human institution such as a college, it might certainly be arguable that the damage wrought by the act of schism had been so mortal that neither of the resulting societies can claim, any longer, to be the original society. Obviously, if that contention could be proved, the original society would no longer be capable of functioning as a society, and would in fact no longer exist as a society. But if it does not exist as a society, it does not exist at all; for to be a society was of its essence. It will have gone into dissolution like a human being who has died. Something, or some things, else may exist instead, but this new thing or things are not the old society. There has been, as Aristotle would say, corruption and generation. A new form, or forms, have assumed the old matter, and the old *thing* has ceased to be. The one clear fact, involved in the very idea of 'a society', is that two societies cannot constitute one society, unless one is subordinate to the governance of the other, as in the instance of a parish dependent on the government of a diocese; or unless (as is the case with the 'houses' in a boarding-school) both are subordinate to a superior governance which includes them both in a wider, actually existent, society.

A nation-state is a society in the political sphere. In order that it should exist, it is not enough that its members should be of the same family or race, that they should speak a common

---

[15] According to *1066 and All That*, what happened in 1570 was that Pope Pius V left the Church of England. There are conceivable theological grounds on which that could be a quite sensible statement. See below.

language and inherit a common culture, or even that their
law-courts should administer the same traditional law. They
must further be of a single polity, acknowledging the same
sovereignty (which, of course need not be that of a hereditary
monarchy), and be subject to a single ultimate but actual
executive. The English, the Scots and the Welsh belong today
to such a political entity, of which the Crown in Parliament is
at once the expression and the organ; they are members of one
state, of a single political society. To this state there once belonged what are now named the United States of America.
No-one in his senses would maintain that the United States and
Britain are today a single state. Their respective members passed
out of political association in the eighteenth century. Since the
Declaration of Independence the United States have ceased to
acknowledge the British sovereignty as having authority over
themselves. They have set up a sovereign executive and legis-
lature which are other than the Crown in Parliament. They
have formed themselves into a new political society. Once again
it is to be observed that these are statements of fact, making no
appeal to the moral order of values. They do not presuppose any
judgment upon the rights and wrongs of the events and
decisions which led to the separate political existence of the
United States. They neither condemn nor condone 'rebellion'.
They merely register its ineluctable consequence, when it
achieves success in the American way.[16]

[16] The process of establishing a political 'schism'—in this case an abortive
one—is aptly described in the following message from *The Times*' 'Own Correspondent', New York, February 5th, 1861 (quoted in *The Times*, February, 18th
1961): 'Disunion has now reached its second stage—reconstruction. A conven-
tion of delegates from the seceding States met yesterday at Milledgeville, with
a view to form a federal slaveholding Union, with the present federal Constitution as its basis, altered or modified to suit the case. . . . I understand that the
programme is: The adoption of the present Constitution without a reserved
right of secession; the choice of a provisional Executive; the creation of an
army . . . and the adoption of the present revenue system of the United States
until a better can be framed. Envoys are to be sent to Europe to secure the
recognition of the new nation, and provisions are to be made for the admission
of the other slaveholding States. From today forward, therefore, the controversy
assumes new proportions. Instead of the great Federal Government mated
against individual States, it is the remains of the old federation, . . . reeling
under the shocks of rebellion against the confederacy of the Gulf States, elate
with unexpected success, and hoping for the immediate accession of the whole
slaveholding States'. The parallel with the Elizabethan Settlement of Religion
is piquant. Note that the American secessionists proposed to carry on with the
existing Constitution, 'altered or modified to suit the case', and—for the time
being—to adopt the pre-existing revenue system. The installation of the 'provisional Executive' would have been the act which gave birth to the 'schism'.

In a changing world a society has to take corporate decisions to adapt its life and secure its ends in succeeding environments. One form of such corporate decisions in the British State is Acts of Parliament. In order to become an Act, and so to be invested with the status of a decision of the State, a Parliamentary Bill, having received the requisite assent of Parliament, has further to receive the Assent of the Crown, externally and officially expressed, as by signature of the relevant document.

Suppose, now, that the Crown were permanently removed from the field of public action. As the British Constitution at present stands, it would seem that the State could then no longer function. In theory, it would disintegrate into its component parts; the various local governments would become severally sovereign in their own areas. The British State would no longer exist; its place would have been taken by a number of smaller political societies. In fact, of course, recourse, would be had to the radical sovereignty of the people, and the permanent demise of the Crown would at once be circumvented and remedied by the conveyance of the supreme authority to some other organ of political life. The point is, that neither the State nor any other society can function or exist without a means of publicly expressing its corporate will, a will which in the nature of the case is determinative for the life of the society's members as such. This means of expressing the corporate will must exist in the historical world, and so be subject to the contingencies of human existence on earth.[17]

[17] It could be argued that the existence of the organ for expressing the public will is even more important than its exercise. The Eastern Orthodox Communion has existed for nine hundred years since the separation of East and West. During all that time, there has been no Ecumenical Council recognised as such by the Eastern Orthodox. Yet the Communion still exists. But it exists, it may be said, because an Ecumenical Council is always theoretically possible for it. The central authority exists, though the sovereign slumbers. Meanwhile, the essence of a society is association. If communion ceased between the parts of Eastern Orthodoxy, it would have disintegrated. As we saw previously (Chapter 1, Additional Note) P. Evdokimov identifies the Church with that Communion. It may be added that the persistence of intercommunion between the autocephalous churches of Eastern Orthodoxy permits an interchange of views, at an official level, between the bishops who, collectively, are the organ of sovereignty, so that a certain diffused sovereignty is exercised even without the periodical convocation of a General Council. However, it does seem to the outsider that the lack of a functioning 'central government' in the Orthodox Communion leads to a looseness of association making temporary 'schisms' all too likely to occur. Nor does Orthodoxy seem well equipped to react decisively as a unity to the changing needs of daily life.

It should be observed that, in practice, it is impossible to provide, in the original charter and constitution of a society, for all the particular contingencies of its future life. Any attempt to do so is likely to cramp and constrain the society in much the same way as the progress of evolution seems to have been arrested in some species whose mechanisms of self-maintenance and defence are too narrowly specialised. Such a species will die out rather than adapt itself to a strange milieu; whereas the human species, with its low degree of specialisation, has proved amazingly adaptable. Thus it has been argued that an unwritten Constitution like the British is superior to a written constitution, as being able to adapt itself more easily to new times and problems. In fact, a human society which finds itself encumbered with a written constitution, which has become obsolete or unworkable through the change of times, will either take steps to abrogate its constitution or will treat it as a venerable dead-letter, an 'Old Testament' which is to be honoured, even if rather in the breach than the observance.

Since our subject is the nature of the Church, it will be well to add here a distinction between two sorts of societies: that which is fully autonomous within its own sphere; and that which exists as subsidiary to another, more embracing, society. A sovereign state is an autonomous society, because in the conduct of its own affairs it recognises no human court of appeal beyond its own. A trade union is not an autonomous society, as is evidenced by the fact that it concedes that there is a right of appeal against its own decisions (e.g. the expulsion of a member) to the courts of the state. Christianity claims for itself an intrinsic authority by divine right over against all political societies. If the Church is a concrete human society in the historical order, it will be an autonomous society, and we shall expect to find that it claims, and even on occasion exercises, the right to expel a member without appeal, from active functioning membership and the privileges thereof.

When Roman Catholics say that the Church which Christ established is a society, they mean that the Church is, by Christ's institution, essentially the sort of thing which we have been describing. And of course they identify this society with their own body. It is desirable to add, as it were in parenthesis, that they do not of course mean that the Church, in its most primitive days, already possessed, in developed actuality, the full structure of organisation, law, and government which is found in the Roman Catholic Communion today. To deny development is no part of their argument. What they contend is that the development has been of and in one continuing society. They share with other Christians the faith that, whatever the Church is, her existence till the end of human history on earth is guaranteed by God. To this major premise they add a minor premise, namely that the Church is essentially a concrete historical society. And they infer, necessarily, that some one among the societies existing on earth today, to the exclusion of all other such societies, is the one Church established by Christ as the ark of salvation, the 'little flock' to which 'the kingdom' is promised. The arguments by which they seek to show that this one society is their own communion do not concern us here.

In strong contrast, Anglo-Catholics accept and proclaim the post-Reformation view that their own Anglican communion is one among several which, together, make up the one Church of Christ. Plainly, then, they do not think that the Church is a concrete historical society in the sense explained above. The Anglican Communion and the Roman Catholic Communion are no more parts of one historical society than two university colleges, sprung by fissure from a previously existing college, are one college. The test in both cases is the same: is there any existing and functioning authority which can legislate as and for both bodies, and can make decisions which will have the force of law in both? In the case of the colleges there is no such existing and functioning authority.[18] Similarly, in the case of the two communions, there is no such authority.

[18] It has been pointed out above that, in the case of the two colleges, there *is* a University which includes them both; they are two colleges, but are one in their membership of the same University; not one *as* a college, but one *in* a University. If the Church is a society, there is no historical authority superior to it, to which it owes allegiance in the order of revealed religion.

It may be that there are Anglo-Catholics who will say that they consider themselves bound by the decisions of the central authority of the Roman Catholic Church. They may not in fact mean more than that they view these decisions as having persuasive force. If they really mean that they acknowledge them as having the force of law within the Anglican Communion, then it is at once supremely relevant to point out to them that the Roman Catholic Church teaches that schism is a grave sin, and that a schismatic is one who refuses to be subject to the Roman See. The Roman See is unwavering in its call to all men to join its own visible communion.

The meaning which we have attributed to the term 'a society' is not a private meaning, invented for the purposes of theological debate. It is the public and accepted meaning of the term. If Anglicans wish to give the term a private meaning of their own, such that they can retain it as a description of the Church of Christ, while denying that the Church is the sort of thing which we have in this chapter described, the least that can be asked of them is that they should state clearly what this private meaning is. They have never done so. But there is more to it than that. By appropriating the term 'a society' (with a private, unstated, meaning) as a description of what they take to be the Church, and by taking along with this term the associated terminology (community, fellowship, institution), Anglicans have been able to present their ecclesiology as being a continuation of the pre-Reformation and patristic tradition of thought on the subject of the Church, when in fact it represents a fundamental breach with that tradition. Thus the real issues in debate have been confused, and it is not easy to resist the impression that many souls may have been misled.

No doubt it will be objected against our argument, that the unity of a society is adequately assured by the unity of its government; and that the Church, though made up of divided communions, has such unity of government because Christ himself is the 'head', the supreme governor, the 'king', of the Church, or of what Maurice called the Kingdom of Christ. To reply to this objection may serve still further to elucidate what Roman Catholics mean when they say that the Church is essentially a visible society.

There is, of course, ample authority for the truth that Christ is the head of the Church. He was already the shepherd of the flock in his earthly life. But his headship, kingship, lordship in the consummated form belongs to that glorified condition which is his in virtue of his resurrection. His headship is not an inert dignity but an active reign and a dynamic of conquest. He 'sits on the right hand of the majesty on high', but is actively engaged 'till all things have been put under his sway'. There is therefore no doubt that he governs the Church.

The question is, whether he governs it in such a way as to constitute it a concrete historical society; and, if so, *how* he governs it to produce this effect.

In speaking of the British State, we remarked that in the permanent absence of the Crown, the State could not function and would, in fact, disintegrate. There is, however, an exception to this general truth. The State could continue to exist and to function if the Crown, foreseeing a prolonged absence, had provided for a regency. The Queen of England can spend months away from this country without serious inconvenience, because she appoints a Council of Regency to act for her in her absence.

Christ is no longer present on earth in the historical way in which he was present during his Palestinian ministry. During the 'days of his flesh' he could rule his disciples, and by his rule constitute them a corporate entity, as a father rules his family, a master his school, a shepherd his flock. But it was destined that he should 'go away'; it was even 'expedient' for them that he should leave them. What is to happen to the 'little flock' during this 'absence' of the shepherd, which is to last till his Second Coming?

We can see no *a priori* impossibility in the idea that the ascended Christ, no longer subject to the limitations of time and place, but rather expressing in his glorified humanity the fullness of his own divine power, might have willed to rule his Church by intervening by direct messages from on high, to meet the changing contingencies of her life on earth. But we are all bound to admit that in fact no such messages are normally received, nor is there any arrangement for their reception. When they are alleged to occur (as it is alleged that St Margaret Mary received an order to effect the institution of a feast of the Sacred Heart) they are usually highly suspect. Nor do they ever take on the force of law in any Christian communion unless the authorities of that communion accept and impose them.

It appears to follow inevitably that, if Christ is the head of the Church, and since he is neither present in it in immediate historical modality nor governs it by direct messages from on high, the Church can only be a historical society *if Christ has authorised a regency,* so that the decisions of the regency are clothed with the authority of the heavenly King. What that regency may be, how it may be constituted, whether it is a democratic government, an oligarchy, a rule by a single regent, or a mixed form of authority, it is beside our present purpose to determine. But unless there is such a regency, the Church is not a historical society in the sense we have explained. And again we may ask: what alternative explanation of the term 'a society' is, or can be, offered? And if Scriptural authority for the belief that such a regency exists be demanded, we may for the moment content ourselves with a reference to Matthew, 18. 18: 'What things soever you bind on earth, shall be bound in heaven; and what things soever you loose on earth shall be loosed in heaven.' In the Semitic terminology of the primitive Christian tradition, there could scarcely be a more emphatic way of affirming that the authority of the officers of the Church is so truly delegated that its exercise carries with it *a priori* the authority of God.[19]

In the end, I think, it will be found that to deny that the Church is essentially a society in the sense that has here been given to the term must lead logically—and that is to say, really —to one of two alternatives. Either the Church is in its ultimate essence a purely invisible thing; or the Church is, though not a society, a visible entity which is *potentially* a visible society— potentially, and, perhaps, ideally. What name can we give to an entity which is potentially but not essentially a society? Perhaps we could try calling it a social tendency. Is the Church a supernaturalisation of that tendency in our human nature which led Aristotle to define man as a political animal? But to name the Church the supernaturalisation of a tendency is to locate her in the sphere of interior grace, and would lead us back to the notion of the essential invisibility of the Church. Or could we identify the Church with that group of external things—the Bible, the Creeds, the sacraments, and an apostolic ministry— which have it in them to exert a centripetal attraction upon believers in so far as they are believers? But this would be to

---

[19] Among Christians who admit the doctrinal authority of the Bible it is not necessary here to examine the question whether this saying was actually uttered by 'the historical Jesus'. It is possible that St Paul had this passage in mind when he bade the Corinthian community to meet together, as though in his own presence, and execute upon the 'incestuous man' the judgment he had already passed upon him. The whole proceeding would be 'in the name of the Lord Jesus' and instinct with his 'power'. Whatever the original meaning of the parable of the 'prudent servant' (Mt. 24, 45-51; see C. H. Dodd, *Parables of the Kingdom*, pp. 158 ff) the early Christians probably understood the servant in question to be the representative, in the Church of the interim between the Resurrection of Christ and his Second Coming, of the 'absent' Lord.

identify the Church with her 'signs'. Or again, could we identify her with whatever social results this attraction has at any time produced among believers? This last suggestion approximates closely to Luther's more mature views upon the visible Church, as also to the minimal interpretation of which the Lambeth Conference's statement is susceptible. It can accept Maurice's description of sacraments, ministry, and so on, as 'signs' of the Kingdom of Christ, that is—in his terminology—signs of the Church; but it adds to this description the idea that these are signs tending to produce what they signify. However, it is hardly our task here to explain the theory of the Church as a potential society, but rather to ask for such an explanation, and to emphasise the fact that it is surely misleading to apply the term 'a society' and its related expressions, to what is only a potential society. For whatever may be the truth about the Church, it is certain that to hold that she is a society entails very different practical consequences from those which flow from the idea that essentially she is not more than a potential society.

We may sum up this discussion by remarking that there is one thing which a society cannot be: it cannot be a dissociated society; because this is a formal contradiction in terms. It may be loosely associated, or closely associated. The bond which it creates between its members may be the basis of much, or of little, common thought, common action and mutual love. And in these senses, the unity of a society is capable of greater or less perfection. But these degrees of perfection all presuppose the existence of the society itself; they all presuppose that the members of the society are associated in a common life. And if the society is a concrete historical society, not only an other-worldly entity or a purely interior grace, then the association in a common life is incompatible with what Christians have called schism.[20]

The notion of association is traditionally expressed in Christian language as 'communion' (koinonia), a word which goes back to New Testament times. There is communion between Christians when they mutually recognise their rights, as

[20] It may be observed that St Paul's use of the word 'schism' to describe disagreements short of external rupture is not the meaning which has become classical in Christian terminology, according to which schism, in the objective sense, is precisely such an external rupture.

members of a common whole, to share in specifically Christian activities in the liturgical order: *communio in sacris*. The high point of this sharing is of course common participation in the central Eucharistic rite (the *missa fidelium*) and in the Eucharistic meal. Participation in this rite and sacrament is not, in traditional thought. *common,* it does not serve to bind the participants into the divinely intended mutual association, if there is an external rupture such that those involved in the rupture are not recognised as having the right to participate in each other's Eucharist. On the traditional view, a 'schismatical' Eucharist, considered objectively, does not either constitute or tend to cement the universal communion of the Church.

In traditional usage, an individual Christian could, for more or less grave reasons, be lawfully deprived of the right to communicate at the Church's Eucharist. Such a one was 'excommunicated'. Whole local communities could be put under this ban. There is some reason to think that it was threatened by Bishop Victor I of Rome against all the communities of Asia Minor. When such a ban had been lawfully imposed and was disregarded to the extent that the 'excommunicated' local community continued to perform the sacred functions of the Church, there was the beginning of a 'schism'. If the Church is a concrete historical society, it is obvious, and it was taken for granted in Christian antiquity, that the activities of such a banned group could make no difference to the continuing existence of the one society whose ban had been disregarded, nor could it in any measure invalidate the acts of that one society before or after the schism.

What has just been said about Christian antiquity requires, of course, to be substantiated in later pages of this book. It is, however, hoped that enough has been said to show that it is a misuse of language to describe as belonging to one society two Christian communions which are, as communions or associations, divided from each other, and between which there is no mutual recognition of rights. It was humorous, but not strictly nonsensical, for the authors of *1066 and All That* to sum up the English Reformation in the words: 'Pius V left the Church of England.' It is something beyond humour when it is argued that the two Christian societies whose division from each other springs from the English Reformation are yet one society.

Chapter 4

THE EARLY COUNCILS (1)

Our review of post-Reformation ideas about the Church has disclosed three groups of answers to the question: Of what nature is the Church militant? At one extreme, there is the theory that she is a completely invisible reality: the invisible link which unites, in the eyes of God, those who are justified or those who are predestined to salvation. Opposed to this theory is the doctrine, propounded as is well known by Roman Catholics if not by some other Christian groups, which—without denying her spiritual aspect, and indeed while insisting upon this as her *raison-d'-être*—yet affirms that she is essentially a real historical entity and in fact a concrete historical society, so that fully active membership of the Church involves full 'communion' with her other active members (a society cannot exist in dissociation). Each of these 'extreme' views—the exclusively spritual theory, and the doctrine that the Church is a single historical society with a spiritual 'inner side'—is clearcut, easily conceived and stated, and (of course) manifestly distinguished from its opposite. Between these two there are various views which all affirm a certain exterior manifestation of the Church in history, yet deny that this constitutes her as essentially a society in the sense in which we have explained that term. Of these intermediate views, some appear to hold that an external unity of all believers is, in itself, a matter of indifference, while others urge that Christians *ought* to be externally united with one another in a single universal communion, so that external unity is of the *bene esse* but not of the *esse* of the Church—it is a goal towards which all Christians and all Christian societies or communions ought to be tending. Some of these intermediate views lay down certain conditions for 'reunion' (e.g. the acceptance of an episcopal ministry), whether on grounds of doctrine or of expediency. But they all agree that the Church in her

3

essence is only potentially a visible unity of intercommunicating members; potentially, and perhaps also ideally, a concrete historical society.

How is a Christian to choose between these varying views on the essential nature of the Church? By what criteria will he accept one of them and reject the other two? If God calls all men to membership of his Church, we cannot avoid the obligation of choice. And it seems clear that the alternatives stated are exhaustive; either the Church is purely invisible, or she is essentially a single historical society; or, if neither of these theories is true, she must be at least potentially a single historical society. The one point about which disagreement is impossible is, that the term Church connotes sociality, whether purely invisible, or actually visible, or potentially visible.

It might seem that the obvious answer to our question, for all except Liberal Protestants, Modernists, and Quakers, would be: Consider what Christ has taught us about the Church. But if this means referring the question to the verdict of 'the Jesus of history' (which would mean, in practice, the verdict of the *science of history*), it is an exhortation which it is not altogether easy to obey.

When we approach the New Testament books, and especially the Gospels, simply as ancient documents, on a par with the History of Thucydides or the Annals of Tacitus, we have to take account of the fact that critical scholarship has not made up its mind, and perhaps will never do so, about the details and extent of the contribution made to Christian origins by the historical Jesus. Part of the difficulty resides in the fact that there is practically nothing that historical science *can* know about Jesus except what is mediated to us through the faith of the primitive Church and her members. We see him through the eyes of the primitive Church, or we see him—virtually—not at all.[1] And it is an extremely delicate critical task to decide the extent to which the faith of the primitive Church and its current interests have affected the gospel tradition. This influence of the Church's mind is almost certainly present in the form, for instance, in which some of our Lord's parables and

---

The meagre references to Christ in such pagan writers as Tacitus may themselves derive from Christian informants. The references in Rabbinic literature may similarly depend on the allegations of the Christian 'heretics' (*minim*).

sayings have been preserved; and criticism has to take account of the possibility that some of the sayings may have been invented by primitive Christians and by them 'put onto the lips' of Jesus. This delicate task is one, it is probably true to say, that historians are not yet prepared to undertake except in very broad outline and with a large measure of conjecture and dispute. The 'quest of the historical Jesus' has indeed discovered the primitive Church; it has not yet discovered Jesus, if we are to trust pure criticism.

There is, it is true, another line of approach to the New Testament, and one no less valid for the believer than the purely critical approach. The books of the Bible are the official, sacred, literature of Christianity, and they are traditionally regarded as inspired by the Holy Ghost. They thus provide us not only with clues in a scientific process of historical detection, but with a norm for faith. They come to us with an authority other than, and superior to, the 'authority' of other ancient literature. Historians, to take a case in point, may dispute whether Jesus actually uttered the words: 'Upon this rock I will build my Church'; but, for the Christian, the fact that these words are attributed to Christ by the author of an inspired Gospel carries a religious weight which is, intrinsically, unaffected by the disagreements or hesitations of historians.

However, it is possible to agree that the Bible is inspired by the Holy Ghost, and to accept the inference that what the Bible tells us is true in the sense intended by the Holy Ghost, and yet to disagree profoundly about the content of the truth conveyed by the inspired books. Such disagreement has been the very stuff of theological controversy down the ages, and has been peculiarly evident since the Reformation. Nor has it, since that date, been confined to disagreement between Roman Catholics on the one hand and Protestants on the other. It has raged between Protestants themselves. Often, indeed, it is due to differences of theological approach—to unstated 'first principles'. But it has also an objective source. The truth which a document claims to convey is not necessarily the sort of scientific truth that is conveyed by the multiplication tables, by the axioms and postulates of Euclidean geometry, or by scholastic metaphysics. If there is one thing that stands out clearly about the New Testament books, it is that none of them asks to be measured by such scientific standards. Each of them belongs to some literary type, and uses the conventions appropriate to that type. To determine the literary types in question, to settle their respective conventions, and to apply the results thus obtained to the exegesis of the several books, is not the task of a casual half-hour, nor is the interpretation to which it leads likely to be incontrovertibly convincing. To this it has to be added that frequently we find ourselves asking, in theology, questions which the New Testament writers did not set out to answer. This does not prove that our questions are irrelevant or unimportant; it may suggest that they were not 'live issues' in the apostolic age. Thus, for instance, it could have been that no-one in that age would have thought of questioning that the Church is essentially a single society—just as, on the contrary, it might today be argued that Jesus could not possibly have entertained any idea of a visible Church.

I do not wish to appear excessively 'agnostic' about the witness of the New Testament. Granted some presuppositions which I think correct, I do not despair of the help which it may give us, and I propose, later on in these pages, to revert to the subject. But it has to be admitted that the required presuppositions would not be universally admitted. It therefore seems worthwhile, before examining the New Testament, to formulate a hypothesis, and on the basis of it to conduct an investigation in another field of data.

The hypothesis is that post-Biblical Christian history contains evidence of the nature of the Church as she was constituted by Jesus Christ. This suggestion is based on the fact, admitted by Christians, that Christ brought to mankind a final revelation and a final endowment of grace or of 'means of grace'; that, therefore, he established a religion that was to endure till his Second Coming. 'Behold I am with you all through the days that are coming, until the consummation of the world' (Mt. 28, 20.) This being so, it seems reasonable to suppose that this religion, divinely established and embodying Christ's grace and truth, has left some trace of itself in world history, and that this trace is likely to be most marked in the story of the particular complex of historical facts which is known by common consent as the Christian religion. So stated, the hypothesis does not seem to be an extravagant one. It is neither unduly narrow, since it does not pretend to *restrict* the 'traces' of Christ's grace and truth to what is usually regarded as the field of Christianity; nor is it prematurely precise, for it does not commit us before-hand to accept without criticism whatever we find in the Christian story as being positive evidence of Christ's intentions. It does not even preclude *a priori* the possibility that, at the end of our examination of the post-Biblical 'Christian fact', we might find ourselves obliged to admit that Christianity made complete shipwreck of the truth almost before the last apostle was dead. But we ought not to presuppose that this is so before examination of the facts.

In the ensuing investigation I shall take it for granted that the Church is a basic constituent of what Christ gave to mankind. I shall not assume any agreement about the right meaning to be given to the word 'Church'—beyond the very vague fact that it plainly refers to some social aspect of the Gospel or to some interior, invisible, social implication of the religion established by Christ. Our investigation will be concerned with the mean-ing actually attached to the word, to the content read into the idea, of the Church in Christian history.

The investigation, which will not be exhaustive but sufficient for our present purposes, will take place within a limited sector of Christian history. I do not propose to expatiate on the idea of the Church current in Western medieval Christianity. What that idea was is not seriously disputed. We may take, in illus-tration of it, a part of the teaching of Thomas Aquinas (thir-teenth century) on schism, which he regards as (objectively speaking) a sin, and treats as such. He says that the name of schism is given to a sin which is, directly and of its own nature, opposed to unity. What a man is doing when he commits the sin of schism is to separate himself from unity. Unity is an effect of charity. Charity, in fact, does not only link one individual with another individual by the spritual bond of love; it links the whole Church together in unity of spirit. Hence, the term 'schismatics' is properly applied to those who, of their own will and intent, separate themselves from the Church, which is the principal unity. Particular unities of some individuals with others are subordinate to the unity of the Church, just as the mutual interlocking of limbs in a physical body is subordinate to the unity of the whole body. The unity of the Church has a double expression: (a) in the mutual connection of the members of the Church, in other words communion (*communicatio*); (b) in the subordination of all the members of the Church to one head. . . . This head of the Church is Christ, whose role in the Church is played by the Pope. Hence the term 'schismatics' is applied to those who refuse to be subject to the Pope, and who will not have communion with the members of the Church who are subject to him. A schismatic as such wilfully disregards the commands of the Church, and refuses to submit to her judgment.[2]

It is clear from this passage that, for Aquinas, the Church is a visible historical society,[3] with visible interconnection between its members, and with a constitutional structure and a sovereign authority. The sovereign authority is Christ. But Christ is not present in the Church on earth under the modalities of actual historical kingship. He is like the householder in St Mark's Gospel: he has 'gone on a journey' from earth to heaven. And like the householder he has provided for the administration of his affairs on earth during his 'absence'; he has 'set his house in order'. Like the Queen when she goes on a foreign tour, he has appointed a regency. The Pope wields sovereign authority in the Church on Christ's behalf and as his representative, with authority delegated by Christ himself. We are not interested at the moment in the claim that it is in the Bishop of Rome that Christ's regency is vested. But we are interested in the idea of the regency, and in the idea that this regency 'brings down to earth' the unitary and all-embracing authority of Christ over the Church. And we are interested in the contention that to withhold obedience from the regency is to offend directly against that unity of the Church which is the effect of Christian charity. We are interested in these matters, because they show that for Thomas Aquinas, the Church is a concrete historical society, indissociable by its essence. And we quote him, not for the light than can be gained on the subject of his personal convictions, but as a witness to the Western medieval notion of the Church.

The Reformation, however, developed as a protest against medieval superstitions and corruptions of the Gospel. A move-

---

[2] *Summa Theologica*, 2a 2ae, xxxix, 1.

[3] The Pope acts for Christ in the Church. Obviously, the Church in which he acts is the visible Church, the Church militant here on earth.

ment which did not shrink from rejecting Transubstantiation, a dogma that had behind it the authority of the Ecumenical Council of the Lateran (A.D. 1215) would not be likely to bow to the authority of Thomas Aquinas.

I therefore propose to go back behind the Middle Ages, and indeed behind the year A.D. 1054, usually counted as the date of consummation of the great and tragic breach between the Christian East and West. And we will start from a period before the still earlier ruptures between the Chalcedonians and the Monophysites and between the Nestorians and the Imperial Church. We might take as a convenient date the accession of the Emperor Theodosius I (A.D. 379) and the First Ecumenical Council of Constantinople (A.D. 381). The Church of that Council is the Church from which all our present forms of Christianity trace their descent; in those days all our forefathers were members of a single communion.[4]

The condition of Christendom in the time of Theodosius was not unlike its condition today, inasmuch as Christians were divided up into a number of separate bodies. There was the Great Church, itself going through crises of communion. But alongside it there were numerous other 'churches': the Montanists, the Novatianists, the Donatists, the incipient Arian or semi-Arian bodies to which the barbarian invaders of the Empire tended to adhere. For our immediate purposes, what is important, is that of all these bodies, only one has left progeny to the present day. All of us, Eastern Orthodox, Copts and Nestorians, Roman Catholics, Anglicans and Protestants are descended from the Great Church which became 'established' under Theodosius I as the official religion of the Roman Empire. If we can determine the ideas about the Church established by Christ, which were the common property of the members of the Great Church of the closing years of the fourth century, we shall have discovered the ideas which stand between all of us and the first origins of Christianity.

[4] This is a slightly idealised picture of the situation at the moment of Thedosius' accession to power. The long agony of the Arian troubles was only drawing to its close, and it was not till 382 that a legation sent to Rome by a second synod at Constantinople secured for the new Bishop of Constantinople the communion of his brother (Damasus) of Rome. The fact of communion was thus established. Its foundation—whether in unity of faith or alternatively in recognition by the See of Rome—was not understood in the same way in the East as at Rome. Cf. Batiffol, *Le Siège Apostolique*, pp. 141, 273-8.

Before embarking on this task it may be well to remind ourselves of a warning uttered by that great exponent of the 'appeal to history', J. H. Newman:

> For myself, I would simply confess that no doctrine of the Church can be rigorously proved by historical evidence: but at the same time that no doctrine can be simply disproved by it. Historical evidence reaches a certain way, more or less, towards a proof of the Catholic doctrines; often nearly the whole way; sometimes it goes only so far as to point in their direction; sometimes there is only an absence of evidence for a conclusion contrary to them; nay, sometimes there is an apparent leaning of the evidence to a contrary conclusion, which has to be explained.[5]

To apply this passage to our own concern, we may say that we are not to expect a clear, unanimous and explicit adherence of the whole of Christian antiquity to an accurate definition and elaboration of the idea of the Church. Our question is rather: In what direction does the mass of the evidence point? And here another quotation from Newman is relevant:

> I will address one word to Chillingworth and his friends—Let them consider, that if they can criticize history, the facts of history can certainly retort upon them. It might, I grant, be clearer on this great subject than it is. This is no great concession. History is not a creed or a catechism, it gives lessons rather than rules; still no one can mistake its general teaching on this matter, whether he accept it or stumble at it. Bold outlines and broad masses of colour rise out of the records of the past. They may be dim, they may be incomplete; but they are definite.[6]

Is the history of Christian antiquity 'definite' upon the broad issue whether the Church is a visible society?

The answer of a Roman Catholic to this question might well be suspected of *parti pris*. I therefore give here the judgments of some non-Roman-Catholic scholars.

The late A. J. Mason, in his essay *Concepts of the Church in Early Times*, has a section entitled: 'The Church was the visible organization which bears that name.' In it he writes:

---

[5] *Difficulties of Anglicans*, Vol. ii, p. 312. By 'doctrine of the Church' Newman means, in the context, doctrine taught by the (Roman Catholic) Church. His statement can, however, be applied to the doctrine that the Church is a visible society, or to any other notion of the Church. It should be added, that of course Newman does not mean that there is no way of reaching certainty about Christian doctrine; but only that the appeal to history by itself is inadequate.

[6] *An Essay on the Development of Doctrine*, p. 7. 'This great subject' was the nature of Christianity as delivered to their converts by the Apostles.

We must proceed to ask whether the fellowship thus (sc. by the word *ecclesia*, Church) denoted was the historical—the 'empiric' body which passes under the name, or whether it is an ideal quantity, whose very existence is known only by faith. In this enquiry the modern scholar is aided by a very remarkable work. The publication of Rudolf Sohm's *Kirchenrecht* may be said to mark an epoch in the study of the doctrine of the Church. The theory set forth in it has not been left uncriticised, but on certain points the assertions of Sohm will hardly be called in question again.

In this work and its sequel Sohm has shown clearly that the distinction between the Church as a religious conception and the Church as a concrete institution . . . was wholly unknown to the Christians of early times. 'Early Christianity had not, indeed, an explicit doctrine of the visible nature of the Church in the religious sense; but in an instinctive and naive fashion the visible community of Christians, as such, was identified with the fellowship of the saints, the elect, the children of God who are led by His Spirit'.

The notion of an invisible Church of the Predestinate, Sohm says, came into men's minds before many centuries after Christ had elapsed. Augustine,[7] Wiclif entertained it. But Luther was the first to whom the contrast between the two things became a religious certainty. No one before Luther had been able to emancipate himself in conscience from the visible Church. Until his time the opposition between the true Church of Christ and the corporate society did not exist, so far as the practical life of Christendom was concerned. All antiquity from the first century to the end of the Middle Ages had failed to draw the sharp and ruthless line of demarcation which ought to be drawn. It was not in a position to do so.

It will be noted that Mason, by implication, associates himself with the views of Sohm as stated above. Later in his essay, he discusses the Church's ancient title of 'Catholic' and remarks:

It must not be supposed that when the Church was called . . . the Catholic Church, the existence of other Churches was implied which were not Catholic. The language of the New Testament held sway over men's minds, and they could not bring themselves to use the word 'Church' in the plural except in a local signification. It did not enter into their thoughts that there could be separate connexions and widely ramifying unions of Christians, to each of

[7] For a different interpretation of Augustine, see Chapter 7 *infra*. For Mason's essay, see *Early History of the Church and Ministry*, ed. H. B. Swete.

which the name Church might be given. Both on the one side
and the other such a use of terms would have been rejected.
From our modern point of view we may speak of the Marcionite
Church or the Montanist Church, or the Novatianist Church,
standing side by side with the Catholic Church, but this was not
the nomenclature of early days. Each body of Christians in its
turn claimed to be the Church, and by so doing denied the claim
of the rest. . . .

Alike at Rome and at Alexandria, in Africa and in the East,
men believed in a great spiritual community, founded by Christ,
through his Spirit working in the Apostles, to which all the
promises of the Old Testament were attached. This community
was necessarily unique. In it, and in it alone, the gifts and graces
of the Spirit of Christ were to be looked for. . . . Nor was this
community an intangible thing. It was a reality of experience,
embodied in a practical discipline. The society was well known and
unmistakable. . . . It had an organised hierarchy for worship
and for the pastorate of souls. This hierarchy maintained unity
between the local branches, and did so in the name and by the
authority of Christ. However far back the history is traced, no
date can be assigned, however roughly, for the appearance of
Catholicism in the Church. The Church was Catholic from the
outset.[8]

With these judgments of Sohm and Mason we may compare
some observations of the great Liberal Protestant scholar
Harnack, who affirms that to speak of the Church is to speak of

assembly, assembly of the called and chosen as a unity; and
this involves a social element, a social element realised already
here on earth, since in the midst of the world the called are the
Church of God and as such have community with one another.
. . . To combine together is not, for those who invoke the name
of Christ, something secondary or inessential in relation to the
idea of the Church; that idea demands such combining together,
and is only realised thereby.[9]

And of the new notions introduced at the Reformation he
writes: 'The Reformation did not only destroy the medieval

[8] Mason's findings are restricted to the Church before A.D. 325. He did not
therefore have to consider whether, for instance, Augustine's views on the
Church, and, in particular, on the validity of sacraments administered outside
the Catholic communion, can be reconciled with the witness of the first three
centuries. See Chapter 7 *infra*.
[9] *Entstehung und Entwicklung der Kirchenverfassung und des Kirchenrechts
in den Zwei Ersten Jahrhunderten*, p. 149.

structure of the Church, but retains also no connexion with the structure of the Church in the second and first century.'[10]

Sohm, Harnack and Mason are weighty names. We may add to them that of C. H. Turner, who wrote of the patristic period:

> There was complete agreement as to the doctrine of the Catholic Church, the visible fellowship of the disciples, the Body of Christ. The separatist communities, at least from the middle of the third century onwards, had with the idea of the Church no quarrel: for the most part the *rationale* of their separate organization was that each of them claimed in turn for itself to be the true embodiment of this unique society.

And of the Fathers of the Great Church, from Irenaeus to Augustine, he remarked: 'On the supreme duty of communion with the visible fellowship of the brethren in the one true fold of the Redeemer there was no shadow of wavering, however many the representatives, or however various the types and local expressions, of the Christian tradition.'[11]

Similar statements can be quoted from contemporary scholars. Thus Dr Greenslade writes:

> The Fathers, together with most early heretics and schismatics, were substantially agreed upon certain principles regarding the unity of the Church. It was held on biblical grounds not simply that the Church ought to be one, but that it is one, and cannot but be one. This unity was predicated of the visible Church, and the visible Church was thought of organically, as one structure, one communion . . . bodies separated from that communion were outside the Church.[12]

With this passage may be compared the following from an unsigned article in the *Oxford Dictionary of the Christian Church* (s.v. *Church*): 'In early times the doctrine of the visible unity of the Church was accepted on all sides. The schismatic bodies which arose (Melitians, Donatists, Monophysites) all considered themselves the whole Church . . . the Reformation led to a reformulation of the idea of the Church.'

It would seem superfluous, in view of such judgments from the pens of scholars who are not Roman Catholics (or Eastern Orthodox), to review the total evidence of the first Christian

[10] Ibid. p. 120.
[11] In *Early History of the Church and Ministry*, ed. H. B. Swete, pp. 194 f.
[12] *Schism in the Early Church*, p. 18.

centuries on the subject of the Church. It may, however, be useful to try to illustrate the operation of the idea that the Church is a single visible society in the story of the great Ecumenical Councils of the fourth and fifth centuries.

A long and disastrous chapter in the relations of Church and State was closed when Theodosius I issued his decree of February 28th, 380, to the people of Constantinople:

> Our will is that all people subject to our merciful sway should be of that religion which the blessed apostle Peter conveyed to the Romans, even as the religion still propagated by him declares, that religion which, as is well known, the pontiff Damasus observes, as does Peter of Alexandria, a man of apostolic sacredness. This religion bids us, in accordance with apostolic authority and evangelical teaching, believe in one Godhead of Father and Son and Holy Ghost in equal majesty and in holy trinity.

A second law, of January 10th, 381, after proscribing places of heretical worship, enjoins perpetual observance of the Nicene faith.

This mention of the 'Nicene faith' carries our minds back to the whole stormy story of the Great Church from the early days of what historians, with some irony, call 'the peace of Constantine'.

Few episodes in political history have been of greater moment for the earthly fortunes of Christianity than the *volte face* whereby, in the early days of the reign of Constantine the Great, Christianity became officially a licit religion. The persecution initiated by Diocletian had been anything but a piece of irrational savagery. It was a logical consequence of the conviction, deeply rooted in ancient political thought, that the State is omnicompetent, so that religion could claim no immunity from the control of the political sovereign. The Roman Emperor was not only the head of the army and the government. He was *pontifex maximus*, the supreme priest of all State religion. To those responsible for the conduct of Roman political affairs the Christians, obstinately practising a religion that was not recognised by the State, and obstinately refusing to practise the State religion, inevitably seemed like adherents of a chronic rebellion.

When Christianity became a licit religion it was automatically assumed by the imperial authorities that the government's relations with it would be of the same nature as its relations had been with paganism. And in so far as Constantine's purpose was not merely to tolerate but to patronise Christianity, if not to adopt it as the religion *par excellence* of the Empire, it could not occur to him that disagreements among the members of the Great Church were a matter of political indifference. These disagreements were not slow in manifesting themselves, and at a very early date we find him attempting to deal with the incipient Donatist schism of Africa.

A second dispute arose to mar the splendour of his final victory over his Eastern rival Licinius and the definitive establishment of his monarchical rule in the early twenties of the fourth century. Alexander, Bishop of Alexandria, had excommunicated one of his priests, Arius by name, and a number of Arius's party, for their refusal to accept the bishop's own teaching on the subject of the divine nature of Christ. But Arius had found wide support among the Eastern bishops, and especially enjoyed that of Bishop Eusebius of the capital city, Nicomedia. By early in A.D. 325 the whole East was aflame with the controversy.

The Emperor's first efforts were to persuade Arius and Alexander to sink their differences, as being concerned with subtleties of theology that ought not to be allowed to shatter the harmony of the Christian world. He addressed a letter to them both:

> I understand that . . . you, Alexander, asked the opinion of your priests . . . upon a point of insignificant detail; and that you, Arius, gave rash expression to a reflexion which ought not to have been entertained in thought, or, if entertained, ought not to have been made public. Hence arose discord leading to the refusal of communion, the rending of the holy people, to the detriment of the harmony of this same body. . . . Never should such questions have been asked and answered. . . . Such investigations ought not to be lightly . . . entrusted to the ears of the people. . . . You know well that philosophers of the same school often disagree on some particular point of their system, and that these disagreements do not prevent them from maintaining among themselves the unity of doctrine.

What could be more statesmanlike than these comments? All down the ages politicians have thought or said as much. What is a point of dogma, compared with external ecclesiastical harmony (and political peace)? Why, in a famous phrase, split the civilised world for the sake of a diphthong?

But the point at issue was, as we can see today, the Godhead of Christ (and, ultimately, monotheism itself), and it soon became clear to Constantine or to his advisers that something more must be done if harmony among the Christians was indeed imperative.

Already in the third century local councils of bishops had met, either (as in the East) occasionally, to deal with some incidental emergency, or regularly, as in the West. To deal with the Arian emergency it would surely be fitting that Christianity's new standing in the Empire should be manifested in a council representing the whole Christian world, an 'ecumenical' council. Under imperial patronage such a council was in fact convened, and it met at Nicaea, near Nicomedia, in the late spring of A.D. 325, though its 'ecumenicity' was rather in idea than in material fact. Those attending it were but a small minority of the whole episcopal body. In particular the West, which had been almost untouched by the doctrinal controversy, was very poorly represented, though the Emperor's personal religious adviser, Bishop Ossius of Cordoba, took a leading part, and the Bishop of Rome was represented by two priests.

Constantine himself addressed the opening session, and assured the bishops that he feared war no more than he did any 'sedition within the Church of God'. The two greatest powers in the ancient world, Christianity and the Empire, thus met for the first time in a 'summit' conference. It was an historic moment.

Arius, it is important to realise, was not a sheer innovator. His teaching, that the Son of God had begun to be, before times and ages, by the will and purpose of the Father, that he was indeed 'perfect God, unique Son, unchangeable', but that 'before being begotten or created or established he was not, for he was not unbegotten', could point to many precedents in earlier theological thinking and writing. In its own day it found, as has been said, many episcopal sympathisers. Yet, when it came to the point, the Council found no difficulty in condemning Arius and his errors.

The question, however, was whether mere condemnation was enough. Was not some positive statement of the orthodox faith called for? The Council directed its attention to this problem. But was it possible to frame a suitable statement, one that excluded Arianism without going beyond traditional, even scriptural, language? The trouble was that the followers of Arius were prepared to accept everything that Scripture said about Christ, professing to find it not inconsistent with their own theology of the Trinity. Bishop Eusebius of Caesarea, the great ecclesiastical historian, hitherto a patron of Arius, put forward the baptismal Creed of his own local church; but this also was judged inadequate. In the end, a traditional Creed was adopted, but it was given precision by some insertions, of which the most important were that God the Son was declared to be 'of the substance' of the Father and 'consubstantial' with him.

The word 'consubstantial' was destined to become the war cry of the orthodox party in the subsequent struggle for the soul of Christendom. But of course it could not be found within the pages of the Bible; it was an innovation. It seems that the majority of the Eastern bishops viewed the term with suspicion, and in fact it left the orthodox flank open, if not to Arian subordinationism, at least to what we should now call Sabellianism. But the Emperor let it be known that the term had his support (it may be doubted whether he understood its implications), and an Arian historian tells us that he threatened to exile any bishops or other clergy who refused to accept it. In the end, the Nicene Creed received the signature of all the bishops present at the Council except two. These two were in fact exiled to Illyricum.

The Creed was immediately followed by what we should call a canon: 'The Catholic Church anathematizes those who say (of the Son of God): There was (a time) when he did not exist; Before being begotten he did not exist; He came into existence out of what was non-existent; He was of a *hypostasis* or substance other (than the Father's); He was created; or Changeable; or Subject to alteration.'

Such, in brief, was the story of the doctrinal decisions of the first Ecumenical Council. One does not need to be a Christian to see that the Arian heresy raised a question of fundamental importance for believers. To say that the Godhead of Christ was at stake is less than the truth. What was really at stake was monotheism, Christianity's supreme heirloom from the Old

Testament, and the key to the possibility of reconciling the faith with philosophy. Christ had been worshipped as God from time immemorial: 'Thomas answered (Jesus), Thou art my lord and my God' (Jn. 20, 28). The Arians did not propose to abolish such worship; Arius himself, as we have seen, could describe the Son of God as 'perfect God'. But Arius would have combined this traditional devotional and cultic attitude with a theological explanation which, when all the terminology is fully weighed, puts the Son in his heavenly nature definitively on the creatures' side of the gulf that divides every finite reality from the divine Absolute. If Christianity had followed where Arius led, or if it had been content to tolerate Arianism within its own borders, it would have become the founder or patron of a new, and superficially attractive, polytheism. Things have turned out otherwise, and in actual historical fact our gratitude for this escape is owed to the Fathers of Nicaea. They saved Christianity from the greatest hazard it had had to face since the so-called Council of Jerusalem (Ac. 15). But what of the means they employed?

Obviously, Arius and 'his errors' had to be condemned. On this point Alexander the bishop had been right, and the Emperor had been wrong. But once again, would condemnation by itself have sufficed? The term 'consubstantial' became the object of a bitter hostility. But behind the conservative dislike of a new word, using—it may be argued—this dislike as an ally and a cloak—there were theological and philosophical tendencies which we can only consider as irreconcilable with the Gospel. Traditional theology was not equipped to meet such a threat; it was itself, in some of its currents, deeply affected by a doctrine of the 'Logos' which was nearer to Philo's Hellenistic Judaism than to St John's Gospel. Nor was the bare letter of Scripture an adequate retort; as has been said, Arianism could quote Scripture to its purpose. The Nicene Creed however could not be interpreted in an Arian sense. And so it was against the standard-bearers of the 'consubstantial', and in the end against the Nicene word itself, that sympathisers with Arianism came to direct their main assault. And despite the newness of the word, despite its somewhat Sabellian potentialities, it was behind the 'consubstantial' and its champions—Athanasius of Alexandria and the occupants of the See of Rome—that the forces of orthodoxy at last rallied and triumphed.

The Nicene Creed, however, was strong not only with the strength of truth. It was reinforced by the anathematism (see above).

To 'anathematise' was, of course, to excommunicate, to expel from the fellowship of the Church.[13] But the word is heavily charged with a meaning that is more than merely juridical; it is a word of profound religious significance. The noun 'anathema' had been taken over by primitive Christianity (cf. e.g. Rom. 9, 3) from the Septuagint Greek version of the Old Testament, where it translated the Hebrew *herem*, a 'banned thing'. To 'ban' an object (or a person) was to remove it altogether from human use and barter, and to devote it to annihilation;[14] and this as a religious act, performed by the sacred assembly of the People of God or by its representatives. Thus the Christian anathematism did indeed excommunicate, but in doing so it claimed to remove its object from the sphere of salvation.

For early Christianity these two effects of an anathema were in fact one, since the Church was believed to be 'the ark of Noe', outside which there was 'no salvation'.[15] And the Fathers of the Council, in pronouncing the anathematism, claim to be the mouthpieces of the Church: 'The Catholic Church anathematizes. . . .' There is here no hint of a distinction between the Church founded by Christ and the visible communion of the Great Church. Other Christian communions of course were known to exist, but they had no representatives in the membership of the Council. The language of the Council implies that these other communions were not part of the Church.[16]

---

[13] When the object of the anathematism is not personal but a doctrine or a heresy, to anathematise means to proclaim incompatible with the true faith.

[14] *Theolog. Wörterbuch zum N.T.*, s.v. *Anathema*.

[15] 'Let no one deceive himself: outside this house, that is, outside the Church, no one is saved' (Origen, *hom. in Iesu Nave*, iii, 5). These homilies are preserved only in Rufinus's Latin translation, and Rufinus sometimes 'improves' on his original. But for the sense, cf. Cyprian, *Ep.* 73, 21: 'Salvation outside the Church does not exist.' It is important to observe that the principle that 'outside the Church there is no salvation' is still maintained by the Roman Catholic Church (and indeed by all Christians, according to their definition of the Church), but that, as will be argued at greater length later in this book (see Chapter 9), its practical implications are modified by the recognition of 'good faith' in those who are not members of the Church.

[16] A Novatianist bishop was present at the Council under the aegis of the Emperor; but it looks as though he had come to seek reconciliation with the Catholic Church. For an earlier example of conciliar anathematism, cf. the Council of Elvira, canon 52: *Hi qui inventi fuerint libellos famosos in ecclesiis ponere anthematizentur*; this was a disciplinary canon.

The Council of Nicaea, with the help of its subsequent champions, not only saved Christianity from the quagmire of polytheism. It manifested, in a historical gesture and at a great moment in human history, when the Church had just emerged from civil proscription and was on the way to becoming established as the official religion of the Roman Empire, that Christianity has a living voice and can articulate its beliefs. It also showed incidentally, or rather it discovered for itself and then proclaimed, that the Bible is not a sufficient 'rule of faith' without the developments that only defined 'dogma' can guarantee. All this it did, and could only do, because it was possessed by the conviction that the Church established by Christ is a human, historical, concrete society, and that therefore Christian communions outside that one visible communion are no parts of the Church.[17]

In defining the 'consubstantial' and in condemning Arius and those who shared his heterodoxy, the Council had exercised what amounted to authority in teaching (*magisterium*) and to jurisdiction in respect of the faith of the Church's members. But its historical importance is not confined to the doctrinal sphere: it also enacted twenty disciplinary canons. 'Hitherto the Church had had no collection (of enactments) resembling a disciplinary code. She had traditions; she showed loyalty to ancient usages. When new problems emerged, local councils dealt with them, but their decisions had only local authority. . . . But the canons of Nicaea were accepted everywhere and at once. They became the nucleus of ecclesiastical law.'[18] The problems which called for these canons were, however, problems of the moment; there was no effort to compile a *corpus* of canon law. We may here advert to a few points of interest for our enquiry.

Canon 2, concerning premature ordination of converts, concludes: 'He who acts contrary (to this canon) will run the risk

---

[17] The word 'consubstantial', though not scriptural, was not entirely untraditional. It had been employed, in the middle of the third century, by Bishop Dionysius of Rome, and had been accepted from him, with some reluctance, by his namesake of Alexandria. Unfortunately, it had also enjoyed the patronage of the heretical Paul of Samosata. It is difficult to explain its introduction to the Council of Nicaea and its acceptance into the Creed, except on the supposition that it was a Western contribution offered, e.g. by Ossius or the legates of the Bishop of Rome, or by both. Constantine gave it his support; but he must have got it from somewhere.

[18] Bardy, in Fliche et Martin, *Histoire de l'Eglise*, Vol. iii, p. 91.

of losing his clerical status, for disregarding (this) great Council.'
It would be too much to say that, at this early date, the distinction between the validity and the liceity of Holy Orders was
clear. But the canon shows an awareness that the clergy, as
representing a visible society, must be under the juridical control
of the visible Church. So, too, Canon 4 provides that a bishop
should be consecrated by not less than three of the bishops of
his province, and that the metropolitan bishop has the right to
confirm the appointment.

Canon 5 affirms that a person excommunicated by one bishop
must not be received into communion by others. It provides,
however, for a review of such sentences, by the provincial
council of bishops. This canon is inspired by the deep, traditional conviction that communion, though it normally comes
under the jurisdiction of the bishop of a local church, is essentially communion with the whole Catholic society. A lawful
sentence of excommunication, though fulminated by a particular bishop, expels its victim from the communion of the
Church at large. The Church is not a federation of autonomous
mystic *thiasoi*; it is a universal society with local embodiments.

Canon 8 legislates for the reconciliation of Novatianists
(Katharoi, as they were called in the East) who may wish to
join the Catholic communion: 'Concerning the Katharoi who
turn to the catholic and apostolic Church, the great and holy
Council resolved. . . .' The Novatianists had left the Great
Church (they themselves would have put it the other way round)
in disgust at its leniency towards those who had lapsed during
persecution and had then repented. The Council has no doubt
that they are outside 'the catholic and apostolic Church'.
Individuals from among their clergy will only be reconciled if
they state in writing that they will conform to 'the decisions of
the catholic and apostolic Church' on the questions which divide
the two communions.

A society, as was pointed out in a previous chapter, cannot
exist without rules, though the rules may be largely unwritten.
The canons of Nicaea were intended and received as written
rules for the society which called itself the Catholic Church. We
may say that the Church seized the first opportunity she had
had since the fall of Jerusalem to formulate her common mind
on the matter of rules, and the result was the birth of Canon

Law.[19] Canon Law is attractive to no one except canon lawyers. Its only justification is that which also justifies the law of the civil State: that without law the common life is impossible. What is, from our present point of view, of interest in these canons of Nicaea is that in their implications, and in their choice of language, they confirm the thesis that the Fathers of the Council believed the Church to be a visible society, of which they were governmental representatives. They spoke as holding indisputable authority in 'the catholic Church'. They identified this Catholic Church with their own communion on the one hand and with the Church established by Jesus Christ on the other. If their understanding of the Church's nature is correct, it does not exist as more than one communion. And they believed that, in Cyprian's words, 'outside it there is no salvation'.

We have not had to give much attention to another aspect of the Council of Nicaea, in which, however, it takes on a rather sinister significance. The whole story of the genesis and convocation, the conduct and the consequences, of the Council can be seen as an important episode in the new relations between the Church and the State. It is not likely that the Council would have been held without the positive co-operation and encouragement of the Emperor. Against his will, it could not have met and transacted its business. It was pressure from him that brought the doctrinal issue to a decision. And the resultant *dogmata* were given not only the sanction of a spiritual excommunication but the civil sanction of exile. This Emperor would shortly transfer his favour from the 'consubstantialists' to their bitter enemies, from one of whom, Eusebius of Nicomedia (later, of Constantinople, Constantine's New Rome) he would receive baptism in his last illness. The implications of Constantine's share in the Council may have been too little noticed by most of those who rejoiced at the defeat of Arius; they were not lost upon the bishop of Nicomedia.

The doctrinal content of the Nicene Creed has not been our direct concern. But indirectly, it is of the greatest importance

---

[19] There is, I think, some evidence that in the persecution period 'rules' had been known to emanate from the See of Rome. At least, Eusebius informs us that Victor I, bishop of Rome about the end of the second century A.D., threatened to excommunicate the churches of Asia Minor unless they conformed to the general custom for determining the date of Easter. It has been maintained that Eusebius misrepresents the facts of this case, but, cf. my 'Eusebius and St Victor', *Downside Review*, Autumn 1951.

for the purposes of this enquiry. The 'great synod' of Nicaea was the first of many ecumenical councils. It had to settle an issue which lies at the heart of the Christian gospel: was the Christ whom Christians worshipped really God? What we have tried to show here is that there is, implicit in its conciliar action and in the modalities of that action, the conviction that the essential unity of the Church is a visible unity, the unity of the visible Church; and that the visible Church was, for the Fathers of Nicaea, 'one structure, one communion', so that 'bodies separated from that communion were outside the Church'.[20] When Christians today, in their liturgical worship or their theological conferences, recite the 'Nicene Creed', proclaiming their faith in a Son of God consubstantial with God the Father, they owe that formula—one of the treasures from the past which we all today share in common—to the conviction concerning the nature of the Church which was implicit and operative in the Council's proceedings.

[20] Greenslade, quoted *supra*, p. 59.

Chapter 5

THE EARLY COUNCILS (2)

Our examination of the story of the Council of Nicaea has shown that the group of bishops there assembled spoke, in their decisions, as representing the Church established by Christ, implicitly identified by them with their own communion. The Council's verdict on the doctrinal issue raised by Arianism, its *dogma*, settled the central point of the Christian religion: Christianity is, and was to remain, true to its monotheistic inheritance from the Old Testament, and the cult of Jesus is not inconsistent with such monotheism, since, as Son of God, Jesus is consubstantial with his heavenly Father. The means adopted to this end took the form of (*a*) proscribing various Arian expressions, (*b*) imposing on the conscience and faith of all the Church's members a word (the 'consubstantial') which is not found in Scripture and was unpopular with many who were basically orthodox in their belief; this word was regarded by the Fathers of the Council as inevitable if their dogmatic purpose was to be accomplished, and in fact it became, in the next half-century, the touchstone of Christological orthodoxy. The proscription of Arian errors took the form of anathematisation, which means exclusion of the professors of such errors from the one and only Church, and so exclusion from the sphere of salvation in Christ.[1] The Council further, in its canons, enacted laws which were to be obligatory for the Church as a whole; it shows no consciousness of any idea that local bishops or regional churches have complete autonomy or that the whole Church of Christ lacks authority or means to determine the details of its universal life.

The forty years from shortly after the death of Constantine to the accession of Theodosius I were a period of ecclesiastical

---

[1] As has been pointed out, this 'exclusion' from salvation has to be interpreted in the light of the notion of 'good faith'. Doctrinal error, held in good faith, does not necessarily entail loss of 'sanctifying grace'.

chaos. The virtual unanimity (on paper) of the Council of Nicaea had covered profound differences and anxieties which were not slow in disclosing themselves. We look back to Nicaea as the first, and in some ways the most glorious, of a series of ecumenical councils; and for centuries prior to the Reformation the doctrinal decisions of such councils had been regarded as final and without appeal. Only by an effort of the imagination can we appreciate the fact that the fourth century had no precedents by which to mould its attitude to the findings of the 'great synod'. There were many who had no intention of doctrinal disloyalty but were nevertheless prepared, in the immediately succeeding decades, to question and even to reject the 'consubstantial'. Arius, we have to remind ourselves once again, was not a mere innovator; there had been currents in previous theological thought which could seem to point to his rather brash and clear-cut conclusions.

The divisive influence of theological differences was exacerbated in this period, and was indeed in some measure caused, by the policies of the State. The Empire was tending to drift asunder into a Western and an Eastern zone, each controlled and administered by its own Emperor, who by no means always agreed with the policies of his colleague. It was unfortunate for the Church that the political line of demarcation followed closely the linguistic and cultural line, which again coincided so closely with the line between the theological East with its centrifugal tendencies and the practical West, whose unification under the lead of the Roman See was, if anything, increasing.

The most disastrous period of all, however, was the decade in the middle of the century when Constantius was sole Emperor and used all his influence and power to impose unity of faith and communion on the basis of a State-approved doctrinal compromise between the orthodox and their Arian or semi-Arian opponents. His death in 361 was followed in the West by a Catholic reaction, led by the Roman See and supported by Athanasius of Alexandria. In the East, the Emperor Valens pursued the ecclesiastical policy of Constantius. There was a strong movement towards orthodoxy taking shape in the East, but the relations between the two halves of Christendom became almost inextricably embroiled by Rome's support of

Alexandria in an unfortunate alliance with Paulinus, the orthodox, but intruded, bishop of a small group in Antioch.

Broadly speaking, it may be said of this mid-fourth-century period, that it was a time of the gravest peril for three closely interrelated Christian values: the autonomy of the Church in face of the State; unity of faith; and unity of communion. The condition of the Eastern half of the Church in the concluding phase of this long agony is illustrated by the fact that when, in 379, the Catholics of the city of Constantinople were given an administrator in the person of Gregory of Nazianzum, they were in possession of only one of the city's churches, and the See of the bishop had been occupied by Arians for forty years. Gregory turned a private house into a place of worship for his flock.

But there was the promise of better times. Under the Catholic Emperor Theodosius I a great council of the Eastern bishops was summoned, and met in the capital city in 381. Retrospectively, this council has been given the title and prestige of an ecumenical council, the second of the seven recognised as such by both Eastern Orthodoxy and the West today. But it was attended only by bishops from the East; the Bishop of Rome himself seems not to have been invited, and sent no representative. In fact, the difficulty caused by the existence of two Bishops of Antioch, one recognised by the orthodox Eastern episcopate, the other by Rome, was now complicated by Rome's reluctance to acknowledge the Eastern promotion, first of Gregory and after his retirement, of Nectarius, to the See of Constantinople.

However, there was no question about the orthodoxy of the Council of Constantinople. We are told that, while adhering to the Nicene faith, it published no Creed of its own; but there survive four canons issued by its authority. The first of these enjoins that 'the faith of the three hundred and eighteen Fathers who met at Nicaea in Bithynia . . . is to remain in force, and every heresy is to be anathematised; especially that of the Eunomians or Anomaeans, and that of the Arians or Eudoxians; also that of the Semi-arians or Pneumatomachi, and that of the Sabellians, and that of the Marcellians, and that of the Photinians, and that of the Apollinarians'. The list is a painful commentary on the troubles of the previous period. One notes again the use of the pregnant word 'to anathematize', which on this occasion takes as its object not the persons adhering to false opinions, but the opinions themselves. The second canon represents a stage in the modelling of the ecclesiastical organisation in the Eastern Empire according to the administrative divisions of the Empire itself; it was perhaps motivated in part by hostility to the See of Alexandria. The third canon enjoins that the Bishop of Constantinople is to enjoy 'the privilege of honour after the Bishop of Rome, because Constantinople is the New Rome'; this was perhaps, in intention, less a trespass on the unique position of Rome than a blow to the pretentions of Alexandria, which was traditionally the second See of Christendom. The fourth canon repudiates the claims of one Maximus (supported for a time, unfortunately, by no less a person than Ambrose of Milan) to be bishop of Constantinople; it 'invalidates' all his clerical creations.

For our purpose, little more needs to be said about the second Ecumenical Council. Shortly after its closure, the new Bishop of Constantinople, Nectarius, received letters of communion from the Bishop of Rome. And when Paulinus, whom Rome had so unwisely recognised as Bishop of Antioch, died, he was given no successor in his own line, and at last both East and West were in agreement as to the lawful occupant of that great See.

The Council of Ephesus (A.D. 431) ranks as the third Ecumenical Council (it is to be carefully distinguished from the council, also held at Ephesus, of 449, which posed as ecumenical but has gone down to history as the *latrocinium*, (the 'robber band'). The story which came to a climax in 431 has a human aspect in which there is much to deplore. It can be seen as a phase in the long disedifying struggle between the Sees of Constantinople and Alexandria. It is possible to feel some sympathy with Alexandria in its dislike of an upstart See whose real eminence was due to political rather than to ecclesiastical circumstances. But it is, on the other hand, with some distaste that one observes the methods employed to humiliate Constantinople by the great Doctor of the Church Cyril of Alexandria, an 'up-to-date Pharaoh', *pharao redivivus*, in the eyes of one of his contemporaries. From another point of view, the story is a further episode in the relations between the Catholic Church and the Imperial Government; as usual, the Council was convoked by the Emperor. It also throws a fascinating light on the question of the respective roles in the life of the Church of a General Council and the See of Rome. Once again, however, the issue for us here is none of these things, but the basic question, whether the Church is a concrete historical society with a structure (whether papal or not) such as a historical society must inevitably possess or generate for itself.

In the broad vista of history, the importance of this Council lies in the attitude adopted by it, and by the Great Church thereafter (but not by the Nestorian communion), to the Christological issue which is summed up in the epithet applied to Our Lady, *theotokos* (she who gave birth to God). Nestorius, upon becoming Bishop of Constantinople, had first sought to suppress within his local church, and then to deprecate, the use of this title. He had come to Constantinople from Antioch, and the title seemed to him hard to reconcile with the theological traditions of the Antiochene school. He thought he saw the danger of a serious confusion of thought. *As God*, surely our Lord had existed from eternity, and could not be said to have been 'born' in the days of Emperor Augustus?

Cyril of Alexandria kept himself well informed about events in the imperial capital. He was quick to see in Nestorius' campaign against the title of *theotokos* a challenge to Alexandrian theology. But the Bishop of Rome, whose information came partly but not exclusively from Alexandria, was also scandalised by the 'new' Constantinopolitan Christology. Rome may not have had much interest in the prestige of the Alexandrian theological school, but she was deeply interested in the status of Christ as the one Mediator between man and God. True enough, as the Antiochenes would emphasise, the Son of Mary was not such a mediator unless he was truly man. But then, neither was he the mediator unless he was also truly God. To reject the title *theotokos* seemed to the Romans to amount to emphasising one aspect of the twofold truth at the expense of the other. After all, in ordinary speech, a mother is not the mother of the human nature of her son; she is the mother of her son. Was the Son of Mary God, or was he not? If he was God, and Mary was his mother, she was obviously 'mother of God'. Deny this—such was Rome's conviction—and eventually you will find that you have made Jesus not one entity but two; your mediator will have lost the basic unity which alone makes it possible for him to *mediate*. Broadly speaking, and with all apologies to the subtleties and qualifications of the Antiochene school, Rome was surely right.

Celestine, the Bishop of Rome, strong in the confidence that he had seized the real point at issue, and no less confident that he had the authority to deal with the matter by himself, decided that Nestorius must either retract or be excommunicated. He then chose as his agent in the affair the unyielding enemy of Nestorius, and the occupant of the great rival see, none other than Cyril. Cyril was instructed to forward the Roman decision, with a ten days' ultimatum attached to it, to the Bishop of Constantinople.

But before Cyril had carried out these instructions, the Emperor, moved perhaps by Nestorius, intervened with a summons to meet in general council, until which 'no innovations must be made by anyone separately'. Celestine accepted this situation with a good grace; he was probably genuine in hoping that the proposed council would find Nestorius amenable. It was just as well. Cyril, in the meantime, had forwarded the Roman ultimatum to Nestorius, together with a list, of his own devising, of twelve propositions to be 'anathematised' by the Bishop of Constantinople. This document, the 'Twelve Anathematisms', would have committed Nestorius to affirm that the incarnation resulted in a 'natural union' of the divine and human elements in Christ. The Antiochene school, whence Nestorius had learnt his theology, knew what it meant by 'nature', and could hardly be expected to see anything but rank heresy in this Alexandrian phrase. The immediate effect of the Anathematisms was to swing the Bishop of Antioch and his party over from the side of Cyril to that of Nestorius.

The Council had been summoned to open its proceedings at Ephesus at Pentecost 431. When the day came, neither John of Antioch and his fellow-easterners nor the papal legates had arrived. Cyril's supporters were present in force, and waited for a fortnight beyond the assigned date. They then opened the proceedings, despite the urgent appeals of the imperial representative and the refusal of Nestorius and his supporters to take part in an incomplete council. In these circumstances, the Cyrillines had no opposition to face in their conciliar session. A single day sufficed for the condemnation and deposition of the bishop of the imperial See. Not unnaturally, the victim protested to his Emperor.

Theodosius II was a pious young man, and, like other Emperors before and after him, he wanted peace in the Church. He refused to recognise the validity of the Council's action, and ordered a reconsideration of the whole affair. Meanwhile, John of Antioch and his group of some thirty Eastern bishops had arrived, and proceeded to excommunicate all the bishops of Cyril's Council. Fortunately, the papal legates now also put in an appearance.

The interested parties were by now all adequately respresented in the city of Ephesus, and but for what had occurred before the advent of the legates, it should have been possible to get them together in a general meeting. As it was, the meeting convened on July 10th was attended only by the Cyrilline bishops and the Westerners. The legates studied the minutes of the session in which Nestorius had been condemned, and on the following day they ratified the condemnation. A few days later John of Antioch and his adherents were also excommunicated; this excommunication was quashed by the Bishop of Rome when it had been reported to him, and in 433 the breach between Cyril and John was healed by their joint acceptance of a formula of union.

Such, in briefest outline, is the story of the third Ecumenical Council. For our purposes, it is of interest to note the terms in which the Council at its first session, before the arrival of the papal legates, expressed its sentence on Nestorius: ' . . . Our Lord Jesus Christ, who has been blasphemed by Nestorius, has defined, through the agency of this most holy council, that he should be deprived of his episcopal dignity and have no part in hierarchical association.' The implication, that Christ speaks in the voice of the ecumenical council, reminds us of the Council of Jerusalem's decree: 'It has seemed good to us and to the Holy Ghost.' There breathes through it the conviction that the visible society, of which the bishops are the official spokesmen, is one with Christ, in the unity that binds the members of a body to its head, that unity which is the privilege of the Church which Christ established.

The Acts of the Council include five canons. Among other things, they disqualify any bishop who should adhere to 'the council of the apostasy', that is, to John of Antioch's party. A metropolitan who so behaves is *ipso facto* excommunicated by the council and suspended; an ordinary bishop is deposed. A sixth canon runs: 'Whoever should decide to contravene in any way the acts of the holy council of Ephesus, the holy council decrees that he should be deposed (if he be a bishop or a member of the clergy), or excommunicated (if he be a layman).' It should be noted that John of Antioch not only signed the Formula of Union with Cyril in 433; he 'adhered to the sentence of the holy council against Nestorius, held him deposed from his See, and anathematised his evil teaching' (Hefele-Leclerc).

The unfortunate Nestorius was given little opportunity to found a Nestorian communion. Relegated from Antioch to Petra, and thence to the Great Oasis, he sank into an oblivion from which he witnessed, twenty years after Ephesus, what he held to be the vindication of his own convictions by the Council of Chalcedon. He wrote a treatise on his story and his opinions, which survives under the grotesque (mistranslated) title of *The Bazaar of Heraclides*. The villain of this book is, of course, Cyril, who is represented as animated by personal hostility. As for the 'Ecumenical Council' of Ephesus, it deserved to rank with the later notorious *latrocinium*. The whole affair could be summed up in the answers to three questions: 'Who was judge? Cyril. And who was the accuser? Cyril. Who was Bishop of Rome? Cyril. Cyril was everything. Cyril was the Bishop of Alexandria and took the place of the holy and saintly Bishop of Rome Celestine.'[2]

But the memory and the Christology of Nestorius have been preserved in veneration to the present day by the Eastern communion which claims the heritage of the ancient church of Persia; the scholars of the Persian church had learnt their faith in the Antiochene school of theology. For these, whom we call Nestorians, the obstacle to union with the Eastern Orthodox, the Roman Catholic, and the various Protestant communions, is radically the adherence of these bodies to the decisions of the Council of Ephesus. That Council has thus, for our present enquiry, the melancholy importance of being the first point from which any of our contemporary divisions originate. It is worthy of remark that the Council defined no doctrine as such;

[2] *Bazaar of Heraclides*, ed. Driver and Hodgson, p. 132.

what it did was to condemn an individual teacher and his (unspecified) teaching. It did, however, incidentally 'canonise' a *dogmatic epithet*: Mary, it taught, was *theotokos*, she who gave birth to one who is God. These roots of the 'Nestorian schism' bring vividly home to us that the price of definiteness of teaching is, in this fallen world, division. They may also remind us that, great as the boon of Christian unity might be, surrender of the dogmatic principle may well be too great a price to pay for it. The issue between dogmatism and liberalism is one that we shall consider at a later point in this enquiry.

The fourth and last of the Councils in the period preceding the fall of the Western Empire was that of Chalcedon. This Council was, among other things, a triumph for the See of Rome and its occupant, Leo the Great. Before examining the Council itself, it may be worthwhile to draw attention to a feature of Leo's ecclesiology which conveniently illustrates the traditional view of the relations of the historical government, the visible hierarchy, of the Church to the abiding headship of Christ in heaven. The bishops, Leo teaches, are the 'rulers' (*rectores*) of the Church, and are empowered for their ruling function by the Holy Ghost.[3] They are the Church's priests; but as men, they are conscious of their weakness. However, they can be sure that Christ himself intercedes perpetually on their behalf, since 'if he has delegated to many shepherds the care of his sheep, he has not abandoned the guardianship of his beloved flock'. Thus Leo clearly finds no inconsistency in believing in the abiding kingship of Christ over his Church, and at the same time in the 'regency' by which his will is carried into execution on earth. Dr Walter Ullmann, in a recent article,[4] has shown, with special reference to Leo's doctrine of the papal supremacy, that the authority of the regency is regarded by Leo as having been transmitted, like an entailed inheritance, from Peter to the contemporary government of the Church. Whatever may be thought of Leo's views on the papacy, his general view of hierarchical authority in the Church is only the expression, with incomparable lucidity, of what was universally believed in his day. It should be added that for Leo the 'flock' which Christ

[3] 'The Church has, as its rulers, those whom the Holy Ghost has prepared (for that task)', quoted by Batiffol, *Siège Apostolique*, p. 419.
[4] *Journal of Theological Studies*, 1960.

cares for in heaven and the bishops tend on earth is the Church which Christ founded. There is an implicit identification of the Church of Christ with a particular historical society.

As we have seen, Nestorius had emphasised the duality of natures in Christ (if we may use modern language to pin-point what was held to be his error) in a way which seemed to threaten Christ's unity and therefore his mediatorship. The problem before the Council of Chalcedon was to give adequate expression to this duality without sacrificing the unity which was so strongly emphasised at Alexandria and indeed at Rome. As usual, the Council was convened by the political power. It had been preceded by the *latrocinium* of Ephesus (A.D. 449), at which the papal legates had been defied by the Alexandrians. The world had been faced, in consequence, with the menace of a rupture between the Eastern and Western halves of Christendom; and this time, Alexandria would have been in the camp opposed to Rome. Leo would have been content, like Celestine before him, to deal with the crisis without a general council. However, he accepted the Emperor Marcian's decision that a council should be held. He stipulated, indeed, that his own legates should preside, but in fact the legates allowed the Emperor's civil representative to do so.

The number of the bishops who attended the Council was unprecedented—over five hundred; but many did not remain till the end of the sessions. At the very start of the proceedings the legates required that the Bishop of Alexandria must not sit as a member of the Council. They averred that such was Leo's decision, and the bishop of Rome is 'the head of the Church'. So Dioscorus, who had distinguished himself among other things by 'excommunicating' the Bishop of Rome, found himself in the position not of a judge but of a defendant. He refused to appear in this role, and was deprived of his episcopal dignity and of 'every sacerdotal function'. The Emperor promptly relegated him to Paphlagonia.

There remained the question of defining the faith against the alleged errors which Dioscorus had been trying to foist upon the Church. The Council had before it, and gave official approval to, a doctrinal statement issued by the Pope himself (the *tomus ad Flavianum*), and the legates would have been happy to leave things there. But the lay officials insisted that something more

should be done, and in the end, with the help of the legates
themselves, the historic Formula of Chalcedon was composed,
accepted, and signed.

The Council then went on, like the Nicene Council before it,
to other business. It passed a number of canons, including the
famous 28th. This canon states that the ancients had rightly
recognised the primacy of the See of Old Rome, because that
city held the (political) sovereignty. But it points out that Constantinople is now the civil equal of Rome, and 'therefore' is,
like Rome, great also in ecclesiastical matters, 'being second
after Rome'. Thereupon it gives the Archbishop of Constantinople the right to consecrate the metropolitans of the (political)
dioceses of Pontus, Asia, and Phrygo-Thrace. There were two
grounds on which Rome might object to this canon: it could be
seen as another attack on the See of Alexandria, traditionally
the second See of Christendom; and it seemed to base the
Roman primacy on secular rather than religious foundations.
One is not surprised to learn that the canon was submitted to
the vote in the absence of the Roman legates, who made a
formal protest the next day. When, after a long delay, Leo at
length ratified the decisions taken at Constantinople, he explicitly excluded this canon from his ratification. It may well
be that the Eastern bishops had no intention of insulting Rome
by passing the canon. But it is another sign of the tendency to
align the life of the Church with political and contingent
realities extrinsic to its own nature and function. The Empire,
at the end of the previous century, had made the Catholic
religion the official cult. It looks as though the Eastern bishops
were beginning to think of it simply in that light.[5]

The sentence against Dioscorus was pronounced in the
Council by Leo's legates. It is given, in the Greek text of the
acta, in the following form: 'The holy and blessed archbishop
of the great and old Rome, Leo, by us and by the present holy

---

[5] On the other hand, there was a tendency to regard the Empire as a divinely
sanctioned 'ecumenical' State, and the Emperor as a quasi-sacred official; if this
were so, Christianity might be looked upon as the State religion without
derogation from its universal quality. But in fact no human civil polity, since
the supersession of the 'Old' by the 'New' Testament, has such an absolute
status as was accorded, in some streams of thought, to the Roman Empire. It
is noteworthy that the synodal letter, in which the Council seeks papal confirmation of the canon, is careful to express the real religious basis of the Roman
primacy. This letter has a rather brief list of signatures.

council, with the thrice-blessed and glorious Peter, who is the rock and foundation of the Catholic Church, the foundation of the orthodox faith, has deprived (Dioscorus) of the episcopal dignity and of every sacerdotal function.'[6] The 'papal claims' in this statement do not interest us here except in so far as it is clearly implied that what Leo was to the Catholic communion of his own day, that Peter was, and by Christ's appointment, to the Church of Christ; and that the concrete visible society (only a fragment of contemporary 'Christendom') that is here exercising jurisdiction over the Bishop of Alexandria is identical with the Church which Christ established.

The Formula of Chalcedon ends with the words: 'Those who dare to compose a different Creed or . . . to offer a different Symbol to (converts) . . . , these the holy and ecumenical council has decreed should be deprived of their office, if they be bishops or clergy, and anathematised, if they be monks or laymen.' Thus the dogmatic determinations of the Council are made part of the dogmatic structure of the Catholic Church.

Just as the Council of Ephesus lies at the root of the division between Nestorian Christianity and the rest of Christendom, so, most unfortunately, a result of the Council of Chalcedon was the split between those who accept it as an Ecumenical Council and those who think that it betrayed the Christology of Cyril of Alexandria. The latter group survive today as the 'monophysite churches'.[7]

Both the Nestorian and the Monophysite communions have had a glorious history. Down the ages, they have borne witness to the name of Christ, and suffered for that name, in partibus infidelium. At the present time, taken separately (and each is

---

[6] Batiffol, Le Siège Apstolique, p. 543.

[7] See Vardapet Kerekin Sarkissian, 'The Ecumenical Problem in Eastern Christendom', Ecumenical Review, XII, 4 July 1960, pp. 436 ff. This (monophysite) author points out, rightly, that wide differences between regional, racial, or other constituents are perfectly possible within a single 'communion'. But what happened in the sixth century (as a result of the Council of Chalcedon) was a division penetrating 'the very heart of Christian fellowship, the bond of unity, i.e. communio in sacris'. It may be observed that the differences between the monophysite churches and the rest of us seem to call for friendly theological discussion. No-one can dispute that the crucial issue (whether the incarnation was 'in' or 'out of' two natures) was one on which, in the terms in which it had to be faced in 451, compromise was impossible. On the other hand, it may be doubted whether the monophysites' Christological faith, as distinct from their theology, is at the present day distinguishable from that of the heirs of Chalcedon.

4

further in Christological dogma from the other than either is from the Eastern Orthodox communion), they form but a tiny minority of Christians. They do, however, from the point of view of the possibility of Christian 'reunion', present a peculiarly acute problem, since each of them is based, formally, on the rejection of the doctrinal authority of a Council which, for the rest of us, is one of the Seven Ecumenical Councils of the first Christian millennium. On the other hand, looking at our own theoretical problem (the nature of the Church), I am not aware that either of them denies the proposition that the Church of Christ is essentially a single visible historical society. In impugning the authority of the Council whose findings they reject, they implicitly regard us as having fallen away from orthodoxy and Catholic unity. Implicitly, each of them regards its own communion as the true and single heir of the promises of Christ to his Church.

For the rest of us, Eastern Orthodox, Roman Catholics, and heirs of the Reformation alike, not only the first two Councils (which Nestorians and Monophysites also recognise) but all four of the great assemblies dealt with in this and the preceding chapter stand in the very centre of the stream of history which links us, through the Church of the New Testament days, to the historical Jesus Christ. They mark the stages in a period, a century and a quarter long, of very turbulent, often disedifying, and yet immensely creative, Christian history. Before Constantine Christianity had been detached from the central current of human affairs; for much of the time, a proscribed religion. It was conscious, indeed, of its supernatural mission and authority. It could have said of itself what Bishop Butler said of conscience: If it had the power, as it has the right, it would rule the world. But very obviously it did not rule the world. The conversion of Constantine, and the change of imperial policy resulting from that conversion, had the immediate effect of giving Christianity the right to exist, and before long it had become the established religion of the Empire, a dominating factor in the public culture of the Mediterranean world.

In face of this extraordinary alteration in its external conditioning, the new religion showed its instrinsic greatness by refusing to rest content with the status of a fashionable myth.

Myth is characterised by its evasion of the question of its own categoric truth; by this evasion, it escapes the scrutiny of the principle of contradiction. Christianity would not practise this evasion; and, if it was not to do so, it must face the question of the intellectual implications of its *cultus*, its devotional practice and liturgical tradition. The Councils, especially the second, third and fourth, took place against a background of intense theological thinking and hard argument. It was proper, if not natural, that the issues upon which they expressed the mind of Christianity were the two great matters of the Holy Trinity and the person and natures of Jesus Christ. Even on these great issues, while the fourth Council benefited by a scientific elaboration of theological vocabulary, the Councils did not offer a fully worked-out system of philosophical theology. What they did do, was to set the great dogmatic limits within which subsequent theological thought must work, and thus they underpin the whole structure of the great medieval schools of theology.

The Councils did not recognise any need to give similar dogmatic expression to the Church's convictions about her own nature. As regards the Church, they give us, not a set of dogmatic formulae, but the picture of the Church herself, as they conceived her to be, acting publicly upon the great stage of human history to give dogmatic formulation to what Christianity believes about God and Christ. As we have seen, the pre-Constantinian Church believed herself to be a unique, visible, historical community or communion. The evidence of the first four Ecumenical Councils is that this belief was carried over into the Constantinian period, and was the factor which enabled the Councils to do their dogmatic work. Take away this conviction about the Church, and you have cut the nerve of conciliar action in the fields of doctrine and discipline alike.

It is characteristic of great formative periods in human affairs that they present a complex of centrifugal forces. The age of the first four Councils was not only an age of definition of doctrine, and of the conflict of theologies behind those definitions. It was an age of dialogue with Greek philosophy, as in the speculations of a Gregory of Nyssa. It was an age of vigorous ecclesiastical architecture and art. An age, too, in which the worldliness that was the inevitable temptation accompanying Christianity's new political and social status was

contrasted with the 'flight to the desert' and the great labora-
tory experiments of the Desert Fathers in Christian asceticism
and prayer. It was also an age of competition and rivalry between great and ambitious episcopal sees, and of unprecedented
problems in the relations between the Church and a State which
wished to consider itself Christian. The conflict between Constantinople and Alexandria was in fact a symptom of the
emergence of a notion that Christianity might be regarded as
the religious aspect of a divinely guaranteed Empire, a notion
that clashed with the traditional view of the Church as a fully
autonomous society to which contingent political conditions
were intrinsically indifferent.

We must not try to pretend that the story of the great
Councils is not darkened by scandalous moral failures. But it
remains to ask ourselves whether anything less than a firm
conviction about the nature of the Church as a single historical
society, and the translation of that conviction into appropriate
action, could possibly have held all these diverse factors together
and preserved the complex totality of Christianity to be the
matrix of a series of new civilisations. Christianity is a message
and a gift to man from God who is truth and spirit, and who
demands to be worshipped in spirit and in truth. But, in the
first place, there is no ground even in the most primitive records
of Christianity for the supposition that the divine message can
be summed up in a simply formulated idea. And on the other
hand, man, the recipient of the message, is 'a little lower than the
angels'. He is bodily, as well as spiritual. And he is social as well
as individual. There are, as von Hügel taught, an intellectual, a
mystical, and an institutional element in Christianity, as in all
human religions. Each element is potentially scandalising; each
needs checks and limits which it will respect. But without the
synthesis of all three elements, human religion ultimately
falters and fails.

It is not easy to write about the Councils of Ephesus and
Chalcedon without coming up against the claims being made at
that period for the See of Rome. In our present study we are not
concerned with those claims in themselves. But one feature of
them comes close to the subject of the nature of the Church.
It was the Roman view, as remarked by Batiffol,[8] that you are

---

[8] *Le Siège Apostolique*, p. 606.

not in communion with the *Catholica*, unless you are in communion with Rome'. There was a strong current of thought in the East which tended to put the matter differently: the basis *two* of Catholic communion was the profession of the orthodox faith. The two views are of course not, in themselves, contradictory. What is important for us is that both insist on the universal communion of believers; though for some Eastern writers this may seem to have represented an ideal rather than an essential necessity. But whatever the vacillations and vagueness of particular writers, the official acts of the Councils are expressions of the belief about the Church which implies that visible fellowship in sacramental communion is of the essence of the Church which Christ founded, that Church which, in the eyes of the conciliar Fathers, was identical with the Catholic communion.

As an appendix to the story of the first four Councils we may refer briefly to the conditions under which communion was restored between the imperial East and the Roman Church in A.D. 519, at the end of the thirty years' Acacian schism. The schism had resulted from the Eastern bishops' acceptance of the Henoticon of the Emperor Zeno, which attempted to placate the Monophysites by passing over the claims of the Council of Chalcedon to ecumenical authority. Pope Felix III had, in consequence, excommunicated the bishop of Constantinople, with whom, however, the great mass of Eastern bishops remained in communion. The reconciliation of the two great Sees was effected early in the reign of the Emperor Justin I, who acceded in 518, and the terms demanded by Pope Hormisdas and accepted by the Eastern bishops, beginning with John of Constantinople, involved the signature of the celebrated Formula of Hormisdas:

> . . . Following in all things the Apostolic See, we also profess all its decrees; and for this cause, I hope that I shall deserve to be in one communion with you, which the Apostolic See proclaims, in which (i.e. probably, in which communion) is the entire and perfect solidity of the Christian religion, promising in future as to those who are separated from the communion of the Catholic Church, that is, those who in all points do not agree with the Apostolic See, that their names shall not be recited during the holy Mysteries.

The interest of this document for us is, once again, not the Roman claims to which it gives utterance, but its witness to the general ancient belief that the Catholic Church is essentially a communion, and its implicit exclusion from the muster-roll of the Church of those who refuse, or are denied, a share in that communion, that common life of a historical society.

Our purpose, in this and the previous chapter, has been to bring out into the open the idea of the Church held in Christian antiquity from the end of the New Testament period till about A.D. 500. It seems indisputable that the dominant idea was that the Church is by its essence a single historical society, with a divinely established structure of government, and with inter-communion of its parts and members. This is the only idea of the Church which can claim to have been both operative and practically controlling during those centuries. If Christ and the New Testament writers meant anything in particular by the Church, if he established the Church as part of his final revealed religion, it can hardly be unimportant that the centuries in closest contact with his apostles took a definite view of what the Church was.

We have now to consider whether that view of the Church can still be maintained in the light of subsequent Christian experience and of the present state of Christendom.

Chapter 6

CYPRIAN AND THE CHURCH

We have remarked[1] that Dr Greenslade, in his important book, *Schism in the Early Church*, states clearly that the ancient notion of the Church was that she 'cannot but be one', and that this unity was predicated of the visible Church as a single structure; so that bodies separated from the one communion were outside the Church. This means that, in the thought of the early Christian centuries, the Church is essentially an indivisible historical society; there could be, and there manifestly was, schism *from* the Church, but there could not be schism *in* the Church.

But Dr Greenslade is reluctant to rest in this ancient view as an adequate and final notion of the Church as founded by Christ. It seems to him to be hardly consistent with the fact of a grievously divided Christendom, coupled as it is with apparent fruits of the Holy Ghost in the life of all the major Christian bodies and their members. His attempt to present an alternative notion is developed largely with reference to the teaching of Augustine on the validity (granted certain conditions) of 'sacraments' conferred by members of schismatic bodies.

As is well known, this teaching of Augustine stands in marked contrast to the line taken, in the Baptismal Controversy, by that other great African, Cyprian. I therefore propose to lead up to Augustine and to Dr Greenslade's own suggestions by a preliminary examination of Cyprian's doctrine of the Church, and the inference, with regard to baptism attempted outside the one Catholic communion, which he himself deduced from this doctrine.[2]

[1] Chapter 4, *supra*.
[2] Cyprian lived and died in the period of the persecutions. Thus the course of our study involves some neglect of chronological sequence. But this book makes no pretence to be a history of the ancient Church.

Cyprian is, indeed, worthy of study both for his own sake and for his position in the Christian tradition. The first four Councils, even when they gave their sanction to Western modes of expressing Christian truth, were predominantly Eastern in their personnel. But Cyprian is a pure Westerner, and a witness to Western ways of thinking about the Church. Nor was his work without influence in the East. He died soon after the middle of the third century. Before the end of the fourth century a collection of his letters in a single volume was on sale in Constantinople. 'Translated in part into Greek, continually copied in the West, appreciated by all readers, the works of Cyprian . . . are invoked by the Council of Ephesus, used by Theodoret, placed immediately after the Bible and the Councils in the Gelasian Decree, and exploited by the canonical collections even in Syriac and Armenian'.[3] Optatus of Africa in the fourth century, and Augustine after him, were deeply influenced by Cyprian's work. And I suspect that at least one of his little books was a favourite volume in the library of the Roman See.[4]

For all his reverence for his 'master', Tertullian, Cyprian was not a great speculative theologian. He was a great ecclesiastical statesman and administrator and an accomplished practitioner of rhetorical Latin style. His ideas about the Church emerge especially with reference to major issues: the threat to Christianity in schism, as distinct from heresy; and the conditions under which converts from schism could be admitted to Church membership. In the early days of his brief episcopate (brief though it was, it was not much longer than his Christian life; for he had been an adult convert from paganism) he had been faced with schism in his own local church of Carthage, and with the wider issues raised by the Novatianist schism. Novatianism

[3] G. de Ghellinck, *Patristique et Moyen Age*, Vol. ii, pp. 203 f.

[4] Cyprian compares the Church to a system of waters, flowing in channels from, and depending on, a single source (*De unitate ecclesiae*, v). In seeking from Rome a decision of the Pelagian question, Augustine wrote: 'We would have you tell us that our little stream of tradition flows from the same source as yours which is so abundant; we do not pour back the waters of our stream to increase the generous flow of your source' (*Ep.* clxxvii, 19). The Pope, Innocent I, replied to the Carthaginians: it is right that all the waters, as though from their native source (sc. the Roman Church) should go forth and flow through the various regions of the world, as pure waters of an uncontaminated spring (in *Augustini Epp.* clxxxi, 2). Cyprian's water-system is the Church; Innocent's is the faith.

originated in the election of a rival to Bishop Cornelius of Rome. It threw the whole Catholic world into an uproar, and became a long-enduring phenomenon in the East.

It goes without saying that the word 'church' (*ecclesia*), in Cyprian's usage, often refers to a local church, duly constituted with its bishop, clergy, and people; he is emphatic that 'a church exists in its bishop, and a bishop in his church'.[5] When it has this meaning, the word can of course be used in the plural. Often, however, the word is used to denote the universal Church. When it does so, it refers to a concrete historical entity, not an invisible 'number of the elect' but a thing of flesh and blood, of bishops, clergy, and laity. I know of no passage in Cyprian's works where the word 'Church' can be shown to refer to, or to include within its meaning, the Church 'expectant' in the intermediate state, or the Church already 'triumphant' in heaven.[6] And on the other hand, there appears to be no occasion when his use of the word includes any person who is still alive and is outside the one communion of the universal Church. For Cyprian, the Church *is* that world-wide association of baptised persons in which he himself is a bishop, though he can make a mental distinction between the Church as sanctifying and the People of God as being sanctified: 'One is the Church, which, having attained the grace of eternal life, both lives unto eternity and gives life to God's people.'[7] So, too, he speaks of the Church as the 'mother' of Christians: 'Of her womb are we born, of her milk are we fed, of her Spirit our souls draw their life-breath.'[8]

This universal Church, although it may seem to the outward eye to be a federation of intercommunicating local churches, held together by the unanimity (*concordia*) of their bishops, and although it is usually held that Cyprian recognised no office in her which exercised the function in respect of the universal Church which the local bishop exercised towards his local

[5] *Ecclesia in episcopo est et episcopus in ecclesia.* Local church and bishop are correlatives.

[6] When Cyprian has occasion to speak of the triumph of the Church, he speaks not of her present triumph in the persons of those who have died and are in heaven, but of the *future* triumph of the Church that is now on earth: 'One who is not in the Church cannot be a martyr. A man will not be able to attain to the kingdom, if he has deserted the Church which is destined to reign', sc. hereafter. *De unitate*, 14.

[7] Ep. lxxi, 1.   [8] *De unitate*, 5 (trans. Bévenot).

community, yet is really, in Cyprian's mind, something more than a federation. Its unity is in reality prior to the multiplicity of the local churches.

In the first place, baptism, as Cyprian repeatedly emphasises, is 'one' for the whole Church. It is an initiatory rite which, though normally administered by, or on behalf of, the bishop of a local church, makes its recipient a member not simply or primordially of the local community, but of the universal Church. This means that you are not a member of the universal Church *because* you are a member of a local church (though the latter membership is normally a *sign* of the former). In reality, you are a member of your local church because baptism has made you a member of the universal Church. Hence, the local churches are not simply a number of distinct religious societies (such as the pagan *thiasi* were). If they had been, then you could, at least in theory, have belonged to one of them without belonging to the whole which each of them represents; but in fact, baptism made you a member of the whole Church, and gave you (provided you had not come under sentence of excommunication) communicating rights in any local community in which, even temporarily, you found yourself, whether as a local resident or a visitor. The effect of excommunication, on the other hand, despite the fact that it was a sentence ordinarily imposed by a local bishop, was that you would not be admitted to communion as a visitor to another local church.[9] In all this, Cyprian's evidence of course simply represents the general ancient Christian tradition on the subject of baptism, a tradition that has survived to the present day. It is all so normal that, as a rule, we do not think about it. Yet it determines one important issue : it shows that the sacrament of Christian initiation implies the priority of the universal Church as compared with the local community. The 'Church of my baptism' is the Catholic Church, and the Catholic Church is not a resultant from relations set up between local communities. On the contrary, the local church derives its character of 'church' from the fact that it is a local manifestation of the universal Church.

This same principle underlies the method by which a man is

---

[9] Cf. Ep. xliv, 1; it may be supposed that the Novatianists here mentioned as visitors at Carthage had already been excommunicated by the local church of Rome. References to the *Epistles* follow Hartel's enumeration.

made a bishop. It may be desirable, and it was the custom in Cyprian's day, that the local church, for the charge of which he is being appointed, should publicly affirm that the candidate is acceptable. But he is actually made (*facere, ordinare*) a bishop by bishops of other churches, usually of course from neighbouring churches. Thus, and only thus, he becomes a member of the association of bishops (*collegium episcoporum*) which tends the universal flock of Christ: 'Though we bishops are a multiplicity of shepherds, yet we tend a single flock.' Episcopacy is not something that springs up locally and is bestowed from below; it is something that belongs essentially and primordially to the universal Church and is given from outside the local community. The bishop, then—if we may make an inference from Cyprian's teaching—is essentially an officer of the universal Church, though he exercises his functions with particular reference to his own local community. The local churches are linked up through their bishops, as we have seen that the individual Christian is linked up through baptism and communion, with the rest of the Catholic Church. The Church is thus radically one by virtue of its single initiation rite, its super-local government, and its unity of communion. It is one by virtue of what we may call the sacramental reality of these rites and links. In its undivided unity it is itself a sort of 'sacrament' (the word had a wider reference in ancient Christianity than it has today): Cyprian can speak of 'the undivided sacrament of the Catholic Church'.[10]

A thing of undivided unity, of which the members are human beings of flesh and blood in a state of probation on earth, initiated into it by a visible rite of baptism, and held together by a government consisting of human beings who are created bishops by public rite itself administered by bishops, can hardly be anything other than a visible human association. The fact of the universal visible unity of the Church is something of which Cyprian is deeply and vividly conscious. It is an indisputable fact to which he can appeal in argument with confidence. He speaks of 'all the churches of the world linked with us by the bond of unity' and 'communicating with us'.[11]

[10] *Catholicae ecclesiae individuum sacramentum*, Ep. lv. 21. The atoms of Democritus, which were theoretically indivisible, are called *individua* by Cicero.
[11] Ep. lxvi, 7.

But Cyprian believes and teaches that this factual visible unity of the Church is more than merely a fact; it is the inevitable expression of a principle and a law. It is not merely an unbroken unity; it is an unbreakable unity. The Church not only *is not* divided, not only *ought not to be* divided; it *cannot be divided*: 'If the Church is not found among heretics, because she is one and cannot be divided . . . it follows that baptism too . . . cannot exist among heretics.'[12] Cyprian was at odds with the Bishop of Rome on the question whether those 'baptised' in schism, and wishing to join the Catholic communion, should be 'baptised' ('again') or accepted as already baptised. He held—wrongly—that baptism could only be administered 'validly' within the Catholic communion. He thought that this resulted from the admitted 'major premiss' that the Church is an indivisible visible unity. It is important to observe that, although the Church rejected Cyprian's inference, it did not question the truth of his major premiss. We shall be concerned with Cyprian's argument later on; at the moment we are interested in his major premiss, which appears to be common ground between him and those who opposed him in the Baptismal Controversy.[13]

Cyprian appeals to Scripture (Ex. 12, 46, oddly enough) as guaranteeing the indivisible unity of the Church: 'The truth of the inspired scripture make it plain that . . . the Church cannot be sundered against itself and divided, but maintains the unity of an undivided household.' This unity is something established by God:

---

[12] Ep. lxxiv. 4.

[13] The collection of Cyprian's letters includes one from bishop Firmilian of Cappadocia, who was violently opposed to the Roman view that (some) schismatical baptisms could be valid. Firmilian appeals to the bishop of Rome's claim that the Roman See is the Rock on which Christ built the Church, and argues that, if a schismatical communion can baptise validly, it follows that there are many Churches, and therefore many 'Rocks': 'I am justly indignant with the open and obvious foolishness of Stephen (the bishop of Rome): he boasts of his episcopal place and claims that he is in the succession of Peter, on whom the foundations of the Church rest; and yet he introduces many other Rocks and establishes the novel structures of many Churches, inasmuch as he lends his authority to the validity of (schismatical) baptism.' Thus, in Firmilian's view, the notion of 'Church' is the same as that of 'communion'; if more than one communion can claim the title of Church, then there are several Churches—which, for a Christian, is an absurd conclusion. *Apud Cypr. Epp.* lxxv, 17. Firmilian will have written in Greek; we have only a Latin version of his letter, and this may have been 'touched up' in the office of the bishop of Carthage before publication.

The apostle admonishes us that we should bear with one another, lest we depart from the unity which God established . . . He, therefore, . . . who separates himself from the bond of the Church and from the fellowship of the bishops can have neither the power nor the dignity of a bishop, having refused to maintain the unity and peace of the episcopate.[14]

When did God establish the unity of the Church? According to Cyprian, it was done in the act in which Christ brought the Church into being: 'Baptism is one; and the Holy Ghost is one; and one is the Church, founded by Christ our Lord on Peter to originate unity and for the sake of unity.'[15] In this passage Cyprian is not concerned with the claim of the See of Rome to be, in a unique sense, the 'see of Peter'.[16] He is concerned with the indivisible visible unity of the Church. His argument, implicitly, is that if Christ had established the Church on several Rocks, there might be a case for saying that the Church could be visibly divided; but in founding her upon Peter singly he gave unity to her as a primordial property that is as necessarily permanent as the Church itself is. Not only did he thus make the Church's unity primordial and permanent, but he *manifested* unity by founding the one Church upon the one Peter. Elsewhere, Cyprian says that the power of forgiving sins was given by our Lord to Peter in the first instance, on whom (sc. Peter) 'he built the Church, and in whom he made unity originate and be visible'.[17] The foundation of the Church on one Rock, Peter, was thus a sort of efficacious sign of her indivisible visible unity, a sign of divine origin which, as such, necessarily effected what it signified.

When, therefore, Cyprian speaks, as he not infrequently does, of schismatics 'rending' the Church, he certainly does not mean what he says. Schism does indeed tear the schismatics away *from* the Church. But it does not tear the Church herself into two parts so that each part remains a part *of the Church* after the rending. Of the two communions with which we are

[14] Ep. lv, 24.   [15] Ep. lxx, 3.
[16] Judging by Firmilian's letter, quoted p. 92, n. 13, *supra*, such a claim was made by Stephen of Rome. Elsewhere, and before the Baptismal Controversy had strained relations, Cyprian, in a letter to Rome, makes at least a polite reference to the special origin of the Roman See, and Church, 'the See of Peter and the original church whence the unity of the bishops took its rise' (Ep. lix, 14).
[17] *Unde unitatis originem instituit et ostendit*, Ep. lxxiii, 7.

presented after the consummation of a schism, only one—on Cyprian's principles—can be the Church.[18]

So far, we have been building up our reconstruction of Cyprian's view of the Church with little reference to his treatise *The Unity of the Catholic Church* (I refer to this, for short, as *De unitate*). Before examining that work more closely, it may be convenient to summarise what we have learnt from him so far:

(1) 'Church' (*ecclesia*), in Cyprian's writings, always means an actual association of baptised human beings on earth, an *historical association*. The local church is an 'incomplete' society, as depending on or forming part of, the universal Church, which it 'represents' in a given locality. The universal Church is a 'complete' society.

(2) The unity of the universal ('catholic') Church is a unity of actual association by intercommunion, a sharing in common sacraments in subordination to a super-local, universal, episcopate; and the individual bishops are linked together by mutual recognition and communion.

(3) This unity is a historical and contemporary *fact*, to which Cyprian can point and from which he can argue.

(4) It is also a unity which *cannot* be broken. To Cyprian this is strictly equivalent to saying that there can only be one Catholic Church. To concede the name 'Church' to more than one communion would be, for him, the same as to say that Christ had founded a multiplicity of 'Catholic Churches', which would be absurd.

---

[18] The fact, of course, is that the metaphor of 'rending' contained in the word schism, though hallowed by long usage, is inadequate to describe what takes place when a group separates itself from, or is excluded from, the communion of the universal Church. You can tear a piece of cloth, and the result will be two pieces of cloth; you cannot tear the Church in such a way that the result will be two Churches, since—on any view—there is only one Church established by Christ. Less inadequate is the metaphor of the 'body', provided it is realised that the term of comparison is the bodily organism of a human being, not (primarily) 'an aggregate of persons or things' (*Concise Oxford Dictionary*). Augustine uses this metaphor, and can point out that a limb cut off from its body will cease to live with the body's life. As St Paul teaches that the Church is 'the body of Christ', it might seem that we should have made more use of this metaphor in our discussion of the Church's nature. But we might have got involved in the very complex question of what St Paul meant—and whether he always meant the same thing—by the metaphor. I have prefered to use the term 'society', which has the advantage of not being a metaphor at all; and, as has been shown in chapter 3, *supra*, a society cannot exist in two separate associations.

(5) This indivisible visible unity is a property of the Church, like the property that a triangle has of having its interior angles equal to two right-angles. Or rather it is a primordial endowment which makes the Church what it is. This property or primordial endowment is essentially supernatural, having been officially bestowed on the Church by Christ himself when he founded her.

The *De unitate* may have originally borne the title *De simplicitate praelatorum*.[19] But it must be the treatise referred to by Cyprian himself as the book in which 'I did my poor best to expound the unity of the Catholic Church'.[20] It offers to the Christian a simple principle or criterion, by which he may escape the diabolical lures of heresy and schism. That principle is the God-given unity of the Church. The claims of heresies and schisms are disproved, without arguing their particular merits or demerits, by the obvious fact that they are outside the visible unity of the Church.

There is, he thinks, scriptural warrant for saying that Christ gave the property of unity to his Church: as the 'Thou art Peter etc.' passage shows, he built his Church on *one* (man). True enough, the other apostles subsequently received the same apostolic powers and commission as Peter. But that subsequent act in no way alters the fact that the Church was *founded* on *one*—founded, we might say, not on the multiplicity of the Twelve but on the singularity of their leader. There was only one *rock* of the Church.[21]

By thus founding his Church on *one* man, Christ showed that the Church herself is *one*. He did not only show it. In this act of foundation he *established* the Church's unity in its fontal origin.[22] He *made* the Church one, and thenceforward she could only be as he had made her, one. The unity of the Church is as visible as the act of her foundation had been—otherwise, of course, this unity could not provide a 'short way' to confute all

[19] If so, the title was singularly inadequate to the theme of the book.
[20] Ep. liv, 4.
[21] *De unitate*, 4. There are two versions of the *De unitate*, and they differ considerably in chapter 4. I hold, provisionally, with Fr Maurice Bévenot (cf. *The Lapsed, The Unity of the Catholic Church, Translated and Annotated*, 1957), that both versions come from Cyprian himself, one being in fact a 'second edition' of the treatise. But in the text I use the less 'Petrine' of the two versions. No one doubts that this less Petrine version comes from Cyprian's own hand.
[22] *Unitatis eiusdem originem . . . disposuit.*

schismatics. If the Church is not necessarily visibly one, you could not be sure *a priori*—and Cyprian rules out any further investigation of the schismatics' claim—that a particular schismatical body was not a part of the Church.[23]

The argument from the promise to St Peter occurs in *De unitate,* chapter 4. The next chapter is a highly stylised description of the universal Church, comparing her to a tree-trunk with attached branches, to the sun and its rays, and to a fountain pouring its waters through a system of channels. The Church spreads her branches throughout the world, pours forth the abundance of her waters everywhere by means of centrifugal channels, enlightens the whole earth with the beams of her radiance. But she remains, nevertheless, one like the radiant sun, the single tree-trunk based on its gripping root, the fountain which gives unity to the whole irrigation-system.

What is Cyprian trying to convey by these comparisons? In each case, the point seems to be that two things are necessary if the desired result is to occur. First, the tree-trunk, the sun, the fountain must survive as active purveyors of their influence. Secondly, the physical link of branches with the trunk, rays with the sun, and channels with the fountain, must be maintained unbroken. In the case of the Church, we can be sure that the active purveyor will survive, for it has the guarantee of God. But schism breaks the physical link with this active purveyor. Cyprian goes on to describe the Church as a Mother, indeed a nursing-mother. But he says not only that we are fed by her milk, but that we are animated by her spirit; the implication is that, if we break away from her by schism, that spirit will cease to animate us, and we shall be (spiritually) dead. Such in Cyprian's view, is the condition of all heretics and schismatics, of

[23] Batiffol (*L'Eglise Naissante*, p. 431) was mistaken in holding that Cyprian, in his use of the 'Thou art Peter' passage in *De unitate* 4, is thinking of the monepiscopal structure of the local church. Elsewhere (e.g. Ep. xxxiii, 1) he does use this passage of Scripture as an argument for *episcopacy* (the point at issue in Ep. xxxiii is episcopacy, not monepiscopacy). But the theme of the *De unitate* is the unity of the *universal* Church, and it is precisely this that Cyprian is engaged in proving in chapter 4; hence the substitution of *super unum* for *super Petrum*. The argument of chapter 4 goes straight on into the next chapter, which is manifestly concerned with the unity of the universal Church. I have given a fuller criticism of Batiffol's exegesis of chapter 4 in 'St Cyprian and the Church', *III, Downside Review, Summer 1953.* J. H. Bernard (in *Early History of the Church and Ministry,* ed. Swete, p. 243, n.1) also comments on the inadequacy of Batiffol's interpretation of the *De unitate.* The fact is, that in only one place in the *De unitate* does Cyprian advert to the idea of monepiscopacy (chapter 8).

all who are outside the unity of the single universal communion of the Church: 'Break off a branch from the tree, it can bud no more; dam off a stream from its source, it dries up below the cut.'[24]

The more 'Petrine' version of chapter 4 of the *De unitate*, as to which it is disputed whether or not it comes from Cyprian's own pen, is not less insistent than the version examined above on the necessary unity of the Church: Christ founded, in Peter, a single 'chair' (See), and so made it clear that 'there is but one Church and one Chair . . . one flock which is to be fed by all the Apostles in common accord. If a man does not hold fast to the oneness of Peter, does he imagine that he still holds the faith? If he deserts the Chair of Peter upon whom the Church was built, has he still confidence that he is in the Church?'[25] The Cyprian of the *De unitate* teaches the same doctrine of the indivisible visible unity of the Church as is to be found in the rest of the Cyprianic writings. In the *De unitate* he applies this doctrine to the topical question of schismatical Christian bodies and their claims. To this same doctrine he would appeal, as to an uncontroverted major premiss, in the dispute over the question of schismatical baptisms.

With a view to stating the point at issue in the Baptismal Controversy, it may be well to explain that modern Roman Catholicism numbers baptism among the seven 'sacraments'. A sacrament is held to be 'a sign, perceptible to sense, and permanently instituted by Christ, to signify and confer grace'.[26] All sacraments are of their nature apt to bestow or increase sanctifying grace, which is the bond of union between the soul and Christ. Some sacraments, as baptism and holy orders, also confer a 'character' which is permanent and cannot be lost; thus a (validly) baptised person can never cease to be a baptised person, and therefore can never again validly receive the sacrament of baptism. Similarly, a validly ordained priest can never lose the 'character' of the priesthood and therefore can never again be validly ordained priest.

---

[24] *De unitate*, 5. For a further discussion of the argument of *De unitate* 4, 5, see additional note at the end of this chapter.

[25] *De unitate* 4 (trans. Bévenot). According to Bévenot, the 'one Chair' here means the monepiscopal authority in each local Church. Against this view, see additional note at the end of this chapter.

[26] Tanquery, *Brevior Synopsis Theologicae Dogmaticae*, ed. 6, p. 571.

To say that a sacrament is 'valid' is, in modern usage, the same as to say that the rite performed was really a sacrament and not merely an empty imitation of a sacrament. And a sacrament is only a sacrament, only valid, if the rite performed was such that the divinely instituted sign was really expressed by a qualified minister whose intention, in performing the rite, was 'to do what the Church does' in administering the sacrament in question. All this amounts to saying that the phrase 'an invalid sacrament' is really a convenient contradiction in terms; it refers to an outward rite which purports to be, but is not, a sacrament.[27]

A valid sacrament is apt to confer, not only 'character' (if the sacrament is one that does confer character), but the grace of union, or of an enhanced union, with Christ. If it does actually confer that grace, then the sacrament is not only 'valid'; it is also 'fruitful'. It could happen that the recipient of a sacrament might genuinely intend to receive the sacrament, and yet might lack the moral dispositions that would make him capable of receiving the sacramental *grace* or fruit. Thus, one could conceive of a man in the worst moral dispositions receiving, and meaning to receive, the episcopate out of a motive of sinful ambition. Such a man (if otherwise qualified) would receive the episcopal 'character' (the word has here no moral connotation) and so would become a bishop. But the sacrament thus conferred would be 'unfruitful'; it would not actually have conveyed that grace of deepened friendship with Christ which Christ intended it to convey.[28] However, this man, endowed with the episcopal character though not the friend of Christ, could validly consecrate others to the office which he himself had so unworthily, yet validly, received.

This modern teaching and language about the sacraments is the outcome of an immense, centuries-long, theological labour. Cyprian is not to be blamed for living at a time before this long work had been accomplished. Indeed, that he can hold the view about schismatical baptism which he teaches, and which is

[27] In the case of an adult recipient, some sort of intention to receive the sacrament is necessary for validity. In modern theory this may, in extraordinary cases, be no more than a 'virtual implicit intention'.
[28] We need not here consider whether it would begin to convey such grace once the bishop had sincerely repented.

rejected by almost every modern Christian body, is a timely reminder of the extent to which the heirs of the Reformation owe some of their most cherished convictions to late patristic and medieval Catholic theology. Cyprian—this again is due to the times in which he lived—applies the principle 'salvation does not exist outside the Church' with a splendid disregard of the distinction (current in modern Roman Catholic thinking) between objective right and subjective light. But if the Church is thus exclusively the sphere of saving grace, then, since sacraments are means of grace (or, as he would put it, rites that 'bestow the Holy Ghost'), it seems to him to follow immediately that there can be no such thing as a sacrament which is given outside the indivisible visible unity of the Church. Doubtless heretical or schismatical bishops claim to baptise converts and to consecrate others to the episcopal office, but the rites by which they purport to do such things are mere shams. Baptism, then (for this was the point at issue in his time), does not and cannot exist outside the Church.

Uncomfortable to modern sentiment as Cyprian's conclusion may be, and inconsistent with modern practice, his logic has seemed powerful to more than one recent scholar. C. H. Turner suggested[29] that Augustine, in defending the validity of schismatical sacraments, 'never really faced the fundamental argument of St Cyprian'. And Dr Greenslade, writing of Holy Orders (but his argument, as he seems to agree on p. 178 *op. cit.* will apply equally to baptism), says: 'Is not the conception of a valid ministry outside the one and only Church grotesque? I shall argue that the Augustinian position provides no point of rest. You may go back to Cyprian if you can face the implications of his teaching, but if you depart from Cyprian, you must go farther than Augustine.' In what respect we may, and should, go farther than Augustine is a matter for later consideration. We shall see that Dr Greenslade pays Cyprian the doubtful compliment of accepting his logic and denying his major premise, the doctrine of the Church as a single indivisible communion which Cyprian shared with virtually the whole of patristic antiquity.

At present, it is important to notice that, on the subject of the 'baptisms' conferred by schismatics, Cyprian, while he had

[29] In *Early History of the Church and Ministry*, ed. Swete, 2nd edn., p. xxxii.

the enthusiastic support of large sections of the Catholic world of his day, found himself opposed by Bishop Stephen of Rome, with whom the church in Egypt was in agreement. It is to be borne in mind that neither Stephen nor Augustine after him had any intention of rejecting or questioning Cyprian's principle, that 'salvation outside the Church does not exist', nor the major premise, that this ark of salvation is a single communion. It would seem that Stephen laid stress on the argument from traditional practice, and probably on what he would have held to be the Petrine origin of the Roman practice: 'Let there be no innovation, but let the traditional practice (be maintained).' But Cyprian, exasperated beyond endurance, was prepared to sacrifice Rome's tradition to logic. Cyprian's envoys, however, were denied a hearing at Rome, and he may have seen looming up the ugly spectre of a major breach in that 'concord of the bishops' which was, for him, an expression of the indestructible unity of the Church. He had previously suggested to others a practical compromise which may do honour to his heart and to his concern for unity, but is hardly logical. Since they would not agree with him about the necessity, of baptising converts from schism who have been 'baptised' in a schismatical body, let each follow his own practice 'preserving the bond of peace and concord among colleagues (in the episcopate)'.[30]

It seems unlikely that Stephen would have agreed to tolerate a diversity of practice in this matter of the baptism of schismatics. He died, however, before the problem was solved, and about the same time Cyprian also died, a martyr for the faith. It would seem that Stephen's successor was willing to let the matter rest. He could do so with an easier conscience, one would suppose, than Cyprian should have done. Though some bishops might insist on 'rebaptising' convert schismatics, Rome and the churches which agreed with her would never have to admit to their communion anybody whom *they* held to be unbaptised. But suppose an ex-schismatic, who had been reconciled to the Church

[30] It is well known that Cyprian, on other occasions, had proclaimed that every bishop is free to administer his local church according to his own judgment, though of course he will have to answer to God for the use he makes of this freedom (cf. Ep. lxxii, 3). Fr Bévenot (*Recherches de Science Religieuse*, April-October, 1957) points out that we have no evidence that Cyprian ever employed this doctrine of the autonomy of the local bishop *in controversy with Rome*. He argues that Ep. lxxii was written before Cyprian realised that Rome was opposed to his policy of 'rebaptising'.

at Rome and admitted to communion without 'rebaptism', arrived at Carthage and sought communion there. In Cyprian's eyes such a one would be an unbaptised person and therefore not a member of the Church at all. But on any Catholic principles, you cannot be a member of the universal Church when you are in Rome and not a member when you find yourself in Carthage.

For the subsequent history of the question, it may be mentioned that the Western Council of Arles (A.D. 314), with particular reference to the African custom of 'rebaptising' converts, which was still in force,[31] and which the Council describes as a 'special law' of those churches, legislates that the practice was to be discontinued. This was perhaps the 'plenary council' to which Augustine later referred as having decided the issue. The possibility of valid baptism conferred outside the Catholic communion was from about A.D. 400 generally accepted in the West, and papal authority was repeatedly vocal in support of this view. It is also arguable that the Council of Nicaea's decision about admitting Novatianist convert clergy to the Catholic ministry may have implied the validity of Novatianist baptisms. Since A.D. 1054 there has been some variety of practice on the matter among the Eastern Orthodox.[32] The Western view, made official by the Council of Trent, is presupposed in the Statement of the Committee on Church Unity of the 1958 Lambeth Conference: 'All those who believe in . . . Jesus Christ and have been baptized in the name of the Holy Trinity are incorporated into the Body of Christ and are members of the Church. Here is a unity already given.'

Our interest here in the fact of baptism conferred outside the visible communion of the Catholic Church is in the question whether the accepted Western view, that such baptism (granted

[31] It is possible that the Africans referred to were not the African Catholics but the Donatists, whose views on sacramental validity were ultra-Cyprianic.

[32] Fr Bernard Leeming, *Principles of Sacramental Theology*, pp. 543 ff., says that the Greeks very generally appeal in this matter to the 'Economy', 'which may be defined as the power in the Orthodox Church to admit as valid, or to reject as invalid, any sacrament administered outside the Orthodox Church. In theory, all sacraments of the heterodox are in themselves empty, invalid, lacking in grace; and hence, in strictness, they ought to be repealed. Nevertheless, the Church may, through reconciliation, revalidate them. . . . It would appear that sacraments administered by heretics without due form, for instance without the Trinitarian invocation in baptism . . . could not, even by "Economy", be admitted as valid.' It looks as though the Orthodox do not make the same clear distinction between validity on the one hand and liceity on the other, as is accepted in the Roman Catholic Church.

right form, matter, and intention) is valid, is ultimately capable of being harmonised with the ancient conviction that the Church is an indivisible visible human association, a single communion, and that all salvation comes to mankind from Christ through this one Church.

It is indeed often argued that since a baptised person has received a sacrament of which the proper effect is to make its recipient a member of the Church, it is obvious that communions consisting of baptised persons are parts of the Church; are they not themselves composed of members of the Church, baptised persons? But it is certain that the conclusion does not follow from the premiss of this statement. The proper effect of baptism is undoubtedly to make its recipient a member of the Church. But in order to know *what this means,* it is necessary first to know what the Church is. If the Church is a single historical society, then baptism's proper effect is to make its recipients members of that single historical society. For example, if the Eastern Orthodox communion is the one Church, and if schismatical baptisms are valid, then baptism by a Roman Catholic will of its nature make the recipient a member of the Eastern Orthodox communion; and although the Roman Catholic communion will aver that baptism has as its effect to make the recipient a member of the Roman Catholic communion, this—on the hypothesis here envisaged—will be no *proper* consequence of baptism *as a sacrament.* If the Church is a single historical society, it is theologically irrelevant that some Christian communions, other than the one authentic Church, also regard baptism as the rite of admission into their own body. A communist 'cell' which happened to consist solely of Members of Parliament would not, because of the qualifications of its members, be 'part' of the House of Commons. Therefore our question, about the bearing of the validity of schismatical sacraments on the ancient view of the nature of the Church, remains open for further discussion.

Additional Note to chapter 5 of *De unitate.*

I am sorry to find myself disagreeing with Fr Bévenot (*The Lapsed, The Unity of the Church,* p. 108) in the exegesis of this chapter. If I have not misunderstood him, he takes it as referring to the derivation of the powers of all contemporary bishops from the original foundation of the Church on Peter; he appears to exclude any reference to the necessity of intercommunion. (Fr Bévenot refers, in support of his view, to *Ep.* lxxiv, 10, where the simile of the irrigation-system recurs, and the point is made that settlement of disputed points of doctrine must be sought by reference to the scriptures as the 'fountain' of truth. But Cyprian need not be supposed to use his 'fountain' metaphor, of which he is fond, with the same application always. In our section of the *De unitate* the 'fountain' is *not*, I submit, a text of Scripture, but the *action* of Christ (cf. Bévenot, p. 102, n. 23) in founding the Church on Peter, and the *actual result* of that action, namely the Church in her indivisible unity.) Fr Bévenot's interpretation of the chapter makes its argument useless for Cyprian's purpose in the treatise. That purpose was, to refute all schisms, without considering the particular grounds for their secession, by pointing to the fact that, precisely *as* schisms, as bodies existing in visible separation from the visible universal Church, they have deserted the unity which is the property of the Church of Christ. The argument only holds together if the unity in question is not merely a unity of common descent (Novatian himself had been consecrated, it would appear, by validly consecrated bishops) but a unity of intercommunion.[33]

It may be well, to prevent misapprehension and the introduction of a controversial irrelevancy, to remark that I am not here arguing that Cyprian believed that the 'Rock' on which Christ had built his Church survived in a special and unique way in the Roman See. I am only arguing that his treatise on unity disintegrates into mere verbiage if he is not affirming that the Church is a unity of indivisible communion; and we have already seen, from his other writings, that such was his conviction about the Church.

[33] For an example from outside the *De unitate* of Cyprian's appeal to the visible unity of the Church as a 'short way with dissenters', cf. Ep. lv, 24: 'As regards Novatian himself, and your request for information about the heresy which he is alleged to have introduced, you must know that, to begin with, we ought not to concern ourselves with the contents of his teaching, since he teaches outside (sc. the Church). . . . Boast as he may, and proclaim his philosophy and eloquence with proud speech, a man who has not clung to brotherly charity and ecclesiastical unity has lost even what he was before.' The implication that charity and ecclesiastical unity are one and the same thing anticipates Augustine's teaching, as it does that of Thomas Aquinas on the nature of the sin of schism (see chapter 4, *supra*).

Obviously, the question might arise: How do you *identify*, among a number of separate Christian communions, the one which not only claims to be but really is the Church which Christ founded? (This is the question which, later on, Optatus tried to decide against the Donatists by appeal to the 'endowments' [*dotes*] of the true Church). But apart, perhaps, from such moments of acute anxiety as when Cornelius and Novatian first put out their respective claims to be the true Bishop of Rome, I think that to Cyprian it normally seemed obvious and beyond argument that the world-wide communion to which he belonged (what he called the Catholic Church) was the true Church, and not any one of the comparatively insignificant 'schismatical' bodies. Had he lived a hundred years later, when the outlines of a State Church were beginning to emerge over against the communion of the adherents of the 'consubstantial', he might have been more aware of the need of a criterion to distinguish among the Christian communions the one that was really the Church; still more, perhaps, during the Acacian Schism about A.D. 500, or after A.D. 1054. As it was, he was a man of his time, confident that, if he could give sufficient emphasis to the truth that the Church is an indivisible communion, anyone of good will would then see that the communion to which Cyprian belonged was the true Church. And we, too, are not here concerned with *identifying* the true Church; our question, stated in our own terms, is the one which Cyprian seeks to answer: Is the Church of Christ a single, historical, society?

Chapter 7

AUGUSTINE'S CONSISTENCY

O NE of the bishops to whom the summons to the Council of Ephesus was sent was Augustine of Hippo Regius in Africa. But the great convert was already dead before the Council met. As he lay dying, the Vandals were besieging his episcopal town, as though to symbolise the ruin they were bringing on the whole structure of the Catholic Church in North Africa.

Augustine towers above all other Western Christian thinkers of the first millennium. Of his predecessors in the East since the last of the apostles died, only Origen can rival him. But great and fascinating and influential as Origen was, and little though he deserves the ill-repute into which he subsequently fell, Augustine is the deeper philosophical thinker and a more profoundly religious one, more utterly penetrated by the apprehension of the nothingness of himself and of all creation when set over against the reality and majesty of God. Indeed, of all the interpreters of Jesus of Nazareth to his fellow-men, it could be argued that he was the greatest since St Paul and St John. He is the link between Christian antiquity and the thought of the Western Middle Ages. The Reformers, in their turn, looked to him as to a prophet. And if, in one aspect, he is the very type of antiquity's preoccupation with the objectivity of the world about us, in another aspect he holds out a hand to our modern, subjective, existentialist, anguish. He is the classic doctor of grace. But he is also an outstanding witness to the authority of the Church. The diverse facets of Christian truth soar up in his spirit towards an Everest peak which has challenged a host of adventurers ever since, and sometimes lured them to disaster. Withal, he had a very human fallibility, and it can hardly be denied that his condonation of secular pressure to 'compel' schismatics to 'come into' the Church has set a deplorable example too readily followed by generations for whom the voice of Augustine was an oracle.

Augustine's conversion and reception into the Catholic Church took place in Milan, whither he had gone to take up a professorship in rhetoric. Fundamentally, it was a conversion from Manichaean dualism through agnosticism to God; and from Platonism to Jesus Christ. But it was also a conversion to a particular religious institution: 'I should not believe the gospel unless I were moved thereto by the authority of the Catholic Church.'[1] Augustine was not a Christian by conviction and a Catholic by accident; for him, the two things were one.

It was when he returned to Africa, the homeland of the Donatists, that he was brought face to face with the problems raised by that powerful schism. Donatism had been a consequence of the last great persecution, when (the Donatists alleged) the consecrator of the Catholic Bishop of Carthage had been a 'traitor' to the Christian cause. They held that, the Church being essentially holy, sacraments, and among them ordination, conferred by traitors were invalid. Caecilian, therefore, the Catholic Bishop of Carthage, was not validly consecrated, was no true bishop. All who communicated with him were involved in his predicament, and therefore the true Church of Christ was simply and solely those who were in communion with the rival, Donatist, Bishop of Carthage, Majorinus and his successors. The Donatists appealed to the authority, which in Africa was enormous, of Cyprian the martyr, with whom they agreed that all sacraments bestowed outside the one communion of the true Church (which, they held, was theirs) were null. Hence they 'rebaptised' converts from the Caecilianist (i.e. Catholic) Communion. They could even appeal to some texts of Cyprian in which he seems to take the view that the godlessness of a minister of itself invalidates his 'sacraments'; but, as Dr Greenslade points out, Cyprian's real argument against schismatical sacraments was not just that their ministers were bad men, but that he who is not within the Church 'obviously' cannot give what can only be given by the Church, namely the Holy Ghost, to give whom is the function of the sacraments.

Against the Donatists, Optatus of Milevis (A.D. 370) had argued, in favour of schismatical (as distinct from heretical)

---

[1] *Lib. c. ep. Manich.* v (P.L. viii, 176). Our own generation, having discovered that the 'quest of the historical Jesus' cannot by-pass the faith of the first Christian generation, is better placed to sympathise with this dictum of Augustine than were the liberal scholars of the nineteenth century.

sacramental ministrations, that, after all, it is God, not the minister, who produces the effect of the sacraments.[2] Augustine took over this argument, and added that, even when Donatists baptised—and, as he conceded, baptised validly—baptism remains not the baptism of the schismatical communion, but the baptism of the Church. The schismatics are using a valid rite, and using it validly, but it is a Catholic rite used illegitimately by them (as though they had stolen and used the Church's seal-ring). Thus we find in him the clear distinction between the ideas of validity and liceity. But perhaps his own great and permanent contribution to the discussion was the distinction he made between the validity and the *fruitfulness* of sacraments. A sacrament, he held, might be valid, yet without fruit for the recipient's personal sanctification, because of the circumstances in which it was administered, namely (in the case of schismatics) the recipient's sinful alienation from the Church.

It remains to add that, as regards baptism and Holy Orders, Augustine held that they not only bore fruit of holiness in the worthy recipient, but also imparted a 'seal' or 'character' giving the recipient—irrespective of his moral qualities—a permanent place or function in the Church. Thus a validly baptised person is, by virtue of the 'seal' of baptism, permanently related to the Church and her sacramental system in such a way that he is always capable (given the necessary moral conditions) of fruitful reception of the other sacraments; whereas an unbaptised person could not validly receive any of the other sacraments until he had been baptised. Similarly, a validly ordained priest is always capable of validly celebrating the Eucharist—though he can only celebrate licitly if he is in a state of friendship with Christ.

Manifestly, Augustine's attitude to the validity of schismatical sacraments is not a development of Cyprian's, but a point-blank denial of it. And while Cyprian and Stephen were concerned mainly with baptism,[3] Augustine, while affirming the validity of schismatical baptisms (provided, of course, that the right form and matter are used, and that the minister has, as we should put it, the intention of doing 'what the Church does'), goes boldly forward to accept the validity of schismatical orders,

[2] Cf. Leeming, *The Theology of the Sacraments*, pp. 512 ff.
[3] If schismatical baptisms were invalid, it would follow that their ordinations of those thus 'baptised' would be invalid also, since all other sacraments presuppose that their recipients have been validly baptised.

with the same proviso. It appears that Augustine's opinion that, other things being equal, Orders conferred outside the Church are valid' has never been explicitly defined by the Roman Catholic Church, but is 'regarded as "common and certain" doctrine by all (her) approved authors.'[4]

Such being Augustine's view about the sacraments, a view that frankly contradicts Cyprian's, one may ask why he adopted it. C. H. Turner, who felt uneasy about the truth of the Augustinian theory of 'the relation of the sacraments to the Church', and found Cyprian's argument to me, 'on the premises of the primitive tradition of the Church all but unanswerable,'[5] had the impression that Augustine was 'in so great a hurry to evolve a theory which would serve his immediate purpose . . . that he saddled the Western Church with a legacy which has at times been found to be very burdensome'. And Dr Greenslade says that Augustine, following Stephen and others, was moved 'partly by theological grounds, some of which have permanent force, and partly by charity', since he wished to 'allow as much Christianity as he could to the schismatics'.[6]

Without any wish to question Augustine's charity—though I think it was directed rather to the easier return of schismatics to the fold than to allowing them, in their schismatical condition, as much Christianity as possible—it seems worth while to suggest that Augustine probably felt himself bound by ecclesiastical authority to his view, at least as regards schismatical baptism. He speaks of 'a plenary council of all the world' as having confirmed the teaching of Stephen on the matter.[7] He does not name this council. It has been suggested that he means the Council of Arles, which, however, was a Western, not an ecumenical, council. Batiffol thinks that perhaps there was no such conciliar decision, of ecumenical character, but that Augustine thought there must have been, to explain the unanimity among Catholics on the point.[8] But in A.D. 385 Siricius, Bishop of Rome, told the Bishop of Tarra-

---

[4] Leeming, op. cit. p. 521. Father Leeming is here writing about 'heresy or wickedness' in the ordaining minister, but presumably means to cover the general case of schismatical ordinations.

[5] The Early History of the Church and the Ministry, 2nd ed., p. xxxiii.

[6] Schism in the Early Church, p. 181.

[7] De baptismo, i. 9.

[8] Catholicisme de St Augustin, p. 163 n.

gona that 'his predecessor Liberius had forbidden the rebaptism of Arians by public decree, and that the whole of the East and the West kept the custom of receiving them only with an imposition of hands.'[9] As regards Holy Orders, Ambrose of Milan (who had received Augustine into the Church) accepted the Orders of converted Arian bishops and priests; following most probably, thinks Leeming,[10] the custom of the West in this matter.

Whatever Augustine's motives, Dr Greenslade does not wish to go back to the Cyprianic view that baptism outside the one and only Catholic communion is null. On the contrary, he would accept Augustine's view that valid baptism is not restricted to the ministrations of any one communion. But he would call in question the principle on which Cyprian based his view of schismatical baptism. For Cyprian's logic seems to him unassailable. Cyprian had said: outside the Church there can be no sacraments; therefore the baptisms administered by Novatianists or other schismatics are invalid. Dr Greenslade agrees that, outside the Church, there are no sacraments. Therefore, he argues, since we agree with Augustine that valid baptism is administered in several different communions, we must conclude that all these communions are in the Church. Thus we

---

[9] Leeming, *Principles of Sacramental Theology*, p. 514.

[10] *Op. cit.* p. 528. It seems probable *a priori* that Ambrose and Augustine, as regards Orders received outside the Catholic communion, were following a Roman lead, or at least a custom approved by Rome. It is precisely in the second half of the fourth century that Western witness to the view that Catholicism involves communion with the Roman Church or See begins to accumulate. The Donatist schism had raised the question: granted that the Church is a single visible communion (which the Donatists; except for Tychonius, were far from denying), *which* communion is the true Church? The Donatists maintained that their own body was the true Church, and their opponents claimed that it was theirs. It is precisely Optatus of Milevis, in his work against the Donatists, who —among other criteria—makes explicit the doctrine that the Catholic Church is the Church which is in communion with the legitimate bishop of Rome (*Optatus*, II, 3, 4. I have quoted and commented on this passage in 'St Augustine's Teaching on Schism', *Downside Review, January, 1951, vol. lxix*). The same doctrine is expressed by Jerome (writing from Antioch, where there were three episcopal claimants) and by a Council of Aquileia of which Ambrose was probably the leading spirit. The doctrine is used implicitly as an argument by Augustine himself in the *Psalmus contra partem Donati*, 227-31. At a later date, though the case of Apiarius shows that Africa was not prepared to accept Rome's practical interventions without question. Augustine held that the Pelagian affair had been settled by decisions taken at Rome. If, then, Africa in Augustine's day looked to Rome as to the centre of Catholic communion, it is likely that Rome's attitude about rebaptising (and perhaps about reordaining) might seem definitive to Augustine. These were indeed practical matters, but they had doctrinal implications.

arrive at Dr Greenslade's ecclesiological conclusion: schism is not always and necessarily schism *from* the Church; there can be such a thing as schism *in* the Church.

That this ecclesiology is in formal contradiction with Cyprian's is of course obvious, and is admitted by Dr Greenslade. Before considering it on its merits, it may be well to emphasise, what Dr Greenslade also fully acknowledges, that Augustine, for his part, had no intention of calling into doubt, by his sacramental theology, the traditional view of the Church as essentially a single communion. Augustine was apparently unaware that a revision of this traditional view was necessitated by his recognition of the validity of (some) schismatical sacraments. As Dr Greenslade well says:

> The earlier recognition of non-catholic baptism had not been intended to introduce any change in the doctrine of the Church; nor was Augustine's recognition of non-catholic orders. The concession arose from a consideration of sacraments in themselves, somewhat apart from the doctrine of the Church, with the result that non-catholic sacraments came to be reckoned valid *extra ecclesiam,* while, in accordance with the standard doctrine of the Church, they could be efficacious only within the Church. Even this statement requires the qualification that non-catholic sacraments really belong always to God and the Church, and must be performed as in the Church.[11]

And C. H. Turner, after mentioning Augustine specifically, sums up an interesting paragraph with the words: 'On the supreme duty of communion with the visible fellowship of the brethren in the one true fold of the Redeemer there was no shadow of wavering, however many the representatives, or however various the types and local expressions, of the Christian tradition.'[12]

Nevertheless, it has been suggested that Augustine is not entirely firm on the question of the indivisible visible unity of the Church. Thus Mr G. G. Willis writes: 'With St Augustine . . . schism is not thought of as automatically excluding a man from the Church, and leaving the Church as united as before: it is a true rending of the Body of Christ itself.' And again:

[11] *Op. cit.* p. 175 f. The statement that, according to Augustine, sacraments could only be efficacious within the Church requires some slight, but theologically important, qualification. See below.
[12] *Op. cit.* p. 195.

Cyprian 'could easily decide whether a man was within or without the Church. Augustine's more subtle theory' of the possibility of valid baptism administered outside the Catholic communion 'could give no such definitive answer to the problem'.[13]

Mr Willis refers us to Augustine, *Ep.* xliii, 8, 21, where the Donatists are in question:

> They baptise outside the Church, and—if it were possible—they rebaptise the Church. They offer sacrifice in dissension and schism, and in the name of peace they greet (presumably in the liturgical words: *Pax vobis*) those whom they exile from the peace of salvation. The unity of Christ is rent, the inheritance of Christ is blasphemed. . . . We charge them with the madness of schism, the folly of rebaptizing, their wicked separation from the inheritance of Christ which is spread through all nations.

The words in this quotation which afford a basis for Mr Willis's opinion that Augustine was not clear that the Church is indivisible are of course: 'The unity of Christ is rent.' If these words are to be taken at their face value, schism rends the unity of the Church, and it could be inferred that thereafter the Church exists in two portions, two communions, e.g. the Catholic communion and the Donatist communion. But Augustine's use of these words is no more to be taken literally than Cyprian's occasional use of similar language; for there is no doubt or question that Cyprian firmly held the visible Church to be an indivisible communion.[14] Since the literal meaning of the word 'schism' is 'cutting', both these writers fell easily into this way of talking, just as today we may talk about 'broken marriages' although we believe marriage to be an indissoluble bond; when they spoke of the Church being 'rent' they were using rhetoric rather than theological argument. Augustine's real mind is made manifest in other phrases of the passage quoted above: 'They baptise *outside the Church*'; 'peoples . . . whom *they exile from the peace of salvation*'; 'separation from *the inheritance of Christ which is spread through all nations*'. We may compare

[13] *St Augustine and the Donatist Controversy*, pp. 116, 123.
[14] Cf. Cyprian, Ep. xlvi, 1: 'It saddens me' that you Novatianists at Rome (to whom he is writing) 'have consented . . . to the rending of the one mind and body of the Lord's flock by schismatical rivalry.' Yet in the same letter he speaks of them as 'separating themselves from the flock of Christ', and begs them to return to 'their mother', sc. the Church. And cf. Ep. lix, 5.

another passage, which Mr Willis himself quotes: You Donatists 'dare to make mention of the blessed Cyprian as though that great champion of Catholic unity were a support of your separation. *First be in the Church,* which it is well known that Cyprian held to and preached, and then dare to name him as a supporter of your views.'[15] In another passage we find Augustine slipping into the rhetorical description of schism as 'rending' the Church, and at once correcting himself: 'It is to the catholic Church that the words are addressed: One is my dove (*Canticle of Canticles,* 6, 8). . . . Why have you torn the dove? *Nay, you have torn your own entrails; for while you have been torn, the dove remains whole.'*[16] 'The dove remains whole' aptly sums up Augustine's view that schism is *from,* not *in,* the Church. On this matter, and it is basic to the question of the nature of the Church, he entirely agrees with Cyprian. All one can say is that his conviction that the (Donatist) schismatics actually (and validly) baptised, ordained, and celebrated the Eucharist, made him feel all the more poignantly the horror of the sin of schism and its consequences: for him, it involved not only 'apostasy' from the true Church, but 'sacrilege' on the part of the schismatics who administered the sacraments or received them.

When, therefore, Mr Willis says that 'there are traces' in Augustine's works 'of the old view of the disastrous effects of being in schism', he is, in my judgment, understating the case. From the second paragraph of the Psalm against the Party of Donatus (A.D. 393), where he says that by schism the Donatists have handed themselves over to the devil, down to his last extant letter on the subject of Donatism (*Ep.* 423, dated A.D. 423), where he tells the nun to whom he is writing (an ex-Donatist) that 'if she died outside the unity of the body of Christ, her virginity would avail her nothing', the disastrous effects of schism are the burden of his voluminous writings about Donatism. Schism, he argues, deprives the reception of valid sacraments of any lifegiving virtue for the recipients;[17] this is surely a sufficiently disastrous result of schism—so much so, that we shall have to return to the question which Augustine

---

[15] *C. Cresc.* II, xxi, 39.   [16] *Tract. in Ioann.,* VI, 11 and 26.

[17] Though sacramental 'character', a non-moral entity, may be conveyed by them, and is in fact conveyed whenever baptism and Holy Orders are validly administered.

thus raises later. Meanwhile, we may illustrate his teaching on the point by the following passage: 'Christian charity cannot be preserved except in the unity of the Church . . . without this charity you are nothing, even though you should have baptism and faith, and, by faith, be able even to move mountains.'[18] For Augustine, the *communio sacramentorum* (visible fellowship expressed and built up in the sharing of common sacraments), that visible single communion which is the Catholic Church, is charity incorporated, we might almost say charity incarnate; and it is the *only* incorporation of charity; outside it 'charity cannot be preserved'. He was emphatic about the sins of Catholics. But however pessimistic he may have been about the holiness of (many) Catholics, he had no doubt whatsoever that the Catholic Church was, exclusively, the one Church of Christ, that Church which is bidden to 'sing unto the Lord a new song; sing to the Lord, all the world'. That song, he holds, the Donatists do not sing, because they are 'separated from that communion'.[19]

It has, indeed, been supposed that this doctrine of the indivisible visible Church, which Augustine clearly held and taught without reserve, is in fact irreconcilable with his teaching on predestination, developed especially in his anti-Pelagian writings. Dr Greenslade says:

> Under pressure both from his doctrine of grace and predestination and from his recognition that many Donatists . . . were not personally offering any barrier to the Holy Spirit and to sacramental grace, . . . (Augustine) allows that many who appear to be outside the Church are really within it. To me it seems clear that he was never able to work out the implications of his own conceptions.[20]

And Mr Willis agrees with Harnack's judgment (derived from Reuter) that 'the thought of predestination shatters every notion of the Church' and renders valueless 'the institution and means of salvation'. I am not here concerned to defend Augustine's teaching on predestination; it may perhaps be remarked that it was not identical with the more extreme forms of Calvanism, and that it was never accepted without reserve by the See of Rome. I only wish to show that the passage referred to by Dr Greenslade

[18] *Contra litt. Pet.*, II, 77.   [19] *Contra ep. Parmeniani*, III, 4, 24.
[20] *Op. cit.* p. 181.

does not imply a modification of Augustine's view of the Catholic communion as the unique ark of salvation, and, more broadly, that Augustine's theory of predestination in no way undermines his teaching about the Church.

The words quoted (and expanded) by Dr Greenslade in the passage reproduced above are from *De baptismo*, V, 38; 'In the ineffable foreknowledge of God many who appear to be outside are (really) within, and many who appear to be inside are (really) without.' It will be noticed at once that Dr Greenslade has added the words 'the Church' to this passage. He has thereby, in my judgment, given a mistaken interpretation of Augustine's meaning. A study of the context will show what Augustine is really conceding, and what he is not.

In this part of the *De baptismo* he is defending—this time against the teaching of Cyprian—the validity of schismatical baptism. Cyprian had applied to the Church (by which he meant the Church 'militant here on earth', the visible Catholic communion), some words from the Canticle of Canticles: 'Thou art an enclosed garden, my spouse and sister, a sealed spring, a well of living water, a garden with fruit of thy fruit trees.'[21] If these words refer to the Church on earth, they seem to suggest a degree of general holiness which disqualified the claim of the 'Catholic' communion. But, Augustine argued, the text cannot be predicated without reserve of the *historical*[22] Church; it refers rather to the 'fixed number of the saints, predestined before the foundation of the world'.

Augustine points out that, of these predestined souls, (1) some are already leading holy lives in the Church on earth; (2) some are living in the Church on earth, but are not *yet* converted from their sins[23]—thus the Church on earth contains sinners as well as saints; and (3) 'some still . . . even wallow in heresies[24]

---

[21] *Cant.* iv, 12 f.: 'My sister, my spouse, is a garden enclosed, a garden enclosed, a fountain sealed up. Thy plants are a paradise of pomegranates with the fruits of the orchard.'

[22] Unlike Cyprian, Augustine does, on occasion, refer to the 'Church' already triumphant in heaven in the persons of those who have died and have already attained their goal. Their number is constantly being added to. They are those in whom the whole purpose of that economy of grace, of which the Church on earth forms part, has been accomplished (except perhaps the full resurrection of the flesh). They are also, of course, as their place in heaven proves, of the number of the 'predestinate'.

[23] Of course, they *will* be converted before their time of probation in the flesh is ended; otherwise they would not be predestinate.

[24] Augustine had himself 'wallowed' in Manichaeism for years. He was not baptised till his early thirties.

or in pagan superstitions; yet even there the Lord knoweth his own. For in that ineffable foreknowledge of God many who appear to be outside are within, and many who appear to be inside are without' (the latter group being those who are members of the visible Church on earth but are not in the number of the predestinate; these, it is implied, will come to a bad end). And Augustine sums up the three groups of the predestinate thus: 'Of all these, therefore, who, so to say, are intrinsically and secretly within, consists the enclosed garden.'

Thus Augustine contends that there are in the total number of the predestinate (each of whom is known at present, as such, only to God) a certain number who are not at present in the Church. When he says that they are (really) within, he is not saying that they are already really within the *Church*; they are 'within' the number of the predestinate, and the number of the predestinate is not the same thing as the Church on earth. In the world to come the glorified Church will coincide with the number of the predestinate; all of them, and they alone, will be its members. But the Church on earth (which is our concern in this examination of the ancient view of the Church, and which was Augustine's concern in his controversies with the Donatists) is only an imperfect representation of the glorified Church; it is like a half-finished statue, from which various excrescences will have in due course to be chipped off. It includes among its members some who will be found to have been not among the number of the predestinate. It also, at the moment, does *not* include some who are already alive and who will in the end be found to have been predestined to heaven. Augustine does not here tell us whether this last group will, or will not, join the Church at some time before they die; it would be entirely consistent with his present argument to suppose that they will, and that only so will they prove to have been predestinate—at present, they are in the condition of Augustine himself before his baptism.

It must be concluded that the passage appealed to by Dr Greenslade shows no variation or deviation from the teaching that is universal in Augustine, that the Church on earth is exclusively composed of those who are within the single visible 'Catholic' communion. Nor, of course, does this passage imply that any one may stay outside the Church because, after all, if he is predestined he will go to heaven anyhow. On the contrary, Augustine may (so far as this passage goes) hold that everyone who is predestined is thereby destined to die in the one Catholic communion, as the only way of getting to heaven.

Harnack's contention, that the Augustinian theory of predestination 'shatters every notion of the Church', is not, of course, based on any single text of Augustine. And it is a far more radical criticism of the internal consistency of his theology than is Dr Greenslade's. It appears to take its stand on the Augustinian teaching that predestination is God's eternal decree to make a particular man one of his elect.[25] Harnack's argument is that, for such a man or woman, the means of grace (including the Church) are of no importance; whether he makes use of them or not, he will eventually be saved all the same; and on the other hand, it might seem to follow that, unless a man is thus eternally predestined, the most assiduous fidelity to the means of grace cannot ultimately have any saving efficacy for him. It seems to be obvious that, if the argument holds water, then not only the visible Church and the sacraments, but the objective redemption and the preaching of the gospel, are equally worthless. And the same must be said about the act of justifying faith. It will be noticed that Harnack himself says not only that Augustine's predestinationism 'shatters every idea of the Church', but that it 'renders valueless the institution and means of salvation'. Harnack's argument, for one who believes in Augustine's theory of predestination, strikes, if it is valid, at the root not alone of the ancient view of the Church, but of Christianity itself.

But in fact, at the level of thought that concerns us here, the argument is devoid of substance. Augustine himself writes: (If God has foreseen the final perseverance of the elect) he has of course foreseen those gifts of divine liberality *whereby* he deigns to redeem us. The predestination of the saints is simply the foreknowledge and preparation of the gifts of God *whereby whoever are redeemed are most certainly redeemed*.[26] In other words, in foreknowing the salvation of the elect, God foreknows the whole process and the various means by which that salva-

---

[25] In this and the following paragraphs I am following closely Batiffol, *op cit.* pp. 520 ff.

[26] *De dono perseverantiae*, quoted by Batiffol, *ibid.* p. 521.

tion will be worked out within the temporal process which we call probation. As an architect conceives the idea of a completed house and then devises the stages of putting his idea into effect, so God conceives the idea of a man's salvation, and 'then' (but there is no before and after with God) devises the means of realising this salvation. Grace is the means of salvation; and therefore the means of grace are, at one further remove, means of salvation. Among these means of grace, according to Augustine, was the objective redemption accomplished in the death of Christ. But among them also, under the over-arching fact of the Cross, were the sacraments and the visible Church. I do not think that Augustine's logic can be faulted at this level of consideration. I do not think that there is any inconsistency between his view of predestination and his belief in the Cross and the Church.[27]

More than this need not here be said about Augustine's theories on predestination. Our only interest in them has been to determine whether they are consistent with the ancient belief about the Church to which Augustine bears such impressive witness. And in fact they seem entirely consistent with that belief, and we have not discovered any evidence that they led the great African into the use of language on the subject of the

[27] I am very far from denying that, at another and a deeper level of thought (which is, however, outside the scope of these pages) the question of predestination is a difficult one. But I venture to suggest that, although these difficulties of course make their appearance in Christian theology with its revealed *data*, they belong essentially and originally to the sphere of natural theology; they are philosophic difficulties at root. They are all forms of the fundamental difficulty of finding room for finite realities, finite causes, finite freedom, alongside the absolute reality of Pure Act. The existence of God, while it is the supreme mystery, yet constitutes, in itself, no *difficulty* for the intellect, since *ex-hypothesi* God is entirely self-explanatory. It is the existence of creatures which is the source of all our difficulties. On the other hand, that creatures do exist and do act, and in particular that we rational creatures act freely, are facts of ineluctable experience, hard to reconcile with the existence of God. It seems probable that only in the beatific vision, when we shall 'know even as we are known', shall we find the answer to the difficulties, of which predestination is one.

Meanwhile, it may be worthwhile to remind ourselves that Christianity, outside perhaps some streams of the reformation tradition, has never committed itself to the whole Augustinian theory of predestination. Batiffol quotes a Roman document of the time of Celestine I, but not improbably composed by the Pope's deacon, the future Leo the Great. In this the prudent advice is given not to despise, but also not to elaborate, those deeper and more difficult questions on which the Apostolic See has not pronounced. 'There is no doubt', writes Batiffol (*op. cit.* p. 534), 'that predestination is included by this document among the "deep and difficult matters" upon which the Roman See does not choose to pronounce.'

Church and her unity that is even formally at variance with the language of Cyprian. It has similarly become clear that Augustine's championship of the validity of schismatical sacraments did not cause him to modify in the slightest degree the traditional view of the Church as essentially a single visible society or communion. I have further suggested that, in diverging from Cyprian on the subject of the possible validity of non-Catholic sacraments, Augustine was not the mere inventor of a new theory, but was simply loyal to the implications of current ecclesiastical practice and the directions of Catholic ecclesiastical authority. Certainly, by this time, the Roman line about schismatical baptism was regarded as obligatory in Catholic Africa and (so far as he was aware) in the whole Catholic world. As regards the Orders of schismatical bodies, we have seen that his father in the faith, Ambrose, had accepted as valid the Orders of Arian converts; and this not improbably indicates that Rome was already taking the same line in this matter also.

At the present day it is regarded as axiomatic, at least by most Christian bodies in the West, that valid baptism is not confined *de facto* to the administration of *any one communion*; and indeed the Roman Catholic Church teaches that an unbaptised atheist can baptise validly. What basis can be found for this conviction?

Most Christians agree that Christ instituted the Church; but there is disagreement about the Church's nature.

Let us suppose, for a moment, that Christ did not endow the Church with any permanent structure or structural principles, nor give any expression to the sacramental principle other than that which may be implicit in the very fact of the Church herself as in some sense a continuation of the idea, itself a 'sacramental' idea, of incarnation. In that case it would seem natural to view the actual sacraments, such as baptism and the Eucharist, as rites created and adopted by the Church herself for the expression and ordering of her corporate life. On this view, the validity of the sacraments would be the validity appertaining to such merely ecclesiastical rites. True, the Church herself would be of divine foundation; and since she may be presumed to hold from Christ the authority to order her own life according to the permanent, and also to the changing, conditions of her historical existence, the 'validity' of the sacraments could be taken to be indirectly 'underwritten' by Christ, on the principle expressed in the words: 'Whatsoever you shall bind on earth shall be bound in heaven.' But the sacraments would have no *immediate* divine authority, no intrinsic validity, apart from the validity derived from their creation by the Church and her authorisation of them. The Church would not merely 'administer' the sacraments; she would be the immediate *agent* in them, just as a man is the agent of his own acts, although God is the 'First Agent'. On this view it might seem inconceivable that 'sacramental' acts performed outside the Church, and without her authority, could have any meaning or supernatural worth.[28] Baptism, let alone ordination, performed by a schismatic would be of no more intrinsic value than a forged British postal stamp.

As regards the Church's ministry, it does seem to be the classical Lutheran view that this is not something created immediately by Christ, but rather something *mediately* Christ's, as having been established by the Church. On this view episcopacy, for instance, may be of the *bene esse* of the Church; it cannot be of its *esse*, and the Church might abandon it or institute other forms of sacramental ministry alongside the episcopal.[29] Perhaps, then, it is not surprising that some non-Roman Catholic theologians feel greater uneasiness about Augustine's attitude to the ministry than about his line on baptism. For baptism and the Eucharist can claim clear New Testament authority for their immediate institution by the historical Christ.

The traditional Christian view, however, has been that expressed by Augustine, that the sacraments are not the Church's creation but Christ's; so that the immediate agent in them is

---

[28] Unless she 'validated' them retrospectively, as some have thought that the Eastern Orthodox communion is prepared to do in certain circumstances. It may be questioned whether this is really the meaning of the Eastern practice of 'economy'.

[29] The Report of the Lambeth (1958) Committee on *Church Unity and the Church Universal* uses language about the 'historic episcopate' which, while not excluding the view that the episcopate is of the *esse* of the Church, seems to me to leave room for the Lutheran idea: 'This ministry we believe to have been given to the Church by Divine Providence from primitive Christian times' (see p. 24, *supra*). The Report seems studiously to avoid saying that the traditional ministry was given to the Church by the *historical Christ from the beginning*.

neither the Church nor her ministers but Christ himself.[30] What are 'ministers'? They are human instruments, but not precisely—as regards the proper effect of the sacraments in the supernatural order—human *agents*. The Church could not invent a sacrament. She can only administer those entrusted to her by Christ.

On this view the sacraments are part of Christ's original, immediate, and permanent endowment of his Church; and this holds good for Orders and the other sacraments as well as for baptism and the Eucharist. They are Christ's gifts to the Church: or rather they are Christ's own things, committed to the care and dispensation of the Church. In this respect, they are like the books of Scripture. These books, considered precisely in their quality as inspired Scripture, possess their intrinsic supernatural qualities and properties immediately from God; these supernatural qualities are not mediated to the Scriptures by an act of the Church. All the Church can do, all she purports to do, is to recognise this divine endowment of the Scriptures. So, too, with the sacraments. Their grace-giving and character-imparting qualities are intrinsic to them and not dependent on the Church, whatever powers the Church may have to determine their external conditioning, and whatever rights she may possess in regard to their administration.

If this traditional view of the sacraments is correct, if the Church is the administrator but not the creator of the sacraments, then it will follow that, just as the Bible can circulate outside the Church and still remain a collection of inspired Scriptures, so too it is not *a priori* certain that the sacraments cannot 'circulate' outside the Church.

Are the sacraments things which the Church has created, or are they creations of the historical Christ, committed to the

---

[30] On Christ as the agent of baptism, cf. Augustine, *Tractatus in Iohannem*, vi, 5-7. The disciples of Christ, to whom was given the commission to baptise, are here called the 'ministers' of the sacrament; but the 'power' of the sacrament was not given to the ministers, but retained by Christ; and it is in virtue of this retention of the 'power' by Christ that all valid 'baptisms' are one, and 'through this power is established the oneness of the Church'. Augustine finds this truth, that Christ is the real agent of Christian baptism, in the words of John 1, 33: 'The man who will baptize with the Holy Spirit is the man on whom thou wilt see the Spirit come down and rest', sc. Jesus; and he goes on: 'Peter may baptize, but it is he (sc. Christ) who baptizes; Paul may baptize, but it is he (sc. Christ) who baptizes; Judas may baptize, but it is he (sc. Christ) who baptizes.'

keeping of the Church? As regards baptism and the Eucharist there can be no doubt that the Bible favours the latter view, which is also the traditional view; and it would be difficult, on Christian presuppositions, to maintain the former opinion.

But if this is so, and if therefore it is not *a priori* certain that sacraments cannot exist outside the Church, on what grounds are we to decide between the Cyprianic and the Augustinian view of schismatical 'sacraments'? If it is not possible to get a clear and indisputable ruling on the subject from Scripture, it would seem that our only means of settling the matter—short of a special revelation—is to refer it to tradition, that is to say to the traditional practice and teaching of the Church: *nihil innovetur nisi quod traditum est,* as Stephen wrote to Cyprian. And the determining tradition will presumably be the tradition of the Church, whatever meaning we may attach to the word 'Church', and however we may identify the Church and distinguish her from other claimants to the title. In other words, we cannot determine who are in the Church by asking the question: Who have valid sacraments? We have to determine what sacraments are valid by previously determining what and where is the Church, and then examining her tradition, her practice, and her teaching on the subject of the sacraments and their validity.

It remains to add that, if the traditional view of the sacraments is the true one, so that *a priori* they can exist outside the Church, and *a posteriori* they do, it is also true that the sacraments were entrusted by Christ to his Church, and that the *right* (as distinct from the power) to administer and receive them is one which can only be given or allowed by the Church. It is this which led Augustine to distinguish the efficacy of the sacraments from their validity. On this subject his thought may be summed up as follows: If you have no right to receive a certain sacrament in your present circumstances (e.g. because you are in a state of schism), and if nevertheless you flout this obstacle and do receive it (thus expressing your state of schism in a schismatical *act* depending on your free will), you obviously cannot expect to advance your friendship with God by this act which is, *ex hypothesi,* an act of disobedience to his will that all sacramental action should be under the aegis of his Church. The fruitfulness of a sacrament is precisely the gift, or an increase of, friendship with God. 'First be in the Church'. Augustine would say. So we are back again at the root issue: are we prepared to accept the ancient view of the Church to which Augustine stands out as a consistent and impressive witness?[31]

[31] For the meaning attached by Augustine to 'being in the Church', cf. Ep. cxlix, 3: 'Many when they are dying are separated from the Church, who, while they live, seem (*videntur*) linked to the Church through the fellowship of the sacraments and catholic unity.' What gives these people the appearance of being united to the Church is their sharing in the sacraments and in Catholic unity. Augustine, if we may judge by his works as a whole, would seem to have held that, unless they had been sharing in external unity, they would not even *seem* to belong to the Church.

Chapter 8

DEVELOPMENT OR REVOLUTION

IF we believe that Christ founded the Church, we may presume that the word 'Church' has an important meaning. Our last four chapters have been concerned with the meaning attached to the word, so far as it refers to the Church in this life, by Christian antiquity in the era immediately subsequent to New Testament times. We have been appealing to history; and this appeal, so far as it goes, has been decisive. Just as we owe to that period of Christian history the preservation and canonisation of the New Testament books, and therefore all our knowledge of the facts of our redemption, so too we find that those centuries of Christianity were in no doubt that the Church is essentially a single historical society characterised by the intercommunion of all its parts and members. In particular, this was the conviction about itself of the Great Church, the communion from which all modern Christian bodies in some sense derive their existence.[1] Antiquity's answer to the question: 'What sort of a thing is the Church on earth?' is intellectually coherent, even if the complications introduced into it by the 'Augustinian' teaching on the possible validity of non-Catholic sacramental ministrations may seem to involve an element of paradox. Intellectually coherent; but morally, it has been argued, intolerable—a logic of the lunatic asylum. Let us now attempt to state this objection.

'We are invited', it may be said, 'to believe that Christ established the Church as the sole repository and guardian of his redemptive grace and truth, and granted to her a permanent

[1] Our historical review went beyond the Councils of Ephesus and Chalcedon, and therefore beyond the points of theological divergence between the Nestorian and Monophysite communions on the one hand, and the rest of us on the other. But the Council of Nicaea, which lies well before both these points, and Augustine, who was dying when the imperial edict summoned the bishops to the Council of Ephesus, both speak clearly for the view of the Church as a single historical society.

existence and authority. And there might be a sense in which we should be prepared to accept this theory, and <u>even to admit the truth of the inference, which</u> antiquity drew from it, that <u>apart from the Church there is no salvation. It all depends on how you define the Church, and whether you look upon her as a means, or only as a result, of grace.</u>

'But then we are told that this Church of Christ is essentially a unique, indivisible, visible and historical society. As such, she is alleged to possess, by Christ's institution, an immutable structure and a divinely-guaranteed and authorised hierarchy. Membership of this society is necessary as a means to salvation, and involves sacramental baptism and adherence to the Church's one visible communion.

'Outside the spatial and temporal limits of this Church and its antecedents through Abel to Abraham and the Synagogue, there is nothing except a humanity which, as it stands, is on its way to irremediable perdition. The Church's missionary endeavours are directed to the individuals who compose this *massa perdita*, this Babylon, this "world which lieth in darkness". Only by believing her teaching, by conversion to her, and by perseverance in her communion till death, will any adult human being be saved.

'All that happens, all that is achieved, in human history outside the visible limits of the Church is worthless in itself: the glory of pagan Greece and the grandeur of imperial Rome, the life of the Buddha, the speculations of the Brahmin, Islamic mysticism and modern scientific integrity. Not only the non-Christian achievements but all the treasures of Christianity itself except when contained within the narrow limits of the one communion, are intrinsically of no value. Thus, if you identify the one Church with the Roman Catholic communion, or with the Eastern Orthodox, then you imply the worthlessness in themselves of the lives and works of a Wesley, a Shaftesbury, a Schweitzer. If any of these pagan or "schismatical-Christian" achievements can be allowed some value, it is only so far as they may have created conditions favourable for the numerical expansion of your Church and the deepening of its spiritual life. Newman, in his lectures on Anglican Difficulties, when he used his great powers of rhetoric, controversy, and sarcasm to tear into shreds the religious system which had claimed his allegiance for the first half of his life, was presumably speaking under the influence of the Holy Ghost; but when, years earlier at Oxford, he was preaching the Parochial and Plain Sermons, and the best and most thoughtful of Oxford's sons were hanging on the magic of his words, he was but a member of the *massa perdita*, a purveyor of merely natural eloquence untouched by the charity of Christ.

'And to reduce the whole position to absurdity, if there are valid sacraments outside this visible unity of the Church—and Augustine says there are—they are divine things with no sanctifying consequences for the recipient (unless, possibly, their efficacy may be "revivified" upon his subsequent reception into the Church). In short, you have turned the idea of the Church into that of a sect, and the spirit of the gospel into sectarianism.'

Such blunt language, of course, is not in the mode of modern scholarship. For a more restrained statement, and for a plea for theological reconsideration, we may turn to Dr Greenslade, who confesses to a 'strong desire to relate the experience of the early Church to the situation of divided Christendom today'.[2] Dr Greenslade criticises the consequences which Augustine drew, or which might seem to flow, from the doctrine that there can be valid sacraments 'outside the Church', and he suggests that, since we can hardly maintain with Cyprian that only one communion administers valid baptism, we had better solve our problems by rejecting the ancient idea of the Church as a single visible society.[3]

First, as regards Augustine. Dr Greenslade holds that on the whole Augustine was right in treating the validity of 'non-catholic' Orders as essentially the same question as that of 'non-catholic' baptism. It is true that baptism is peculiarly necessary to the salvation of the individual, so that there might seem to be a case for making it as widely accessible as possible. But this consideration is irrelevant if—when Augustine's views on the effects of schism are accepted—baptism outside the Church, though it may be valid, is yet totally inefficacious for salvation.[4]

Dr Greenslade has two arguments against Augustine's sacramental teaching with reference to schism. First, he never really

[2] *Schism in the Early Church*, p. 8.   [3] *Ibid.* pp. 178 ff.
[4] Even schismatical baptism can, on the Augustinian view, give sacramental 'character'. But this will not save an individual without charity, and charity, Augustine would seem to say, does not exist outside the Church.

answered the reasoning which led Cyprian to conclude that sacraments cannot exist apart from the authority of the Church.

Secondly, Augustine's handling of the distinction between sacramental validity and efficacy (or, as we have preferred to say, fruitfulness) involves 'an intolerable doctrine of divine grace':

> The Donatist priest celebrates (the Eucharist) as the Church does and with the same intention; Christ, the true minister, responds and acts; the sacrament is valid. Are we seriously to believe that a 'valid' eucharist can take place which is totally inefficacious, in which no grace is given, in which Christ is present sacramentally to no one? . . . Or are we to think that sacramental grace is bestowed *inutiliter,* or that it is stored up, to become operative when the communicant enters the Church? That is to make grace a stuff instead of the gracious personal presence of God.[5]

On the other hand, the Cyprianic view that valid sacraments can be had in only one communion is rejected by Dr Greenslade on empirical grounds:

> Today . . . most of us find it impossible to deny that the Holy Spirit has been working in communions outside the Church as it is defined by Cyprian, and indeed that he has so worked not only by God's uncovenanted mercies but through their ministries and through the covenanted sacraments which they administer. We cannot wholly return to Cyprian.[6]

Thus, it is argued, we can neither accept the pre-Augustinian position pure and simple, nor can we rest satisfied with Augustine's modification of it. Cyprian's doctrine is contradicted by the manifest facts of spiritual life existing in more than one Christian communion; Augustine's sacramental theology, divorcing validity in some (often occurring) objective circumstances from any sort or degree of spiritual fruitfulness, is incredible. What, then, is the answer to the problem of schism?

Dr Greenslade's solution of the difficulty would recognise as true two complementary propositions:

> There is a continuous, historical, concrete society, founded—or . . . refounded—by Christ, and to this society certain means of grace have been entrusted. Membership of this Church comes about by baptism, normally, and this Church is always in a real

---

[5] *Schism in the Early Church,* p. 178.   [6] *Op. cit.* pp. 181 f.

sense one, even visibly one. What has to be reconsidered in Cyprian is the identification of that one Church with a single communion. . . .

Again what is good in Augustine has to be preserved—the recognition that in some sense the . . . schismatics and heretics . . . were Christians and possessed a ministry and sacraments. What has to be reconsidered in him is, first, the particular idea of apostolic continuity which he shared with Cyprian, and, secondly and more specifically, his refusal to give any substantial recognition to the efficacy of their sacraments . . . Augustine ought to have recognised that the Donatists had not gone out of the Church, that they remained part of the Church. . . . Then we have at least preserved the sound Cyprianic principle that there is no ministry or sacrament outside the Church.[7]

This quotation gives us the core of Dr Greenslade's contention: the Church, though historical, concrete, and continuous, is not to be identified with a single communion essentially; it is, or may be, made up of several separated communions.

Two comments seem to be called for. (1) Dr Greenslade says that the Church is a continuous, historical, concrete *society*. The idea of a historical society has been examined at some length in Chapter 3 of this book, and the upshot of that examination seems to be that if the Church is such a society there is no escape from the conclusion that it must be identified with a single communion. A dissociated association is a contradiction in terms. I will only add here, in illustration, that to maintain that the 'Caecilianists' (Catholics) and Donatists of Africa in the year A.D. 400, taken severally in their corporate quality as two rival communions, were two 'parts' of the same continuous, historical, concrete *society*, is to use language in a way which I do not understand; would Dr Greenslade hold that the British Labour Party and the British Communist Party are both parts of the same concrete political party? Or that the United States of America and Britain are a single political state? Nor is it merely a question of language, important though language may be when we are trying to discriminate between two ideas of the Church. Dr Greenslade might, indeed, retort: Well, you mean one thing by a continuous, historical, concrete society, and I mean another. The question is, what is meant by

[7] *Op. cit.* pp. 181-4.

a society whose constituent parts are mutually independent societies. What sort of an entity is this concrete, historical, thing which includes within it the Roman Catholic communion, the Eastern Orthodox communion, the Anglican communion, and many of the various Protestant sects? When God became man, he took upon him a nature which we can define. When Christ founded the Church, did he found anything definable? Or did he merely found a movement of humanity with some centres of magnetic attraction such as the Bible and the sacraments? If the latter, is it not perhaps a hindrance to clear thinking to call this movement a society?

(2) It will be observed that Dr Greenslade's reasoning is the same as Cyprian's, but is used to produce an opposite conclusion. Sacraments, they both say, cannot be had outside the Church. Therefore, said Cyprian, all so-called sacraments outside the one Catholic communion are null. But Dr Greenslade says: therefore, wherever there are valid sacraments (and Augustine is right in holding that they can be had in several communions), there is the Church. The logic of the argument is in either case unassailable. It is the starting-point of the argument which is questionable. By what authority, or in virtue of what experience, does either Cyprian or Dr Greenslade know that sacraments cannot be had outside the Church? As we have argued in the previous chapter, the question whether valid sacraments can be given and received outside the visible limits of the Church is one which, failing a clear statement in Scripture, can only be answered, on the basis of Scripture and tradition, by whatever person or body has authority to interpret and expound the sources of revelation.

These comments, of course, leave untouched Dr Greenslade's objections to the traditional combination of a 'Cyprianic' doctrine of the Church and an 'Augustinian' doctrine of sacramental validity. Many will agree with him that, if he has given a complete account of the traditional position, some theological reconsideration is desirable. The question would then arise: are we to seek a development of theology, or must we acquiesce in a doctrinal revolution? It seems clear that Dr Greenslade's own suggestions amount to a revolution: we are to give up the ancient idea of the Church as being essentially a single communion.

The notion of theological development should in itself present no difficulties for a Christian. There was development in the individual thought of an Augustine or an Aquinas. There is development in the thought of the Church as a whole, as through the ages she ponders the implications and the mutual relations of revealed mysteries. Development is found within the pages of the New Testament itself.

It is true that a doctrine or a theological inference that has behind it the consensus of antiquity has in consequence, to put the case at its lowest, a very special claim upon the Christian mind. And such seems to be the status of the view that the Church is essentially a single communion. But, it might be argued, even a consensus of antiquity is not always to be taken at its face value. We have only to compare the modern interpretation of biblical inspiration and its corollaries with the ancient attitude to the Bible, to realise to what lengths legitimate development may go. Jerome and the great Dominican biblical scholar Lagrange both believed in the inspiration of Scripture, but seem to have drawn very different inferences from that belief. Is not the doctrine of the Church susceptible of an analogous development?

But development is one thing, and revolution is another. Dr Greenslade, and in this he is of course the mouthpiece of very strong currents of Christian thought, proposes that the ancient belief that the Church is a single communion should be given up. If we wish to determine whether this would amount to a doctrinal revolution, or only to a theological development, I suggest that we may ask ourselves four questions: Is the witness of Christian antiquity, or at least of that part of it, the Great Church, from which all modern Christian bodies descend, morally unanimous in the view that the Church is essentially a single communion? Was this conviction one that was indeed held *de facto*, but still inoperative in the life and official proceedings of the Church? What would be the consequences of abandoning it? What alternative view of the Church is available or conceivable?

(1) We need not waste time over our first question. The moral unanimity of antiquity is widely admitted, even in circles which do not share antiquity's belief on this point. In particular, Dr Greenslade, as we have seen, does not dispute it.

(2) An opinion may be held as a fact, and yet may exercise no determining influence on life and action. In the Middle Ages, there may well have been a moral unanimity of belief that the sun moved round the earth, not *vice versa*. But this belief made no practical difference to the life or theological thought or to the official proceedings of the Church. But the belief that the Church is essentially a single communion was very far from being 'inoperative' in the official life of Christian antiquity. It will be enough to mention two points in illustration. When the Great Church received into its communion converts who had held ministerial office in schismatic bodies, it was prepared, on occasion, to admit them to its own clerical ranks without 'reordination'. But it showed by its whole attitude and mode of procedure in this matter that it denied any legitimate standing to the schismatical bodies from which these converts had come. Secondly, as we have seen, the ecumenical councils acted as the authoritative representative organs of the whole Church of Christ. They did not regard their competence in matters of faith or discipline as being in any way jeopardised or diminished by the fact that the schismatics were not represented in their deliberations and decisions. They pronounced anathema on doctrines contradicting their own definitions or on persons adhering to such doctrines. The conviction that there is but one communion of the Church of Christ was the life-blood of the ancient Church and the presupposition of the dogmatic formulae in which it articulated its corporate mind.

(3) What would be the consequences of abandoning this conviction? We can to some extent anticipate them when we realise the fact, mentioned in the previous paragraph, that it was this conviction that enabled the Great Church of antiquity to meet and surmount its practical and doctrinal problems, and to give definition to the traditional faith which we inherit from that Church. If Arianism, Pelagianism, and Eutychianism were cancers in the corporate life of the ancient Church, it is hard to see how they could have been expelled except by conciliar or papal action such as was in fact employed against them; and such action implied the truth of the ancient concept of the Church.

This lesson from antiquity can be reinforced by an inference, drawn by some Anglo-Catholics, from their theory that the unity of the Catholic Church was broken by the schism of 1054 and again by the English Reformation. With a Church thus broken into three separated parts it is impossible, they point out, to convene an ecumenical council. And they infer that there is, in these circumstances, no possibility of defining articles of faith not defined by the ecumenical councils of the first millennium. Thus, to take an illustration, not only is the Lateran Council's definition of trans-substantiation (A.D. 1215) not binding as such on Christian consciences, but there is at present no way of securing an authoritative definition of the doctrine of the Real Presence. In other words, the kind of dogmatic development which was characteristic of the early centuries, a development which enabled the Church to keep abreast both of the challenges of new heterodoxies and of her own growth in the understanding of the deposit of faith, has been arrested for nine hundred years. If the Church is to recover its 'living voice', this could only be by the 'reunion' of Canterbury, Rome, and Constantinople. Dr Greenslade, who would not wish to be taken as a spokesman for the Anglo-Catholics, would extend the designation 'parts of the Church' to a far more extensive group of bodies than those recognised as such by this Anglo-Catholic theory; and if the 'reunion' of Canterbury, Rome and Constantinople seems a rather distant prospect, the wider reunion necessary to enable the Church, on Dr Greenslade's view, to speak as she spoke in the days of Nicaea and Chalcedon is proportionately more remote.

But if the Church is not essentially a single communion, then even the decisions of the early ecumenical councils may be called in question as lacking the authority which they claimed. They pre-supposed the truth of the view of the Church which Dr Greenslade (with the Anglo-Catholics) denies. If the pre-supposition was erroneous, then the decisions lack cogency. If Donatists, Arians and Semi-Arians, Pelagians and Nestorians were parts of the Church established by Christ, then the general councils of the Great Church were not ecumenical. The Church —whatever we mean by the Church—may have once again to ask itself whether Arianism, Apollinarianism, Pelagianism, and the other dead heresies are valid interpretations of the gospel. To some this may appear a not unwelcome consequence. Its immediate relevance, however, is to show that the proposed 'reconsideration' of the nature of the Church must undermine a great deal more of ancient and traditional Christianity than its belief that the Church is a single communion.

It has indeed been suggested that we can do without the authority of ecumenical councils (not to speak of Popes), since the 'consent of the faithful' is a sufficient criterion of orthodoxy. 'It is the consent of the faithful of the whole Church'—to quote a religious newspaper—'which demonstrates that a dogmatic statement (such as the definition of Chalcedon) is certainly true and part of the essential Christian faith'. And again, the individual Christian 'may be confident that he is in error' if he finds that his judgment on a point at issue is at variance with that of 'the vast majority of Christians of every age'.[8]

This infallibility of the consent of the faithful is admitted and affirmed by Roman Catholic theologians. They call it 'passive infallibility' in distinction from the 'active infallibility' of the 'teaching Church', i.e. the bishops in ecumenical council and the Pope defining *ex cathedra*. By the faithful these theologians mean of course the members of the Roman Catholic communion.

But the criterion is not practical until we have determined the nature and identity of the Church, and are thus in a position to know who are meant by 'the faithful'. The consent of the faithful only serves to determine, for instance, the truth of the formula of Chalcedon, if we artificially limit the 'vast majority' of Christians so as to exclude not only many modern liberals (some of them scholars or thinkers of the greatest eminence) but also the Monophysite communion from its origin till the present day. But if we begin imposing artificial limits on the 'vast majority', there will at once be a strong case for rejecting the idea of the 'divisibility of the Church' on the ground that the vast majority of Christians in all ages have accepted a view of the Church which this idea contradicts. The case for such rejection is strengthened when we reflect that this idea, that the Church is not essentially a single communion, appears to be a rationalisation *post factum* of the situation which we inherit from the Reformation. The Reformation itself was motivated not by a development in the theory of the Church, but by the strong affirmation of justification by faith and of

[8] *The Church Times* (date uncertain).

the supreme authority and sovereignty of God. Meanwhile, the theory of the Church's intrinsic divisibility has made no considerable progress in the two great communions, that of Rome and that of Constantinople, which did not accept the Reformation. These two communions have the first fourteen hundred years of Christianity (since the end of New Testament times) on their side, and today they account for over two-thirds of the total number of Christians. On the other hand, if we extend the meaning of the term 'the faithful' so as to include all 'baptised persons', we shall find that no consensus of the faithful rejected Arianism or Nestorianism in their own day. If these 'heresies' have found so little support in subsequent ages, this may have been due to the effect of conciliar decisions and policies of repression based on them which, if the consent of the faithful excludes the authority of the teaching Church, may be considered suspect.[9]

As was suggested above, to some it may seem that it is no great loss to be compelled to admit that there is no way of ascertaining the Church's mind on the great doctrinal alternatives with which Christianity has been faced in the past, or which she will have to face in the future, even if these alternatives are as ultimate as the choice between Arianism and the Godhead of Christ, Pelagianism and the primacy of grace, the unity or duality in person of the Mediator. There are probably those who would argue that doctrinal determinateness, if not actually incompatible with the gospel, is at least irrelevant to it. Did not the great Ambrose say 'It was not by intellectual argument that God chose to redeem his People'? Thus we are driven, in our attempt to grasp the nature of the Church, to contemplate the great fundamental alternative: a faith which can be at least partially conceived, propounded and preached, or thorough-going

---

[9] In short: (1) The criterion of the consent of the faithful presupposes that we know who are meant by 'the faithful'. (2) If, as is necessary, 'consent' is interpreted as meaning the consent of the 'vast majority' or a moral unanimity, then it will be difficult (unless we pack our cards beforehand with this end in view) to deny that the consent of the faithful sanctions the authority of the 'teaching Church'. (3) It will also be difficult to avoid the conclusion that there is a consent of the faithful in favour of the view that the Church is a single communion. (4) To these points may be added the consideration that the consent of the faithful is in itself inarticulate; it does not *formulate* dogma, but at best it prepares the way for dogma and sanctions dogma when it has been formulated. We can hardly do without a *magisterium*; and unless the Church is a single communion it seems impossible to have an effective *magisterium* or 'teaching Church'.

liberalism. And if we decide in favour of thorough-going liberalism, we shall be compelled to admit not only that Christianity has been on the wrong track ever since the first Christian Pentecost, when it went forth with the historico-dogmatic affirmation that Jesus had risen from the dead and was thus guaranteed by God to be the Messiah, but that Jesus himself made no claim, even by implication, to be exercising a Messianic function or, if he did make such a claim, was mistaken, not perhaps as to the fact of his function, but certainly as to the relevance or legitimacy of claiming it. Such liberalism, if it succeeds in being a religion at all, is not the Christian religion, and hardly offers a basis for Christian reunion. It is worthy of remark that the World Council of Churches, the great organisation of the Ecumenical Movement, takes as its basis the acceptance of the Lord Jesus Christ as 'God and Saviour'—a thoroughly dogmatic, strongly anti-liberal basis, so far as it goes.

Dr Greenslade, of course, is not a thorough-going liberal, if a liberal at all. He suggests that we can distinguish some doctrines, some things to be believed, the acceptance of which would constitute a religious communion as a Christian body and (it would seem) a 'part' of the Church.[10] He mentions the authority of the Bible, with the (disputable) corollary that nothing be held to be an article of faith unless it is either contained in or can be proved from the Bible. To the Bible he adds the Apostles' Creed (the Nicene Creed, it would seem, is also desirable). Besides these beliefs, he mentions, secondly, some institutions, the rejection of which by a religious communion may make it doubtful whether it is part of the 'visible Church militant': the ministry, and the sacraments of baptism and holy communion (the acceptance of the rite of Confirmation is viewed as of doubtful necessity). In the present condition of divided Christendom, Dr Greenslade is not prepared to require an *episcopal* form of ministry or—I think—any recognisable form of 'apostolic succession' in the ministry.

It will be observed that this list of requirements, in order that a religious communion may rank as part of the Church, is not very extensive. It includes, for instance, no statement of Christology beyond what can be inferred from the Apostles'

[10] *Schism in the Early Church*, pp. 216 ff.

Creed and the New Testament, both of which the Arians would have been willing to accept.

We may concentrate our attention on one point: the requirement that every part of the Church must accept the authority of the Bible. This cannot mean the acceptance of the books of the Bible merely as historical documents. Dr Greenslade means that the Bible is to be an authority for faith, and indeed the only such authority. Why, however, should the Bible be thus accepted? Historically, we accept it as the word of God because the early Church so decided. But can we accept the verdict of early Christianity on this point—a point so vital in a set of proposals which omits all reference to the authority of the Church—if we reject its witness to the nature of the Church? If, on the other hand, appeal is made to the fact that not only early Christianity but all subsequent Christians have accepted the authority of the Bible, we have first to face the difficulty that in modern times the Bible has been under such heavy fire from the critics that some have thought it necessary to empty the notion of biblical inspiration of any meaning that could give the Bible final authority for faith; and indeed, its authority has perhaps survived only by reason of the strong backing given to it by ecclesiastical authority. In the second place, if our appeal is to the verdict of all Christians, will it not be logical to make 'the Church' mean just 'the totality of Christians'?

(4) And so we come to our fourth question: What are we going to put in the place of the discarded notion of the Church as a single communion? Even if we could agree with Dr Greenslade (or, for instance, with F. D. Maurice) on the requirements to be met by any body claiming to be a part of the Church, what is the *nature* of this Church, what sort of a thing is it, seen as a unity and not merely as its several parts? To this question I find no answer in the statements of those who think on the lines expounded by Dr Greenslade. They do not wish to fall back on the idea of a strictly invisible Church. But they nowhere define what they mean by 'the Church'; or if they make the attempt, they use the term 'society' in a way which can only raise the further question: What is a society that is not associated? Whether the constituent members of the Church are taken to be all baptised persons, or alternatively a group of religious communions, it seems impossible—once we have discarded the

ancient view that the Church is a single communion—to make 'the Church' mean anything more than this totality of individuals or communions in its tendency towards social aggregation. The Church herself, as logically distinct from her members, is a social tendency.

It may be said—substantially, it has been said—that we must have a new theory of the Church, but we must be patient while this theory is being elaborated. We must have it, it may be argued, because neither the theory of the invisible Church, nor the Anglo-Catholic Branch Theory, nor any extension of the Branch theory such as is adumbrated by Dr Greenslade, as an alternative to the ancient view of the Church as essentially a single communion, will, in the long run, hold water. And we cannot go back to the old theory, because it is contradicted by the facts that stare us in the face; the 'lesson of history' is that the unity of the Church, if it once existed, has been lost—not lost in its metaphysical essence (which remains to be determined), for the Church is a thing, and everything has its unity —but lost in its outward manifestation in terms of a single communion of believers. In particular, to accept the idea that the Church is essentially a single communion would mean that we must either 'unchurch' the great Eastern Orthodox communion, or alternatively identify the Church with that communion and therefore 'unchurch' the great Roman Catholic communion; and is it not paradoxical to accept either of these options?

In reply to this suggestion, it may be noted, in the first place, that since New Testament times there never has been complete visible unity of all Christians in a single communion. The first Epistle of St John shows that it did not exist when that document was being composed. If, then, the lesson of recent history is that the Church is divided, is it not the lesson of history as a whole that she has never, since the death of the last apostle, been united?

More important is the fact that the possible variations on the theme of the nature of the Church have already been exhausted. In other words, we know already that the future can provide us with no theory of the Church's nature of which we are not already aware. The Church either is, or is not, a purely invisible entity. And if she is a visible entity, she is either essentially a single communion or she is not. In the latter case —since the very word Church connotes sociality—she is a visible entity that is potentially a society; and that potentiality is either written into her nature as an ideal at which Christians are to aim, or it is not. There is no possible synthesis between the notions of the Church as essentially an actual single communion and of the Church as essentially a potential single communion. Nor of course is there any possible synthesis between the notion that the Church is in no way visible and the notion that she is actually and essentially visible. There is no possibility of a new ecclesiology, though there may be a possibility of development within the limits of one of the existing ecclesiologies.

Thus there can hardly be much dispute about the answers to our four questions. There was a moral unanimity in Christian antiquity on the subject of the Church's nature. This conviction was not an inert item in the mind of the Christians, unrelated to their corporate and official decisions and actions; it was, on the contrary, the dynamic principle behind the dogmatic development and the disciplinary procedure of the Church. To abandon this belief about the Church's nature would mean, logically and perhaps practically, that we should be tending towards thorough-going liberalism. The only possible alternative belief, short of accepting the idea of a purely invisible Church, is the theory that the Church is a potential society; and this, as we shall argue in a later chapter, would be tantamount to substituting for the realised eschatology of the gospel an unrealised eschatology.

If genuine development entails the subsumption of past positions in a higher synthesis, while revolution means the rejection of the past, these answers seem to indicate that what Dr Greenslade offers us is not a genuine development. In any case, it seems worth while to ask ourselves whether it is not possible to sketch out a development of the theology of the Church which would leave the positive elements of the ancient view substantially intact, would meet the difficulties that have been advanced against the ancient belief, and would be able to point to seeds of itself in ancient Christian thought. To this question our next chapter will be addressed.

Meanwhile, it may once again be desirable to emphasise that though, for the sake of convenience, we have fastened our attention on Dr Greenslade's book, our argument has in fact a wider scope. From our point of view, Dr Greenslade is the able and scholarly spokesman of a school of thought. There is doubtless much diversity of opinion among the adherents of this school on such subjects as sacramental efficacy and ministerial validity. It includes some who hold that sacraments are efficacious signs, and others for whom they are mere, but venerable, symbols. It includes a party which believes that episcopacy is of the *esse* of the Church, and a larger number who are not prepared to say more than that it is of her *bene esse*. But they are all agreed that the Church is not essentially an indivisible visible society, a single communion. They all agree that if there may be such a thing as schism *from* the Church, at least there certainly is schism *in* the Church.

To the extent to which this school of thought appeals to the evidence of history and to the apparent distribution of grace, we have now to ask ourselves whether these appearances and evidences can be satisfied in some less radical way. And here there is a consideration of some importance. Can it be maintained that the grace of holiness is confined within any particular Christian limits? If it seems clear that holiness is found in more than one Christian communion, is it not also sufficiently clear that it exists sometimes outside all Christian adherence and recognisably Christian belief? If so, there is a challenge to us to look for a solution of our problem in a hypothesis which, while doing justice to the specifically Christian facts, would cover this wider range also.

Chapter 9

OBJECTIVE REDEMPTION AND GOOD FAITH [1]

THE first movement of the human quest for experience, knowledge, and understanding is outwards towards the object, and—in the first instance—the material object. The child, and humanity in its childhood, is aware of its surroundings before it is reflectively conscious of itself. *Incipe, parve puer, risu cognoscere matrem.* The Wise Man's maxim: Know *thyself* (*nosce teipsum*) is addressed to such as are adult or on the threshold of maturity. It is only by a relatively difficult process of reflection that we begin to learn the subjective conditions of our objective experiences. Since Descartes, and his *cogito, ergo sum,* we have been more and more initiated into introspection and psychology. In contrast, the Middle Ages, with their predominant interest in the metaphysics of being, were carrying on the mainly objective attitude and interests of antiquity. There has been, over the centuries, a gradual interiorisation of the Western outlook, partly perhaps due to a growing Christian maturity, partly reacting on Christian thought itself to make it more 'subjective'.[2]

[1] This chapter is concerned with the relation to salvation, and to the Church and her sacraments, of those who have reached 'the age of reason'. By the age of reason is meant, here, not the age at which an individual is legally presumed to have attained to the use of reason and therefore to adult moral responsibility, but the age at which any given individual does actually so attain (if at all). Those who die before reaching this age may, for our present purposes, be described as infants. The salvation (or otherwise) of infants, whether baptised or unbaptised, raises special problems which are not examined here.

[2] Perhaps the greatest of Greek love poems is Sappho's, translated (but no one can really translate her burning, incandescent, words; Horace tried and failed) by W. Headlam in *The Oxford Book of Greek Verse in Translation*:

> Blest beyond earth's bliss, with heaven I deem him
> Blest, the man that in thy presence near thee
> Face to face may sit, and while thou speakest,
>   Listening may hear thee,
> And thy sweet-voiced laughter:—In my bosom
> The rapt heart so troubleth, wildly stirred:
> Let me see thee, but a glimpse—and straightway
>   Utterance of word

The ancient Christians, with their strong insistence on the objectivity of the Christian reality, were, in general, men of their own age. And not least typical was Cyprian, with his sublime disregard for all discrimination between objective right and subjective light: 'If escape was possible for those outside the ark of Noe, it will be possible for those outside the Church. . . . Let none suppose that good men can leave the Church.'³ All salvation, they correctly held, comes to man from the objective redemption effected by the actual death of Christ upon the Cross, and his actual resurrection. And the salvation thus accomplished is brought home to men by the Church, which is at once the Body of Christ and a particular historical reality presented to man through his senses and entered by the outward rite of baptism. The whole 'institute of redemption' was as much independent of man's subjectivity as earth and sky and the laws of nature.

Augustine, like Cyprian, is usually very 'objective' in his theological statements. He tends to argue according to the 'normal' (not necessarily the most frequently verified) scheme of things laid down in the given revelation and the instituted means of grace, and to mention no exceptions to the rules, which might cover such subjective 'abnormalities' as inculpable

---

> Fails me; no voice comes; my tongue is palsied;
> Thrilling fire through all my flesh hath run;
> Mine eyes cannot see, mine ears make dinning
> Noises that stun;
>
> The sweat streameth down,—my whole frame seized with
> Shivering,—and wan paleness o'er me spread,
> Greener than the grass; I seem with faintness
> Almost as dead.

Here the passion of love is expressed by an almost overwhelming record of its physical effects: the throbbing (physical) heart; the voice dumbed and the eyes blinded; fever, sweat, shivering and swooning paleness. Contrast Donne's *The Extasie*:

> When love, with one another so
> Interinanimates two souls,
> That abler soul, which thence doth flow,
> Defects of loneliness controules.
> Wee then, who are this new soule, know,
> Of what we are compos'd, and made,
> For, th'Atomies of which we grow,
> Are soules, whom no change can invade.

Donne does not forget the body ('But O alas, so long, so farre Our bodies why do we forbeare?'). But his awareness of love has a dimension beyond what Sappho knew. For him the bodily experience is instrumental to the 'interinanimation of two souls'. ³ *De unitate*, Chapters 3 and 9.

ignorance or error held 'in good faith'.[4] To a very large extent we all argue in the same way. Thus we say that it is sinful to appropriate what is not one's own. Usually, we do not think it necessary to add that, of course, there are cases when a man does actually take what is not his own without committing sin in the eyes of God; he has 'objectively', but not 'subjectively', broken the moral law. Or again, we say that idolatry is sinful. To give a creature such worship as may be given only to the Creator is idolatry. But we do not usually trouble to point out that a man who adores a piece of bread which he innocently but erroneously thinks has become by consecration the Body of Christ, has not committed a sin.[5]

Speaking thus objectively, Augustine tells us that schism is 'a most horrible sacrilege'. Elswhere[6] he says that it is clear from Scripture that 'there is nothing graver than the sacrilege which schism is'. He can use this strong language because, for him, schism is a sin precisely against charity, the supreme evangelical virtue, which unites us to God in Christ and, at the same time, unites us with one another in the universal unity of the visible Church. If we take this objective standpoint, it is obvious enough that a man who receives holy communion schismatically, thus committing a voluntary act of 'horrible sacrilege', can hardly be supposed to receive grace through that act of reception. And the same will be true about schismatical baptism; except that baptism, besides (when it is well received) bestowing the grace of Christ's friendship, also imprints on the soul the 'seal' or 'character' of a Christian, and *this* effect is produced independently of the moral state of the recipient. So Augustine can write (in 'objective' terms): 'Outside the Church there is no salvation. Who denies the truth of that statement?

[4] Inculpable ignorance is called by Roman Catholic moral theologians 'invincible ignorance'. Unfortunately, this term seems to suggest to many people the notion of 'obstinate ignorance', which is precisely the opposite of its technical meaning. Inculpable (or 'invincible') ignorance is such ignorance, whether of the moral law or of the moral implications of a given situation, as is not due to any guilty failure, on the part of the ignorant person, to acquire the necessary information. We are all under an obligation to take reasonable care to learn our duties and to sum up the moral requirements of the situation in which we find ourselves. Any ignorance which remains after such reasonable care has been taken is inculpable; if, in consequence of it, we overlook some duty, we are not guilty in conscience of the misdemeanour which, in objective fact, we commit.

[5] There is an interesting discussion of moral ignorance in Aristotle's *Ethics*, Book II.   [6] *Contra Ep. Parm.* ii, 25.

Hence none of the things that belong to the Church (e.g. the sacraments; we might add, the Bible) have power unto salvation outside the Church.'[7] And he goes on to point out that to say that sacraments outside the Church have no power unto salvation is not the same as saying that valid sacraments cannot be *found* outside the Church.

All this is perfectly logical, so long as we restrict ourselves rigorously to the objective standpoint, according to which schism is a sin, and the use of the sacraments outside the Church is sinful.

But why is it that sacraments outside the Church are powerless to salvation? Is it because they are *given* outside the Church, or because they are *received* outside her? The question is a vital one.

If we say—and it seems to be manifestly true—that schismatical sacraments are, from our objective standpoint, inefficacious or fruitless because they are *received* outside the Church, then we can go on to ask: *why* does reception outside the Church deprive the sacraments of saving fruitfulness? The answer will clearly be: Because a person outside the Church is in the gravely sinful state of schism, and no sacraments avail to salvation for one who is in a state of grave sin.

But at this point the question may very reasonably be asked: Is it a frequent occurrence for a person who receives baptism or holy communion to be in 'bad faith' about his ecclesiastical allegiance? If he is not in bad faith, then, though schism is present as a fact, it is not present as a sin. He is 'inculpably ignorant' of the fact that membership of the Christian body whose sacramental ministrations he is accepting does not constitute membership of the Church. He does not know that he is receiving a sacrament 'outside the Church'. That being so, he is not interposing the obstacle of the (subjectively) grave sin of schism; and as (*ex hypothesi*, for we are not here considering invalid sacraments) his baptism or holy communion is valid, it will also, other things being equal, be efficacious or fruitful.[8]

It is to be remarked that, if this view of the possible fruitfulness of schismatical sacraments may seem to some to be a

[7] *De baptismo*, III, 24.
[8] The 'other things' that have to be 'equal' are the same for him as for one who is within the Church: he must not have his conscience burdened by any other unrepented grave sin.

development, its seeds are to be found in Augustine himself. He is, to begin with, perfectly aware that schismatics are not all equally guilty of the *sin* of schism. There are, in fact, many who are, objectively, in a condition of schism, but are hardly, or not at all, guilty of deliberate sin in the matter. Thus, with reference to Donatism (which he counts as not only a schism but a heresy, since it has become 'inveterate'), he writes:

> But they are not to be reckoned among heretics who defend their opinion, false and perverse though it be, with not obstinate passion; especially if it is an opinion which they have not conceived with bold presumption but have inherited from parents who had been deceived and fallen into error; and if (further) they seek the truth with anxious care, being ready to correct their views when they have found it.[9]

Here is a generous recognition of the fact that the adherents of a schismatical communion, or many of them, may be in good faith, and therefore not necessarily receiving the sacraments with a guilty conscience. A modern Roman Catholic can obviously apply such considerations to, for instance, the great mass of the members of the Eastern Orthodox communion. Perfectly unaware that their own communion is 'outside the Church', they have no schismatical intent. They live serenely, like their parents before them, in the conviction that they are within the unity of God's Church. Their objective condition of schism carries no taint of subjective sin, of guilt. They therefore place no obstacle of sinful 'schism' to the fruitfulness of the sacraments validly administered to them. There is nothing here to prevent these sacraments having their normal effect of giving or increasing sanctifying grace.

We are assuming that the reason why sacraments outside the Church are ('normally') unfruitful is that they are *received* outside the Church, not that they are *given* outside her. Here, too, we can claim the authority of Augustine. He envisages the case of a Catholic receiving a sacrament (baptism, apparently, so that the man should be described as a Catholic catechumen) from a schismatic:

> Take someone in extreme necessity (presumably, faced with the prospect of imminent death), who cannot find a Catholic from whom to receive (the sacrament). Suppose that, while preserving

[9] *Ep.* xliii, 1.

his interior intention of unity with the Catholic Church, he
receives from someone outside Catholic unity what he would have
received within the unity of the Catholic Church. If such an one
forthwith departs this life, we do not consider him as other than
a Catholic. And if he escapes death, when he returns by bodily
presence to the Catholic community from which he never departed in his heart . . . we have no hestitation in praising him,
and are quite right to do so, for what he has done.[10]

Obviously, Augustine holds that such a man has not only
received the 'seal' of baptism but the spiritual fruit of the grace
of God, and this at the time when he received the sacrament
from a schismatic's hands. What determines, then, the possibility of a valid sacrament being unfruitful is not the state of the
minister but that of the recipient. If the recipient is 'in good
faith' ('preserving his interior intention of unity with the
Catholic Church') and if circumstances warrant his reception of
a sacrament even from one whom he knows to be in schism,
then the sacrament, provided it is a 'valid' sacrament, can also
be fruitful; and this, notwithstanding the fact that the minister
may be in 'a state of sin' by reason of his schism.

We are not here directly considering the situation of those
who have not reached the age of reason. But we can find a
further illustration of Augustine's idea of the obstacle to sacramental fruitfulness in his teaching on infant baptism. An adult
is required to make an act of faith in the revealed doctrine of
the gospel, an act of faith which is externalised in the profession
of the baptismal Creed. An infant cannot do this. But nevertheless he receives the sacrament, and receives it 'unto salvation'
(i.e. both validly and fruitfully), because he does not 'oppose the
obstacle of any opinion against the faith'.[11] Doubtless, Augustine
is here speaking of an infant receiving baptism at the hands of
a Catholic. What is interesting, however, is that here again the
question of the fruitfulness of a sacrament is determined by the

[10] *De baptismo*, I, 3. The Canon Law of the Roman Catholic Church provides
that any priest, even if he be a heretic or schismatic, may validly absolve any
penitent in danger of death. Such absolution is in most cases not only valid
but lawful, though 'to avoid scandal' the penitent may be under an obligation
to employ the services of an approved priest if one is available. Clearly, it is not
the *giving* of a sacrament outside the Church which, in Roman Catholic teaching, renders it unfruitful, and clearly there are circumstances in which the
reception of a sacrament from a schismatic can be fruitful.
[11] *Ep.* xcviii, 10.

subjective condition of the recipient. The same principle would appear to be applicable to infants receiving baptism from schismatics. These infants plainly have no heretical sentiments or schismatic loyalties. They thus 'oppose no obstacle' to the grace of the sacrament. And we can imagine such an infant growing up in a schismatical communion with the rest of his family, learning to practise its rites and to defend its tenets, yet never sinning gravely 'against the light'. The case must be verified in innumerable instances. Having been validly and fruitfully baptised, such a one will receive the actual graces to which baptism entitles him,[12] and may reach a high degree of holiness.

Generalising from these passages of Augustine, and from the 'Augustinian' view that there can be valid sacraments 'outside the Church', we reach a very important conclusion. So far from such sacraments being usually inefficacious or unfruitful, they will always be fruitful, provided only that the recipient is 'in good faith' and has 'supernatural contrition' for all his grave sins. To deny their fruitfulness in any given case is to pass judgment on the conscience of the recipient.

It remains, indeed, theoretically possible that 'a "valid" eucharist can take place which is totally inefficacious, in which no grace is given' because none is received.[13] But the occurrence is sufficiently unlikely; and it could happen not only in a schismatical body but within the Church herself.[14] It can equally (if not more easily) happen that the inspired Bible, read attentively by a believing sinner, may have no spiritual efficacy for good on the reader, but rather may increase his condemnation. None of these considerations imposes any strain on, or modification of, the principle that the Church is a single visible communion; since 'good faith', in the case of a schismatic, means that he is inculpably unaware that the ministrations which he is accepting are schismatical. The bearing of all this on the principle that 'outside the Church there is no salvation' will be considered later. For the moment it is enough to recall that Augustine had no suspicion whatever that he was being unfaithful to this

---

[12] 'The sacramental grace conferred through baptism carries with it the right to actual graces for the correct conduct of a Christian life; this is certain', Tanquery, *Brevior Synopsis Theologiae Dogmaticae*, edn. 6, p. 596.

[13] Cf. Greenslade, *Schism in the Early Church*, p. 179.

[14] For instance, a priest might (sinfully) celebrate the Eucharist in a state of unrepented grave sin, and might be the only communicant.

6

principle, and to re-echo his own words: 'Outside the Church there is no salvation; who denies it?'

So far we have been considering the fruitfulness or otherwise of valid sacraments outside the Church. The conditions of the problem raised by invalid sacraments are somewhat different. We may take it for granted that a rite which purports to be a Christian sacrament must conform to certain conditions, apart from which it will be 'invalid'. Thus the Lambeth (1958) Committee on Church Unity and the Church Universal speaks of baptism 'in the name of the Holy Trinity'; no-one would suppose that baptism in the name of a pagan goddess would be a 'valid' Christian baptism. Again, it is held by Roman Catholics, Eastern Orthodox, and many Anglicans, that a valid Eucharist supposes that the celebrant of the rite is in possession of holy Orders (priesthood) derived from the apostles. We are not here to discuss in detail the conditions of validity, but merely to point out that a Christian communion may have rites which it regards as sacramental but which do not fulfil the conditions of validity established by Christ. It must be obvious that, if sacraments convey grace sacramentally, 'invalid sacraments' do not so convey it. The question, however, arises whether reception of 'invalid sacraments' in good faith may, other things being equal, be the occasion of the reception of grace.

Let us suppose an improbable, but not absolutely impossible, occurrence, assuming, for the argument's sake, that only a validly ordained priest can validly celebrate the Eucharist. It could conceivably happen, through a concatenation of accidents, that the place of a sick parish priest was taken at the altar, one Sunday morning, by someone who, unknown to the priest and his flock, is in fact not validly ordained. This impostor 'consecrates' the 'eucharist' and distributes what he has apparently consecrated to the faithful at the time of communion. They, in all good faith, receive what they think is holy communion with the same devotion as on any other occasion. They have no reason to suppose that they have not each received holy communion validly; although in fact this 'eucharist' was invalid and they have not received a sacrament. Does anyone believe that they will not have received any grace from the almighty love of God? Need we even, though we may hold the highest view of the sacramental system and have no doubt of the theological principle known as *ex opere operato*, maintain that they would have received *more* grace if the supposed priest had been really such? For the good order of the Christian economy as an objective historical fact, God requires us to conform our Christtian practice to certain objective conditions. But to imagine that God has bound himself so exclusively to these conditions that he either cannot or will not act outside them in such circumstances as we have suggested, is, it may be thought, to have a sub-Christian idea of God.[15]

Once again we can appeal to Augustine for support. The problem of invalid sacraments is a special case of inculpable failure to participate in the sacramental life of the Church. One case of such failure had already been faced before Augustine's time: that of individuals already convinced of the truth of Christianity but not yet baptised, who died a martyr's death while still only catechumens. What was the reaction of antiquity to this problem, in view of its principle that 'outside the Church there is no salvation', and of the doctrine that initiation into the Church is by way of sacramental baptism? It was the inevitable development of the doctrine of 'baptism by blood'. Unbaptised martyrs for the true faith were 'baptised in their own blood'— which is a polite way of saying that, though baptism is necessary, conditions can arise in which persons who die unbaptised, and therefore outside the Church and the whole sacramental system, will nevertheless be saved by Christ and will be members of the company of the blessed in heaven.

Augustine, in accepting this traditional view, develops it still

[15] Once again we may generalise. In a Christian communion in which, through defect in the 'sacramental sign', or through loss of a valid ministry, the 'sacraments' administered are invalid, we may, without divergence from traditional doctrine, suppose that those who receive these 'sacraments' in good faith receive grace in so doing. They will not have received it sacramentally, but it will really have been grace, tending towards sanctification. It may, however, be pointed out that, like the Incarnation from which they derive, the sacraments are a divine condescension to our human condition, and that therefore we may suppose that their fruitfulness is in some way related to psychological dispositions. The normal (collective and individual) psychological *milieu* of the sacraments is the life of, and in, the unity of the Church to whom Christ entrusted them. A 'schismatic' environment will, on this view, of necessity be something less than fully 'catholic', something 'provincial', with corresponding psychological consequences. There is an obvious danger that whereas sacraments are intended both to root us more deeply in the universal Church and to expand our individual horizons to the scope of her vision and mission, schismatical 'sacraments' may in fact, when frequented within the ambit and the presuppositions of a 'schismatical' body, root us more deeply in the limitations of the latter. Similar considerations apply to valid sacraments in a schismatical communion.

further: 'I infer that not only martyrdom for the name of Christ can supply for lack of baptism, but faith and interior conversion also, if difficult circumstances make it impossible for sacramental baptism to be administered.'[16] Augustine would be among the first to protest against any tendency to regard the sacraments as unimportant. If you can get to the sacraments, especially to baptism, you must of course do so. But if, through no fault of your own, you cannot receive grace sacramentally, then God has his own ways of dealing with your predicament.

The principle involved in this 'development of doctrine' is further applied by Augustine to the pre-Christian period. It was already generally recognised that before the establishment of the Christian dispensation in the blood of Christ, the grace of God was available unto holiness for the members of the Old Testament People of God through the divinely ordained rites of Judaism. But Augustine points to Job, as to one who was outside the Chosen People and the system of covenantal rites, and who yet was saved:

> It is true that there was no other people who could properly be called the People of God. But (the Jews) cannot deny that there were individuals in other nations belonging, not indeed by earthly but by heavenly association, to those true Israelites who are citizens of our heavenly fatherland. The holy and admirable Job is a clear case of this. He was no stranger 'in their midst', but born of Edomite stock; he was born and died in Edom. Yet he is so praised in holy writ that no man of his times can be compared with him for righteousness and piety. . . . I doubt not that God means us to infer that men may have existed in other nations also who lived godly lives and pleased God, thus belonging to the spiritual Jerusalem.[17]

Thus it seems clear that Augustine admits in principle the view that 'baptism of desire', to use a modern theological expression, can supply for sacramental baptism, in cases where the latter is impossible, so far as regards baptism's saving efficacy.[18]

---

[16] *De baptismo*, iv, 29.

[17] *De civitate Dei*, xviii, 47. Augustine goes on to say that such men must have received a revelation of the future coming of the Mediator.

[18] What baptism of desire (and 'invalid baptism') cannot do is to confer baptismal 'character'. In other words, it does not make the recipient a full member of the visible Church. Hence, it never dispenses from the need to receive sacramental baptism if and when such reception becomes possible.

Job, unbaptised martyrs, and catechumens dying prematurely, are all instances of the physical impossibility of receiving sacramental baptism (though whether Job is to be viewed as having been under a physical impossibility of participating in the Jewish rites is perhaps not clear). But the principle involved in these cases seems capable of extension to those for whom baptism is a 'moral impossibility'. A moral impossibility, as regards baptism, might arise through a sincere, 'inculpable', conviction that sacramental baptism is illicit as implying beliefs which one conscientiously rejects. Such a conviction might co-exist with a completely genuine will to respond fully to all the demands of the God of righteousness, so far as these demands come home to one's personal conscience. In such cases, there would be what modern theologians call an 'implicit' desire for baptism. One would desire to fulfil God's will perfectly. God's will is that all should be saved through sacramental baptism. But of this detail of God's will one would be inculpably unaware; it would be included in the generality of one's will to obey God, but not in one's conscious specification of the contents of God's will. It would be an implicit desire.

And if the doctrine of desire as a substitute for actual reception of the sacrament (when the latter is impossible) holds true for the basic sacrament of baptism, it will undoubtedly hold also for holy communion. Hence, incidentally, the emphasis laid by Roman Catholic spiritual writers, on 'spiritual communion' when sacramental communion cannot be had. This fact is of importance for those who are under an unjust sentence of excommunication. As Augustine says: 'Divine providence often allows . . . even good men to be expelled from the Christian association. When they bear this wrong, with the utmost patience, for the sake of the unity of the Church, and do not contrive novelties of heresy or schism . . . the Father who sees in secret crowns them in secret.'[19] If members of the Church, whether excommunicated or for some other reason unable to receive the sacrament of holy communion, may yet hope to receive grace through the devout practice of 'spiritual

---

[19] *De vera religione*, 11. It may be pointed out that if such a person, being a priest or a bishop and sure of the injustice of the sentence of excommunication, presumed to contravene the sentence by continuing to celebrate and administer the sacraments, he would be 'contriving schismatical novelties' and committing grave sin.

communion', it does not seem difficult to believe that a 'schismatic', receiving with similar devotion what he honestly but mistakenly thinks to be valid sacraments, will 'find grace with God'.

We have moved outwards from the question of the fruitfulness of valid sacraments received outside the Church, to that of the grace that may be received by those who, in good faith, make use of 'invalid sacraments', and thence to the possibilities of justifying and sanctifying grace first for those physically so placed that they cannot receive the sacraments, and secondly for those who inculpably but conscientiously reject all sacramental ministrations. We have supposed throughout that the Church is a single visible communion and that valid sacraments are possible 'outside the Church'—a combination of hypotheses which to Dr Greenslade seemed untenable. At each stage of the argument the determining factor has been the physical impossibility of reception or alternatively 'good faith'. The key to a solution was given by the ancient Church's conviction that 'baptism of blood' suffices in place of sacramental baptism when the latter is impossible. At each stage of the argument we have been able to quote Augustine in support of our suggestions, except indeed for the case of 'moral impossibility' and 'implicit desire'; and since the purpose of both Church and sacraments is to recreate man in the moral order, it would seem natural to suppose that moral impossibility based on good faith would not be more spiritually disadvantageous than physical impossibility.[20]

We have now to consider the objection that the positions put forward in this chapter are irreconcilable with the universal ancient Christian conviction that 'there is no salvation outside the Church'. And indeed, it might seem that to admit the possibility of the salvation (by virtue of the notion of 'implicit desire for baptism') even of non-Christians is to contradict the New Testament teaching that 'there is no other name given

---

[20] For the modern Roman Catholic view, cf. Tanquery, *Brevior Synopsis Theologiae Dogmaticae*, edn. vi, pp. 602 f.: 'Perfect contrition or charity, with at least an implicit desire of baptism, makes up in adults, as regards remission of sins, for sacramental baptism; this is certain.' He explains that this 'implicit desire' is included in 'the general determination to fulfil all God's commands'. Perfect contrition is sorrow for one's sins based on the love of God above all things. It is itself implicit in an attitude of complete obedience to conscience, or the 'general determination' spoken of by Tanquery—since the God of holiness obviously requires us to deplore, for his sake, our past sins.

under heaven whereby we may be saved' than the name of Christ. Can these objections be met?

In the first place, it must be said that if the principle that there is no salvation outside the Church meant that only such as have been admitted to the Church by sacramental baptism can go to heaven, it would certainly be untrue; and it is in fact contradicted by the ancient conviction that unbaptised martyrs for the faith could be saved. We are therefore bound, in any case, to seek an interpretation of the principle along somewhat different lines.

The principle undoubtedly implies that God's whole redeeming purpose for mankind has been expressed, 'incarnated', in the 'grace' and 'truth' which 'came to us' through Jesus Christ (Jn. 1. 17) and salvation is 'not to be found elsewhere' (Ac. 4. 12). Exception having been made for divine revelations and dispensations which antedated the Incarnation, the positive values of which have all been taken up into, and absorbed by, the Christian dispensation—so that none of them now has any standing in the supernatural order independently of Christianity—the Christian religious system is the only one that can truly claim to have divine authority and to embody God's saving purpose to mankind. The 'word' of universal human redemption has been 'made flesh' as Jesus Christ.

Again, the principle certainly means that the Christian religious system, the benefits contained in and flowing from the redemption objectively effected by Christ, are contained full and entire only in the divinely authorised embodiment of that religious system in the one Church of Christ. Elements of this complexus of aids to salvation are indeed discoverable outside the unity of the Church. The Bible seems to be an incontrovertible instance of this, since it can be read outside any Christian allegiance whatever. But when so found, these elements, as Augustine argued with reference to sacraments administered by schismatics, are still 'things of the Church'— ecclesiastical property, so to speak, that has got into unauthorised hands. The fact that the 'possessor' of this property is 'in good faith' may be unquestionable; it does not make it any less true that the good which these things of the Church do derives ultimately from the Church from which they derive and to whose care they were originally entrusted.

Thus there is an aspect in which, as Dr Mascall very well puts it,[21] the principle that there is no salvation 'outside the Church' applies to 'the channels or instruments of grace', as distinct from the individual recipients of grace. It means, in this aspect, that all salvation comes *by way of* the Church.

This, however, does not, I think, exhaust the meaning of the principle. It means, or implies, in the third place, that membership of the Church is the 'normal' condition of salvation. Exceptions to this norm, however numerous (and they may actually amount to a majority) remain exceptional.

Fourthly, then, and consequently, the principle carries the implication that such membership is, objectively speaking, of universal obligation. This obligation is as grave as salvation is important.

But all this does not mean that there are no exceptional circumstances in which one who dies unbaptised, or baptised but outside the Church, may yet attain salvation. The circumstances, as we have seen, may amount to a physical impossibility of receiving the sacraments; and of this there are two typical cases: the martyrdom of an unbaptised believer, and the death before baptism of a catechumen. Or the circumstances may consist in a 'moral impossibility' of receiving baptism or entering into the communion of the Church, as when a man is honestly convinced that such a step is forbidden by his conscience; we may add to these cases those where the honest conviction takes the mitigated form: 'I am not morally *bound* to take this step.' Moral impossibility is the same as what we have called 'good faith'.

In either case, whether, that is to say, the impossibility is physical or moral, we are, it should be observed, faced with an abnormal situation. Normally, it is necessary for salvation that a man should be in the Church (and this, in the view of Christian antiquity, means within the visible fellowship of the one visible communion of the Church) at the time of his death; and normally it is not right to delay the steps necessary to attain this active membership. There is, here, an obligation of the gravest kind, from which no power on earth can dispense him. If a man knows that he is not in the Church, he is bound to enter it; and if he judges that it is seriously probable that he is

[21] *Christ, the Christian, and the Church*, p. 149.

not in the Church, he is bound to take all reasonable measures to clear up his uncertainty.

Before leaving this subject, it may be worth while to point out that the New Testament is, on the whole, very 'objective' in its insistence on the Christian religion as the unique source and condition of salvation, as on the similar status, in pre-Christian times, of Judaism ('Salvation is to come from the Jews', Jn. 4, 22); yet it is not without passages which imply the principle of 'good faith'.

When, in St Luke's Gospel, Jesus is asked to say who is 'the neighbour' whom we are to 'love as ourselves', he chooses—not as the *object* of fraternal love but as the one who *exercises* it— a Samaritan, one, that is to say, who is 'in schism' from Judaism. There is no hint here of 'religious indifferentism', as though it did not matter whether one was in the covenantal fellowship or not. It is made clear elsewhere in the Gospels that Jesus enjoined obedience to the 'established religion' of Judaism. But where the Jewish priest and Levite of the parable failed, as regards the 'second commandment' of the Law, the Samaritan did not fail.

The principle of inculpable ignorance is stated explicitly in another passage of St Luke's Gospel: 'It is the servant who knew his Lord's will, and did not make ready for him or do his will, that will have many strokes of the lash; he who did not know of it, yet earned a beating, will have only a few.'[22]

Still more striking is a passage in St Matthew's Gospel: 'There is pardon for all the other sins and blasphemies of men, but not for blasphemy against the Holy Spirit. There is no one who blasphemes against the Son of Man but may find forgiveness; but for him who blasphemes against the Holy Spirit, there is no forgiveness, either in this world or in the world to come.'[23] A literalist exegesis has led to a great deal of agonised anxiety about the nature of the 'unforgivable sin' here mentioned. It should hardly be necessary to say that there is absolutely no sin which God will not forgive if the sinner repents (and grace for repentence will always be offered while the power of choice remains, though it may be rejected by the sinner). There can surely be no doubt that

---

[22] 12, 47 f. The saying looks like the remnant of a parable. It should not be inferred from 'only a few' that inculpable ignorance is, after all, slightly reprehensible!   [23] 12, 31 f.

what our Lord is doing here is, by means of the resources of Jewish rhetoric, to draw violent attention to the gravity of the attempt which had been made (see the context) to represent his own miracle of exorcism—so manifestly, it is implied, a work of divine power and a manifestation of the Spirit of God —as a work of the devil. *Had his opponents only been 'blaspheming the Son of Man'*—had they, 'in good faith', found it impossible to accept Christ's claims for himself—then their 'sin' would have been forgivable, even though it amounted, objectively, to a denial of the content of the Christian revelation in the historical person of Jesus. But they had allowed themselves to be led on from this denial to 'blaspheme' against the Holy Spirit—to defame as evil, nay as diabolic, what their own consciences, would they but have listened to the voice of conscience, would have told them was manifestly good. *This* was a sin against the light; it had put them in *bad* faith. The passage as a whole is a tremendous warning against the spiritual dangers of that sectarianism to which, whatever our Christian 'denomination', we are all prone. But it is also a reminder, if we are to take the 'forgiveness' of those who 'blaspheme against the Son of Man' seriously, that outward rejection of Christ (or his Church) is not necessarily subjectively culpable.

The truth is that, in the end, we shall all of us, Christians of whatever denomination, and non-Christians also, be judged not by the ready-reckoner of external adherence but by the criterion of a charity which is always essentially interior:

> Then the King will say to those who are on his right hand, Come, you that have received a blessing from my Father, take possession of the kingdom which has been prepared for you since the foundation of the world. For I was hungry, and you gave me food, thirsty, and you gave me drink; I was a stranger, and you brought me home, naked, and you clothed me, sick, and you cared for me, a prisoner, and you came to me. Whereupon the just will answer, Lord, *when was it that we saw thee hungry, and fed thee, or thirsty, and we gave thee drink . . . ?* And the King will answer them, Believe me, when you did it to one of the least of my brethren here, you did it to me.[24]

Here, once again, it would be absurd to read 'indifferentism' into the Gospel teaching. We shall be judged not only by love of

[24] Mt. 25, 34-40.

neighbour but by love of God. And love of neighbour includes not only the 'corporal works of mercy' but the 'spiritual works of mercy' also, although the latter are not mentioned in our passage. God is truth, and the love of God implies seeking (if need be), accepting, and professing the truth revealed by God and taught by his Church. To give to others the truth of God is likewise a 'spiritual work of mercy'; and to give the truth one must first have it. Both love of God and love of neighbour require us to belong to the Church of God, which is the incorporation of charity in Christ who was God and man. Still, the ultimate criterion is charity itself. In the end, the worth of right faith and of Christian allegiance and evangelism is the worth of the love of God and man by which they are inspired.

Unless one is prepared to deny that anyone outside the Church can have charity, it seems that one will be driven in the long run to some such interpretation of the principle that 'there is no salvation outside the Church' as that which has been suggested above. And if, on the other hand, one would wish to affirm that the possession of charity implies that its possessor is 'in the Church', one will be driven—short of 'blaspheming the Holy Spirit' by denying charity where it manifests itself—to dilute the notion of the Church to a degree far beyond what Dr Greenslade contemplates; to such a degree, in fact, that the term 'the Church' will mean nothing more than the purely interior and unverifiable harmony of men of good conscience.

We have been discussing the principle that there is no salvation outside the Church mainly from the point of view of its implications for the salvation (and sanctification) of individuals. It may well be, however, that this approach fails to do justice to an important aspect of the principle, which will emerge when it is viewed at its greatest depth. We must not attend so exclusively to the subjective, which is also the individual, side of man's experience as to forget the objective side whereby human life is capable of a social dimension requiring institutional embodiment.

What is at stake in history in this world is man's salvation and sanctification; apart from this, history has, ultimately, no meaning. But 'man' may mean the individual considered as a centre of incommunicable experience; or, and with full justice, the word may mean humanity in its collective life. In philosophic language, man has the unity of a natural species: *homo sapiens, animal rationale*. In biblical language, man has the original unity of 'the first man, Adam'. For the philosopher, history is the flowering of the potentialities of this single species, an efflorescence to which no single specimen can contribute more than a tiny, if indispensable, element; the contribution of each flows into a common pool of human tradition, upon which we all draw. For the Christian, history (considered in abstraction from Christ) is the unfolding of all that was 'mystically' contained in Adam and his personal story and fall. Christ, on the other hand, the *totus Christus* of Augustine, Christ *in capite ET in corpore*, Christ in his life as the Son of Mary and in his life as the Church, first precontains and then actualises all that was already in 'the second Adam from heaven', all that will be in the full efflorescence of redeemed humanity.

If it is true that God has a 'purpose' for each human individual ('since it is his will that all men should be saved, and be led to recognise the truth', I Tim. 2, 4), it is also true that he has a 'purpose' for humanity at large, for the 'progeny of Adam' considered as a totality, as a potential society of mankind. This purpose falls within 'his loving design, to give history its fulfilment by resuming everything (in Christ), all that is in heaven, all that is on earth, summed up in him' (Eph. 1, 9 f.). This divine purpose for humanity at large takes into its scope the whole of humanity, all that is descended from the first Adam ('God was in Christ reconciling the whole world to himself', II Cor. 5, 19). God has no purpose in the world except what is summed up in this universal purpose. And as the life of man considered in this collective aspect is necessarily expressed in historical events, this divine purpose is objectified in the historical life of Jesus and the historical life of the Church. There is no other salvation for collective man than that which is found in and given by the Church. Whatever is actualised in human history, however remote in time and place and apparent inspiration from the Church, has just so much worth—in the final assessment—as it has of positive relationship to the Church. And as it is this relationship which gives everything its worth, so also it is from the Church, the other term of the relationship, that everything derives its value. Think away the Church from the total human situation and story, and there is no ultimate value in any of it;

for to think away the Church is something that can only be done at the price of thinking away Christ, the very *raison-d'-être* of history. In Christ and in the Church, 'history has reached its fulfilment' (I Cor. 10, 11). The Church is the leaven that works in the whole lump. History is supernaturally alive, alive 'unto salvation', to the extent that the Church is alive, directly or by implication, within it.

I have been leaning heavily, in the above paragraph, on a profound chapter on 'Salvation through the Church' by H. de Lubac.[25] The following quotation is from the same chapter:

> The human race is one. By our fundamental nature and still more in virtue of our common human destiny we are members of the same body. Now the life of the members comes from the life of the body. How, then, can there be salvation for the members if, *per impossibilie*, the body itself were not saved? But salvation for this body, for humanity, consists in its receiving the form of Christ, and that is possible only through the Catholic Church. . . . Is she not responsible for realising the spiritual unity of men—in so far as they will lend themselves to it? Thus this Church, which as the invisible Body of Christ is identified with final salvation, as a visible and historical institution is the providential means of this salvation.[26]

[25] *Catholicism*, Chapter vii.

[26] *Ibid*, pp. 110 f. Lubac refers to a magnificent sentence of Augustine (Ep. cxviii, n. 33): 'The whole summit of authority, the whole illumination of reason, for the remaking and refashioning of the human race has been established in that one saving name (of Christ) and in his Church.'
A few notes on the quotation from de Lubac may be useful. (1) The 'body', of which, he says, we are members by our fundamental nature, is the collective totality of mankind conceived as a whole of interdependent parts. Man, he implies, is already such a body, before we bring redemption and its consequences into the picture. But, apart from redemption, this 'body' is Augustine's *massa damnata*, the city of Babylon, a city of the confusion of tongues. So considered, it might be truer to say that man is a potential body, labouring under a dimly felt absence of organisation and unity. Sin is, of its nature, disintegrative. The *actualised* body of humanity is the Church. (2) We are united not only by our nature and our common destiny, but by our common theatre of existence and the interrelatedness which is made possible by that common theatre. Each of us is an epitome of man's whole past history and carries within him the possibilities of man's future history. (3) When de Lubac says that 'the Church as the invisible Body of Christ is identified with final salvation', he is using a mode of speech which we have tried to eschew in these pages. By the 'invisible Church' he must mean the Church as she will be after the Last Judgment; as such, she is of course invisible to us here and now, just as our individual glorified selves, *as* glorified, are invisible to us at present. But there is a real identity and continuity between the Church after the Last Judgment and the Church now visible as a historical institution; just as there is identity and continuity between our future glorified selves and our present historical (and visible) selves.

The salvation of humanity is conditional upon that 'spiritual unity' which the Church exists to realise. This spiritual unity must be an outwardly expressed unity, a concord of minds manifested in and dependent upon a fellowship in outward association. The Church exists to give the world that unity. This has been God's purpose through her since her birth in Christ's resurrection. But 'no-one gives what he has not got'. If the Church is to give an 'incarnate' unity she must herself possess an incarnate unity. If this giving of unity is not just an accidental result of her contingent history but the essential function for which she was established by God in Christ, then she must possess this incarnate unity by her essence; 'action flows from essence', as Aquinas says (*actio sequitur esse*). And if her task and function are to continue 'until the consummation of the world' (Mt. 28, 20), her incarnate unity must be permanent, though always capable of increased perfection. The goal of Christian unity *cannot* be the 'reunion' of *the Church*.[27]

In our previous chapter we saw that Dr Greenslade had brought three objections against the ancient view of the Church as essentially a single communion. (1) Taking for granted the 'Augustinian' doctrine that valid sacraments can be found in more than one Christian communion, he argued that Cyprian was nevertheless correct in maintaining that valid sacraments cannot be found outside the Church; Dr Greenslade therefore inferred that each of several communions must be a 'part' of the Church. (2) He took it as a consequence of Augustine's view of sacraments 'outside the Church', that this would mean that these sacraments, administered in schismatical communions,

[27] The argument is often put forward that, as the Church is, by credal definition, 'holy', yet, in her phenomenal existence in her members, manifestly, at best, only imperfectly holy, so also, though 'one', she may be expected to be only imperfectly one. It is, however, open to question whether the Creed, in describing the Church as 'one', means simply that her members are 'united'. It is arguable that the real meaning of 'one' here is, not 'united' but, *unique*; that is to say, the Creed may be affirming that there is only one Church, not several such. There is no possibility of varying degrees of *uniqueness*. The Church cannot be more or less unique, or imperfectly unique. The Creed is saying, I suggest, that there is only one Church founded by Christ. This is common ground among Christians, and it leaves unsettled what *sort* of a thing this unique Church is. When that point has been settled, it is very likely that we shall find that the Church, though absolutely unique, is less *united* than she might be. Similarly, a single political party may be less united than it might be and yet remain a single party with a single executive. Once, however, unity reaches and passes the breaking-point, there will be two parties instead of one. But there can never be two 'holy catholic Churches'.

would be valid, indeed, yet totally inefficacious, and this seemed to him an intolerable supposition. (3) He pointed to what seemed to him to be manifest evidence of grace, flourishing in more than one communion, and indeed apparently flowing from the 'sacramental' ministrations of more than one communion; and, since the Church is the sphere of the operation of the Holy Spirit, he inferred that the limits of the Church could not be confined to any one communion. On the basis of these objections, he advocated a 'theological reconsideration', such as would lead to the view that the Church, while visible, is not necessarily visibly united in communion, her presence and visibility being assured by the presence and functioning of various Christian endowments and beliefs, such as the Bible and acceptance of the Bible's authority, a regular (but not necessarily episcopal) ministry, and the two chief sacraments.

We, on the other hand, have argued, in the first place, that Dr Greenslade's suggested theological restatement amounts not to 'development' but to 'revolution'; and that the belief in the Church as a single communion is so bound up with other features of the ancient Church, and in particular with its definitions of Christian doctrine, that to surrender it as false would lead, logically, to what we have called 'thorough-going liberalism', of a sort which Dr Greenslade himself would repudiate and which has been virtually repudiated by the World Council of Churches.

It remained to see whether the ancient view could be retained and at the same time an answer could be found to Dr Greenslade's objections. (1) We claimed that the question whether valid sacraments can be found outside the Church is one which cannot be answered *a priori* but depends on tradition as expounded by legitimate dogmatic authority (the 'teaching Church'); in default of such authority, the answer to the question is 'anybody's bet'. (2) We have shown, I hope successfully, that the Augustinian view does not imply that all 'schismatical' sacraments are *ipso facto* totally inefficacious. The fruitfulness of a valid sacrament depends not on the objective status or subjective innocence of the minister of the sacrament, but upon the subjective conscience of the recipient. This raised the whole issue of 'inculpable ignorance' or 'good faith'. (3) A generous, but perfectly justifiable, use of the principle of 'good faith' enables us to explain the many signs of grace manifest in the members of more than one Christian communion without surrendering the view that only one of these communions can be the objective Church of Christ.

It appears to me that Dr Greenslade's three objections have been fully met. Moreover, our own 'theological reconsideration' has enabled us to find room for the presence, and the fruits, of grace not only in a diversity of Christian communions, but outside the ambit of historical Christianity altogether, and this without prejudice to the real meaning and the importance of the principle that Christ is the only Mediator, the 'one name' whereby we may be saved, and that 'outside the Church there is no salvation'. Christianity is thus shown in its true light as the re-affirmation at a supernatural level of all the real values of human history from the beginning of time.

Chapter 10

THE NEW TESTAMENT (1)

BEFORE turning to an examination of the New Testament, to see if it will throw any light on our problem, we may first review the ground that has already been covered.

Christians are agreed that membership of the Church which Christ founded involves some passing beyond the solitariness of the individual believer. The Church is some sort of social reality or social aspect or tendency in Christianity.

More precisely, there are in the long run three different ideas about the Church. (1) It is held by some that the Church is a completely invisible reality of the interior or mystical order, with no manifestation of its presence, recognisable as such, in the field of sense perception. (2) It is often affirmed, or implied, that the Church's presence is, indeed, made manifest in history by partial embodiments, effects, or consequences, among which is, or may be, a tendency for Christians to come together in external groupings, or even to move towards the fullness of Christian fellowship in a single universal Christian society of the future; but that it is not of the *essence* of the Church that she should be such a single communion. In the end, this view, like the first-mentioned, must mean that the *essential* unity of the Church is confined to the invisible order; and, if her unity is essentially invisible the Church herself is *essentially* an invisible reality—just as, for the Platonist, a human being was essentially a soul. (3) A third view is that the Church is essentially one historical society, and can therefore only exist as a single Christian communion. This view corresponds to the traditional Jewish-Christian view of man as essentially a soul-and-body reality—a view which is also Aristotle's. Aristotle held that the soul is the 'form' of the body, so that a man is an informed body or an embodied soul; he is neither the body in abstraction from the soul, nor the soul in abstraction from the body.

As between these three views of the nature of the Church, the broad witness of Christian antiquity, and especially of the Great Church from which all modern Christian communions derive, was, from the end of the New Testament period, unhesitating: the Church was essentially a single communion, and schism is not (to use a modern phrase) *within* the Church, but leaves the schismatics in a state of separation *from* the Church. This view may be thought to be implicit in the claim of Eastern Orthodoxy to be, exclusively, the Church. It is the view that is basic to the Roman Catholic claim. And it is at least interesting that some of the more extreme, fundamentalist, or even 'fringe' Protestant bodies appear to claim each that its own communion is exclusively the People of God. More common, in the communions whose separate existence dates from the Reformation, is adherence to the second of the three views about the Church listed above. Such adherence may be combined with a 'high' view of the ministry and the sacraments or, alternatively, with Evangelicalism. We have suggested that this view, which holds that the visible Church is divisible, is not an authentic development of the older theory of the Church but is rather a 'rationalisation' of the state of division in which Christendom found itself as a result of the Reformation; it was not so much that men 'went into schism' because they had outgrown the traditional view of the Church, but rather that they found themselves 'in schism' and therefore rejected the traditional view.

On the whole, it has been characteristic of the heirs of the Reformation to appeal from the medieval Church and its traditions to the Bible. It is true that the appeal has sometimes been enlarged to take in the witness of the Fathers and their interpretation of the Bible (this was, for instance, the standpoint of the 'Anglo-Catholic' divines of seventeeth-century Anglicanism and of their followers in the nineteenth century). But we have seen that, as regards the nature of the Church, the Fathers, who claimed to be faithful to the teachings of Scripture, were themselves convinced exponents of that view of the Church which has commonly been rejected in post-Reformation circles.

The question may, however, be asked, whether the Bible, viewed in itself and apart from the meaning attributed to it by the Fathers, has anything to tell us about the nature of the Church. Does it exclude any one of the three views listed above? Does it point unmistakably to one of them as the original Christian view? And if it offers no answer to our question which is clear and beyond dispute, does it at least seem to favour one view in preference to the others? It is an important question for two reasons. In the first place, the New Testament reflects the life of Christianity at the most primitive stage to which we can attain, and in reflecting that life it also reflects the thought of the early Christians. Secondly, the Bible has, for most Christians, as it certainly had for Christian antiquity, a doctrinal authority in addition to its historical value. Was post-Biblical Christian antiquity, in its view of the nature of the Church, faithful to the facts and teachings of that primitive age, the age of the apostles and evangelists; or does it present a major divergence from, or corruption of, the original Christian deposit?

From the new teaching, the new wine, the new covenant of the Synoptic Gospels, on through the new creation and the new man of the Pauline writings, to the mediator of a new covenant in Hebrews, the new commandment of I John, and the new name, the new Jerusalem, the new song, and the new heaven and earth of the Apocalypse,[1] newness is one of the keywords of the New Testament: 'Behold, I make all things new' (Ap. 21, 5). And to the extent to which we can reconstruct from our sources the story of Christian origins, we appear to be witnessing something analogous to the emergence, in the evolutionary process, of a new species. What is a species? For our present purpose, we may accept the answer given in a recent book: 'it is an intelligible solution to a problem of living in a given environment. . . . Though later species are solutions to concrete problems in concrete circumstances, though they are solutions which take into account and, as it were, rest upon previous solutions, still a solution is the sort of thing that insight hits upon and not the sort that results from accumulated, observable differences.'[2] A new species, then, is like a new insight, a new theorem, a new *logos* or *ratio*. Life manifests itself in adaptation to environment. As environment changes, so life

[1] Mk. 1, 27; Mt. 9, 17; Lk. 22, 20; II Cor. 5, 17; Eph. 2, 15; Heb. 9, 15; I Jn. 2, 8; Ap. 2, 17; 3, 12; 5, 9; 21, 1.   [2] B. J. F. Lonergan, *Insight*, p. 265.

must change its adaptations or perish. A new species is an adaptation to a new, often a wider, sometimes a higher, environment; or a more successful adaptation to an environment that remains the same.

Christianity, however, was characterised by no alteration in man considered as a biological species. Yet it was emphatically a new adaptation to environment. And, like the biological species according to evolutionary theory, it was an adaptation arising upon a previous adaptation. It is a solution of the problem of living that 'takes into account, and, as it were, rests upon' a previous solution—in this case, the Jewish religion in the orthodox form that worshipped in the Temple and acknowledged the official Jewish hierarchy. And just as a new biological species does not reject everything that characterised its predecessor, but incorporates the essence of the previous solution in its own 'higher viewpoint' solution (man, though rational, is a rational *animal*), so Christianity accepted much from Judaism, and in fact was, it would seem, regarded, at first and from the outside, as merely a variety of Judaism.

Writing of the emergence of the living cell from the situation provided by 'mega-molecules', Teilhard de Chardin says: 'This discovery was doubtless prepared over a long period . . . ; but for all that it was sufficiently sudden and revolutionary to have immediately enjoyed prodigious success in the natural world.'[3] Lonergan, who compares a new species to a new 'insight', draws attention to the thrill that accompanies a new insight: 'this feature is dramatized . . . by Archimedes' peculiarly uninhibited exultation' when he rushed from the baths crying Eureka.[4] Copernicus is said to have gone into a sort of prolonged ecstasy on attaining his solution of the problem of the planetary movements.

There is something sudden and prodigious in the phenomenon of primitive Christianity, sprung from an empty tomb in the homeland of Jewish faith in the early thirties of the first century A.D., and spreading like a forest fire through Judaea to Samaria, on to Damascus and Antioch, and thence to Asia Minor, Greece, and beyond, driven as though by a hidden instinct or by the Spirit of God towards the capital of that Graeco-Roman world,

[3] *The Phenomenon of Man*, English translation, p. 86.
[4] *Op. cit.* p. 4.

where the leader of the first Twelve bore witness with his life some thirty years after the crucifixion. As the author of Acts makes the Thessalonian Jews say, with pardonable exaggeration: 'These men who have turned the civilised world upside down have turned up here also' (17, 6).

This outward expansion of Christianity, while it reveals no doubt the presence in the world of favourable dispositions for a 'new revelation', was the expression of a tremendous inward energy of conviction, thought, and practical initiative. The New Testament literature itself is an evidence of this. Its technical shortcomings have often been noted by rhetorician and stylist. But there is nothing in the remains of contemporary Latin, Greek, or Jewish literature which prepares us for this titanic upsurge of creative genius. It is a collection of astonishing variety in view of its small compass; but this variety is controlled by an underlying unity of exultant, dynamic, faith and hope.[5] This faith may indeed be called an insight, and the rapture of a new insight is the sign-manual of primitive Christianity:

> The first age of the Christian Church was characterised by a vivid enthusiasm which found expression in ways which recall the simplicity of childhood. It was a period of wonder and delight. The floodgates of emotion were opened: a supernatural dread alternated with unspeakable joy. Thus we read at one moment that 'fear came upon every soul', and at the next that 'they did eat their meat with exultation and simplicity of heart'. 'Great fear' results from a manifestation of Divine judgment: 'great joy' from a Divine manifestation of healing power. Thus 'the Church went in the fear of the Lord and the consolation of the Holy Spirit'. The Apostles openly rejoiced as they left the council that

[5] The effect of this new creative dynamism was thus described by Wilamowitz-Möellendorf: 'At last some one speaks in Greek from a fresh, inner experience of life; that is Paul's faith; he is sure of the hope within him, and his ardent love embraces humanity—a fresh life of the soul bubbles up wherever he sets foot. . . . For him all literature is a plaything, he has no artistic vein, but all the higher must we estimate the artistic effects which he all the same achieves. . . . In the Hellenic world of conventional form, smooth beauty, this absence of form in a style which is yet quite adequate to the thoughts and feelings expressed, has a quickening force. What stylistic effect could heighten the intimate charm of the Epistle to the Philippians? . . . The whole of Greek classicist literature stands thereby condemned that the imitation of the classics was productive of new classics only in Latin,—in Cicero, Horace, Virgil. The Greek language, when it came straight from the heart, had to be devoid of art, as it is in Paul, in Epictetus, in Plotinus' (quoted by H. J. C. Grierson, *the Background of English Literature; Classical and Romantic*, p. 274. The quotation refers to St Paul's Epistles, not to the New Testament as a whole.)

they had been allowed to suffer for the Name; Paul and Silas in the prison at Philippi prayed and sang hymns to God, so that the prisoners heard them. Nowhere in literature is the transition from passionate grief to enthusiastic delight more glowingly portrayed than in St Paul's second epistle to the Corinthian Church.[6]

In examining the New Testament we have to bear in mind that the rapture of enthusiasm evoked by the birth of a new life and the discovery of new horizons is rarely allied in the same mind with the lucidity of calm reflection upon experience. To determine, from the New Testament itself, the 'idea' and the ideas latent in primitive Christianity requires a fresh effort of critical and synthetic thinking beyond any that went into the composition of the New Testament books themselves. We must not be surprised if we find ourselves asking questions which did not occur to the minds of the Twelve and their immediate converts.

It is significant for our present purposes that the one great crisis in the inner history of primitive Christianity, of which we have relatively ample evidence, was a crisis of universality and unity. Humanly speaking, it looks as though the whole movement might have foundered on the issue whether Christians were to be a Jewish sect or to become a Catholic Church.

Christianity was not, in its essence, a revolt from the religious system of the Old Testament, but an evolutionary transformation of it.[7] It sprang from a personal adhesion to Jesus of Nazareth as to 'him that was to come', the Anointed of God for whom the time had become ripe. This adhesion was, from the first and already in the historical lifetime of Jesus, the pivotal fact in the new movement; it constituted the differentia of Christian faith—it was, in fact, the same thing as to 'believe in' Jesus. No longer was it enough to be physically descended from Abraham and Jacob, or to be circumcised and obey the Jewish Law and customs. To refuse allegiance to Jesus was the great refusal. If he was 'the expectation of Israel', then to reject

---

[6] J. A. Robinson, *St Paul's Epistle to the Ephesians*, pp. 121 f.
[7] It should be noted that, while 'evolutionary' here implies an intrinsic, and not merely temporal, continuity with the Old Testament, the term 'transformation' allows for that new intervention of God which Christianity has always affirmed to be its own starting-point.

his claim entailed, in principle, the loss of every privilege appertaining to membership of God's Chosen People. And it was
required that the inward acceptance of his claim by faith should
be externalised in 'confession' of his name.

Thus Jesus and 'the good news from God' introduced an
element of crisis of which the consequences begin to appear
already when, in face of the growing opposition of the Jewish
'establishment', the Twelve are chosen and commissioned, and
Peter is promised 'the keys of the kingdom of heaven'. A further
consequence is the prophecy of the destruction of Jerusalem and
the Temple; the visible focus of the old religion has lost its
raison-d'-être, if Jewish officialdom has rejected the Messiah.
The new, the believing, Israel was to be released from the bonds
of Palestinian locality and of the Jewish hierarchy. And if
Christianity was to have its 'proselytes', as pre-Christian Judaism
had had, then faith in Jesus as the Envoy of God would be the
qualification for their acceptance.

However, the apostolic body, despite the pull of Galilee,
established itself, after the resurrection of Christ, at Jerusalem
under the shadow of the still existing and functioning Temple.
In the nature of the case, the overwhelming majority of the
earliest converts were Jews. The author of Acts even affirms that
'a great multitude' of the priests began to listen to the gospel
(6, 7). The faithful did not abstain from Jewish public worship.
We are told that St Paul himself regularly sought out the synagogues of the Diaspora.

Although not, theologically speaking, a schism, the early
Christian body was outwardly very like a schism from orthodox
Judaism. There is almost a law of history that a schism, after
its first enthusiasm of revolt, tends to revert to some part of
the orthodoxy from which it had recoiled. Some such tendency
seems to have come into play in Palestinian Christianity. It was
the other side of a natural failure to persevere at the exacting
level of the new insight. Men found it difficult to shake themselves free from the prestige of the Temple and the Torah, and
from the habits engendered by the racial principle. It would
appear that the remembered words of Jesus did not, on the face
of them, seem to answer all questions with the decisiveness of
Pauline polemic. And was not Jesus himself the Son of David?
Should not James, 'the Lord's brother', be regarded as the heir

to the restored Davidic monarchy? [8] If Jesus had come to perfect Judaism, would it not be paradoxical to jettison the requirements of the Torah which he had not himself rejected?

Against these reactionary tendencies there argued the logic of events in the actual expansion of Christianity; and the question of principle was settled, according to the presentation of facts in Acts (15), at a conference in Jerusalem. Christianity would be, not a Jewish party or sect, but a catholic religion standing on its own feet.

But the victory of the Catholic principle, the principle maintained with such vigour by St Paul 'the apostle of the Gentiles', might have been a pyrrhic one. Could the Jewish conservatives and the Gentile radicals remain united in a single fellowship? For years the issue seemed to hang in the balance; and it may be that it is above all to St Paul that the early Church owed not only its catholicity of principle but its success in retaining Jew and Gentile within a single communion:

> For all his claims to independence, the apostle (Paul) kept his eyes fixed on the community of Jerusalem. He saw the approval of the apostles of Jerusalem as an indispensable condition of his work's value in God's eyes (Gal. 2, 2). The church of Jerusalem, he held, had shared her own spiritual wealth with the Gentile churches (Rom. 15, 27; cf. 9, 4). The traditions of Jerusalem had the force of law. The Lord's Supper must be celebrated as at Jerusalem, and the customs of Jerusalem must be observed at Christian meetings. And was it pure charity which made Paul so constantly concerned for the poor at Jerusalem? Eventually, this was a piece of apostolic policy. With his foundations in Galatia, Macedonia, Achaea and (the province of) Asia at his back, he determined to bring home to them, by means of a great general monetary contribution, the supremacy of the church of Jerusalem—while on the other hand, Jerusalem should thus be brought to grant unreserved fellowship to those Gentile churches. . . . The contribution was to be a manifestation of solidarity, and to elicit from Jerusalem a public declaration of agreement. And Paul got what he sought. . . . This was a give-and-take of capital importance, by which the Church's unity was safeguarded. [9]

Perhaps the celebrated practical charity of the ancient Roman

---

[8] We are told that after James's death there were, at the head of the Jewish Christian church, other kinsmen of the Lord: Symeon, son of Clopas; then two grandsons of Judas. Cf. Cullmann, *Le Problème du Pseudo-Clémentin*, p. 251.

[9] L. Cerfaux, *Le Théologie de l'Eglise suivant saint Paul*, pp. 199 f.

church towards other communities in need was inspired by this
same motive of cementing unity.

Bearing these facts in mind, we may now turn to a document,
the Epistle to the Ephesians, which was written after the
struggle for unity was over but is doubtless marked by the
effects of it. Modern scholarship has not made up its mind
whether this is a genuine work of St Paul or not.[10] If it is, it
must date from about the year A.D. 64. If it was written after
St Paul's death by an imitator, Dr Mitton thinks that it is
probably from about A.D. 87-92. We need not here decide between
these alternatives, the more so as Dr Mitton finds himself able
to write:

> Even if this epistle must be viewed as a pseudonymous work,
> it is not unworthy to bear the name of Paul. Not only is it built
> up of largely Pauline materials, but it faithfully represents the
> Pauline message, edited a little to make it immediately intel-
> ligible and applicable to the time for which it was prepared, but
> so true to the spirit of Paul and his insight into the Gospel that
> it has deservedly been regarded as the quintessence of Paulinism
> . . . in it all the most important elements in Paul's interpretation
> of the Christian message find their proper place, and some receive
> their clearest and most memorable expression.[11]

To this it may be added that, for Christians, the epistle has of
course, independently of the views of historians as to its authen-
ticity and the decade of the first century to which it is to be
attributed, the authority of inspired Scripture.

In seeking in this epistle for the light which it may throw on
the primitive idea of the Church, I propose to follow mainly
J. Armitage Robinson, whose commentary is now nearly sixty
years old, but is a magnificent model of exegesis, in which
objectivity and docility to the text expounded amount almost
to genius. For our purposes, it has the added advantage that

[10] E. Percy (1946) favours the Pauline authorship. C. L. Mitton (who apparently
did not know Percy's study) decides against it (1951). P. Benoit (1956, reprinted
in *Exégèse et Théologie*, 1961), says: 'The chief objection against the authen-
ticity of *Ephesians* is literary: the formulas of *Colossians* are in it repeated,
combined or doubled, adapted and sometimes distorted (*gauchies*), applied with
an element of servility which it is difficult to attribute to Paul himself. Perhaps
we must see in it the hand of a disciple working under the apostle's direction
and using the recently-written *Colossians* for help in his composition.' But
Benoit is inclined to recognise in both *Colossians* and *Ephesians* 'if not the sole
hand of St Paul, at least his mind and heart' (*Exégèse et Théologie*, p. 152).
[11] *The Epistle to the Ephesians*, pp. 268 f.

Robinson was a member of a communion which makes no claim to be exclusively the Church of Christ. Yet this great Anglican scholar, who speaks of this epistle as at once 'the crown of St Paul's writings' and 'St Paul's greatest epistle',[12] sees, as everyone must see, that Christian unity is one of its predominant themes, and writes: 'The truth of the corporate life which was revealed to (St Paul) was never more needed than it is today. Our failure to understand his life and message has been largely due to our acquiescence in disunion. As we rouse ourselves to enquire after the meaning of unity, we may hope that he will speak to us afresh.'[13]

We may begin by transcribing Robinson's account of the 'main drift' of the epistle:

The Apostle begins with a disclosure of the great purpose of God for the world—the gathering into one of all things in the Christ. He prayed that his readers might have the eyes of their hearts opened to see and understand this purpose and their own share in the realization of it. He showed that while hitherto they, as Gentiles, had stood outside the sphere of the special development of this purpose, they were now no longer outside it, but within. For a new beginning had been made: Jew and Gentile had been welded together in Christ to form God's New Man. The proclamation of this oneness of mankind in Christ was the mission that was specially entrusted to St Paul, and for which he was in bonds. That they should know and understand all this was his earnest prayer, as their knowledge of it was an essential preliminary to its realization. Having been given this unity, they must keep it. They had been called to be parts of the One Man, to be limbs of the Body through which Christ was fulfilling Himself; and this consideration must rule their life in every detail. Here was the ground of the distinction of functions in the various members of the Body: some were given by Christ to be apostles, others to be prophets, and so forth, to fit the saints as a whole for the service which they were called to render, and to forward the building of the Body of Christ; till all should meet in one grown Man, who should at length have reached the complete stature of the fullness of the Christ. Here too was the ground of the commonest of obligations: the reason, for example, why they should not lie to one another was that they were members of one another. The positive duties of social life found their

---

[12] *St Paul's Epistle to the Ephesians*, pp. vii, 33.   [13] *Op. cit.* p. viii.

sanction in the same doctrine of unity in Christ: the reason why wives should be subject to their husbands, and why husbands should love their wives, was that husband and wife stand to each other even as Christ and the Church; in a relation of authority and obedience, and yet in a relation of perfect oneness—not twain, but one. Children and parents, slaves and masters, were in like manner to exemplify the ordered harmony of the new life in Christ.[14]

Though Robinson does not mention it here, it is of course the case that the 'body of Christ' which is here spoken of is, for the writer of the epistle, the Church (i, 23).

Thus God's purpose could only be realised as a unity: the unity of men, considered as men, in Christ. This realisation amounted, in the mind of the author of the epistle, to a 'new creation': 'we are his workmanship':[15]

> Mankind had started as One in the original Creation. But in the course of the world's history, through sin on the one hand, and on the other hand through the revelation of God to a selected People, a division had come in. Mankind was Two and not One. There was the privileged Jew, and there was the unprivileged Gentile. It was the glory of grace to bring the Two once more together as One in Christ. A new start was thus made in the world's history. St Paul called it a New Creation.[16]

The polarity of the thought here is worthy of observation. The central idea is that of the new human unity which is the Christian fact. This unity is, on the one hand, fully divine in its cause: 'we are God's workmanship'.[17] As the author of the epistle had said two verses earlier: 'It was grace that saved us, with faith as its instrument; it did not come from yourselves, it was God's gift, not from any action of yours, or there would be room for pride.'[18] Unity therefore is a divine gift. On the other hand, considered as the effect of this divine causality, unity is a reality of the historical order: 'a new start was thus made in

---

[14] *Op. cit.* pp. 130 f.

[15] Eph. 2, 10. Cf. Gal. 6, 15: 'neither is circumcision anything, or uncircumcision; but (there is) a new creation.'

[16] J. A. Robinson, *St Paul's Epistle to the Ephesians*, pp. 52 f.

[17] Eph. 2, 10. Knox translates: 'we are his design'; but the Greek word (*poiema*) means 'something made', as, for instance, a poem.

[18] It could be argued that, in this passage, the author is thinking of the several Christians as individuals, not of their corporate unity in the Church. But 2, 14 (Christ 'has made the two nations one') shows that, for him, the unity of the Church is something given in the redemption, not a merely human achievement.

the world's history.' Man's unity before the Fall was, for St Paul, a historical fact; the fact of Adam at peace with God and with himself in Eden. The division entailed by the Fall, and by the Old Testament revelation to 'a selected People', was again a historical fact: the Jews, as a fully concrete People and polity, stood over against the equally historical Gentiles, in a relationship of historical opposition. The result of the redemption is that this opposition in the historical order is overcome *in the historical order*. The notion that the end-product of redemption, so far as this world is concerned, is a purely invisible Church is alien to the whole thought of the epistle. The point is made by Robinson in his exposition of 1, 4: 'He has chosen us out in Christ':

> It has been said that in the word 'us' we have 'the language of charity', which includes certain individuals whom a stricter use of terms would have excluded. That is to say, not all the members of the Churches to whom the letter was to go were in fact included in the Divine Selection.
>
> To this we may reply: (1) Nowhere in the epistle does St Paul suggest that any individual among those whom he addresses either is or may be excluded from this Selection.
>
> (2) Unworthy individuals there undoubtedly were: but his appeal to them is based on the very fact of their Selection by God: 'I beseech you, that ye walk worthy of the calling wherewith ye have been called' (4, 1). . . . Just as the Prophets looked more to the whole than to the part, so St Paul is dominated by the thought of the whole, and of God's purpose with the whole. It is a new Israel that Christ has founded—a People of privilege. . . .
>
> We take it, then, that by the word 'us' St Paul means to include all those Christians to whom he intended his letter to come. It is reasonable to suppose further that he would have allowed his language to cover all members of the Christian Church everywhere.[19]

If we ask more particularly what, in the historical order, redemption meant for the new converts from heathenism, the epistle answers that it meant incorporation into the 'commonwealth' or 'polity' of Israel, God's Selected People:

> In those days (sc. before your conversion) there was no Christ for you; you were outlaws from the commonwealth of Israel,

[19] *St Paul's Epistle to the Ephesians*, pp. 26 f.

strangers to every covenant, with no promise to hope for, with the world about you, and no God. But now you are in Christ Jesus; now, through the blood of Christ, you have been brought close, you who were once so far away. He is our bond of peace; he has made the two nations one, breaking down the wall that was a barrier between us, the enmity there was between us, in his own mortal nature. He has put an end to the law with its decrees, so as to make peace, remaking the two human creatures as one in himself; both sides, united in a single body, he would reconcile to God through his cross, inflicting death, in his own person, upon the feud. . . . You are no longer exiles, then, or aliens; the saints are your fellow-citizens, you belong to God's household.[20]

This fellow-citizenship with the saints does not mean a purely interior, mystical, oneness of the predestinated or of those 'in a state of grace'. It means fellow-membership of a concrete historical union of baptised believers, considered as identical with the Old Testament organised polity of Israel.

The historical, flesh-and-blood, character of the 'commonwealth of the saints' is clearly implied by the fact that the 'foundation' on which the new Israel is built is not the faith or charity of its original members, but 'the apostles and prophets' themselves.[21] On a flesh-and-blood foundation you do not build a purely 'mystical' structure; you build a concrete fellowship of

[20] Eph. 2, 12-19 (Knox). In the last verse quoted, a better translation would be: 'You are the fellow-citizens of the saints.' The Gentile converts have not incorporated 'the saints' in *their* polity; on the contrary, the Gentile Christians have become members of a polity already existing, the polity of the People of God, viewed as a single continuous entity through its Old Testament and New Testament periods.

Robinson comments: ' "The saints" was a designation proper to the members of the ancient People of God. They were a "holy nation": they were "saints" by virtue of their national consecration to Jehovah. The designation was naturally retained by St Paul, when the Chosen People was widened into the Catholic Church. To quote Bishop Lightfoot's words: " . . . All who have entered into the Christian covenant by baptism are 'saints' in the language of the Apostles. Even the irregularities and profligacies of the Corinthian Church do not forfeit it this title" ' (*St Paul's Epistle to the Ephesians*, pp. 66 f.). Thus the moral imperfections of the members of the Church are, in New Testament linguistic usage, irrelevant to the nature of the Church as 'holy'. This is a consideration which may be noted in connection with the credal designation of the Church as 'holy': the imperfection of her members does not mean that she is only potentially holy; on the contrary, her actual holiness is continually operative to impart itself to them. Similarly, the Church is always actually one, and tending to deepen the fruits of unity in her members.

[21] Despite the venerable authority behind it, the view that, according to Mt. 16, 18, the Church was to be built upon the *faith* of Peter is exegetically indefensible. When the saying is thought back into Aramaic, it is plain that Peter (Kepha) is intended as the rock (kepha) on which the Church is to rest.

actual human beings. And it is this actual historical entity which is destined to be the dwelling-place of the Spirit of God (Eph. 2, 20-2). In a later passage, the epistle enlarges the list of those who have functions assigned to them in this historical fellowship: 'Each of us has his special grace, dealt out to him by Christ's gift. . . . Some he has appointed to be apostles, others to be prophets, others to be evangelists or pastors, or teachers. They are to order the lives of the faithful, minister to their needs, build up the frame of Christ's body, until we all realise our common unity through the faith in the Son of God' (4, 7-13).

The idea of a purely invisible Church is, therefore, plainly inconsistent with the thought of this epistle. Of the three notions of the Church which have been held, this one, at least, is excluded by biblical authority.

What of the second of our listed notions of the Church? Can the idea of the Church as essentially not an actual society or communion but a potential universal fellowship be reconciled with the Epistle to the Ephesians? Is this idea implicit, for instance, in the phrase just quoted: '*until* we all realise our common unity'? Does not the epistle elsewhere admonish us to 'preserve the unity of the Spirit in the bond of peace', as though this unity, though actually a fact in the writer's time, was yet a contingent blessing, depending for its preservation on the uncertain good will of the Christians, and capable of being lost at least temporarily?

In reply to this question, it may first be remarked that such passages as those just quoted do not compel us to think that the author of the epistle would have admitted the theoretical possibility of a divided Church. Already, in our examination of Cyprian and Augustine, we have seen that writers who have no doubt of the Church's visible indivisibility can yet on occasion speak of schism as 'rending the Church'. Similarly, the author of Ephesians might have urged his readers to 'preserve the unity' without meaning to imply that this unity could be lost by the Church herself, but only—at most—that *they* might cease to belong to the Church in her unity. Assuming that the Church is essentially a historical society, it remains true that it is made up of actual, imperfect, human beings, united in an actual fellowship, and each preserving his membership by human acts of external communion which are the expression of his reason and his will.[22] All such acts presuppose human freewill. From the human point of view, they both express and cement the unity of the Church, of which the 'bond' is charity. Since human beings are free, such acts might cease in the case of a given individual, or a local church or group of churches, and a state of schism would result for these defaulters. Merely from the human point of view, there is a statistical possibility that *all* such acts of communion might cease, in which case the Church would have ceased to exist (since a society can only exist as a historical social unity). It is not, precisely, because the Church is a society, that those who hold the ancient view of her believe that her unity is unbreakable; it is because, being a society, she has no other mode of existence except as a single communion, and God has guaranteed her existence. Because this society, under God, depends on the collaboration of its members, it is proper for the epistle to urge its readers to 'maintain' the unity. And as the existence and unity of the Church flows, under God, from the free actions of her members, it is clear that she will grow in *perfection* as those acts increase in number and in worth. But all such growth of the Church presupposes the *existence* of the Church. This Church which, from the human side, seems to depend on the free decisions of its members, is, on the divine side, the Body of Christ and therefore, in the eternal providence of God, immune from the possibility of disintegration; the Body of Christ, now that he is risen from the dead, cannot die; on the contrary, Christ, in his own person, 'has inflicted death' on the divisive principle which had held sway in human history since the Fall. It is integral to the redemption, that the Church, Christ's body and the temple of the Holy Ghost, exists; and in Christ 'the whole fabric, *being* bound together, grows into a temple dedicated to the Lord' (2, 21 f.)—it is already a temple, yet a temple that grows like a body.

[22] We know something of these acts of communion as they were performed in the ancient Church, whether by individuals or by local Christian churches: hospitality to visiting Christians, and their admission to eucharistic communion in the church they were visiting; a great epistolary intercourse between the bishops; material acts of charity to distant Christian communities, for which the church of Rome was specially celebrated; later on, a formal system of 'commendatory letters' accrediting a visitor from one church to another, and letters of communion or 'synodical letters' between bishops.

If, however, there is nothing in the epistle which of necessity implies that the Church can exist in any other mode than as a single historical society, it may be suggested that the deepest thought of the author points to the conclusion that this *is*, essentially, its mode of existence. The moral exhortations of the epistle are not the core of its intention, but, as in the Pauline *corpus* generally, they are practical deductions or riders from the doctrinal teaching. The core of the epistle is the proclamation of a 'gospel' ('the gospel according to St Paul', to use Dr Mitton's happy phrase), of good news that has come from God: the news of the redemption of man already effected in Christ and through his historical acts and sufferings and his actual resurrection. This redemption was not just the salvation of a number of individuals. It was the redemption of mankind. It took outward, historical, shape in the overcoming of the divisions imported into mankind and its history by the Fall and its consequences. It created a new human unity in act. This unity (actual, though so far extended to only a tiny fraction of the world's population) was not basically an achievement of human good will; it was basically a gift of God, part and parcel of that 'salvation by faith' which has God as its author. And this new human unity was a catholic 'polity' or commonwealth, not merely a new 'race' of redeemed men, but an organised living-together of the redeemed in a fellowship that has flesh-and-blood functionaries to implement its common life. Though a new polity, it was yet also old, since it was the polity of Israel universalised and released from those laws and regulations which in effect had made the old Israel a national affair; but it was as tangible an entity as the Old Testament polity. This new polity *is* the Church. To say that it could cease to exist *as a single polity* is to suggest that the Church could cease to exist. To say that the visible unity of the members of the Church is not essential to membership and to the Church's being, is to say that the 'gift of God' has not really been given with any permanent guarantee, but only held out as an ideal for men to aim at.[23]

[23] We have, in the preceding paragraphs, of course gone beyond the words of Robinson in his exegesis of the epistle; though I trust that we have not contradicted him. The following quotations from his *The Vision of Unity* (1908), a collection of four sermons and a paper, may be of interest: '(St Paul's gospel) was pre-eminently the gospel of the exalted Christ, and (may we not

We may here quote some words of the Anglican scholar, Bishop Eric Graham, in his commentary on Ephesians in the S.P.C.K. one-volume commentary (1928):

> The essential place of the Church in the divine scheme of redemption—as the Israel of God continuous in its life with the old Israel—is never absent from the mind of St Paul (cf. Rom. 12, 5; I Cor. 12, 12 ff.; Col. 1, 18-24); but nowhere else does he treat the theme so fully as in Ephesians, or make it so abundantly clear that redemption implies not merely a personal and individual reconciliation with God, but also membership in a corporate society of divine origin—the Church of Christ.
>
> What, then, is the Church? It is a visible society, consisting of all those, whether Jews or Gentiles, who through Christ have access in one Spirit unto the Father (2, 13-8; 4, 5, 25). But it is more than a mere society, just as its origin is more than human. It is an organic union, answering to and manifesting the unity of God—Father, Son and Holy Spirit (4, 3-6). . . . But the most frequent and characteristic of St Paul's metaphors in this connection is that which represents the Church as the Body of Christ (1, 22 f., 4, 4, 16, 5, 23, 28-33); i.e. it is His outward and visible manifestation; the organ of his self-expression; the instrument whereby He works. Moreover, it is an essential part of Himself, just as his 'natural' body was in the days of His flesh; without it He would be incomplete, not, of course, in His perfect Deity, but as the Incarnate Saviour of mankind (pp. 539 f.).

say?) the re-embodied Christ: Christ died, Christ rose, Christ ascended, Christ is supreme in the unseen world; and the same Christ is still living and working in the visible world today. He is not bodiless; He has feet and hands, eyes and lips; He sees and speaks, He comes and helps, in and through His larger and ever-growing body; that body into which His disciples are baptized, within which *they are held united* by the sacred food which is His body. . . . (Paul) could never allow the possibility of a broken Christianity, which should admit of two churches—Jewish and Gentile. The Gentile was co-heir and concorporate with the Jew, or he was nothing at all; he was a member of the body, or else he was still an alien, without hope. . . . The unity of Christians, *and therefore Christianity itself*, was at stake in the controversy'—the italics are in both cases ours. Cf. later in the same volume: 'Christianity is to St Paul the embodiment of the unseen spiritual Christ in a visible society through which He still carries on His work in the world. The Church, he says, is the body of the Christ.' Needless to say, Robinson held that in our own day something has happened of which St Paul could not admit the possibility: not two but many separated 'churches' existed, the unity of the body was broken, that unity with which the fate of Christianity itself was bound up. But if the unity of the Church is, according to St Paul, of the essence of Christianity, and if the Church *is* a visible society, the correct interpretation of the present state of Christendom, for one who accepts the authority of the Bible, is surely that there has been schism *from* the Church.

7

Thus this Anglican scholar agrees with the Anglican Dean Robinson that, for the author of our epistle, the Church was an actual society of which not only 'holiness' but unity was a feature. Neither of them appears to have faced the implications of their exegesis. Yet if, to quote Bishop Graham, redemption implies membership of the Church; and if the Church is 'a corporate society of divine origin'; if, moreover, the Church, this 'visible society', is 'an organic union manifesting the unity of God', are we not driven to ask ourselves, with some urgency, whether the Church is *essentially* a visible society, or only something capable of taking that shape, and whether her manifestation of the divine unity is an occasional phenomenon, or part of her divinely guaranteed, permanent, function towards the world? And if it really is the Church's function, as such, to *manifest* the divine unity, does she not do this precisely by exhibiting her own unity as a society? 'I have given them the privilege which thou gavest me, that they should all be one (thing), as we are one (thing) that while thou art in me, I may be in them, and so they may be perfectly made one (thing). *So* let the world know that it is thou who hast sent me' (Jn. 17, 22 f., Knox, 'Privilege', here, represents 'glory' in the original).

We may now review the results of our examination of the Epistle to the Ephesians. We have seen that modern scholarship is uncertain as to its authorship, although there can be little doubt that it is in an authentic line of theological development from the epistles which there is good reason to attribute to St Paul.[24] But we have also emphasised that, for a Christian, the authority of the epistle need not be made to depend simply on its alleged apostolic authorship. It is one of the canonical and inspired books of Christianity.

It has become abundantly clear that the teaching of this epistle can hardly be reconciled with the view of the Church as a purely interior and invisible entity. It is further clear that, for the writer of the epistle, the Church was *in fact* a single visible society or fellowship of parts and members recognising each

[24] As already noted, Dr Mitton, who favours the view that the epistle is a pseudonymous work, is yet inclined to date it well before the end of the first century A.D. O. Perler has made out a strong case for the suggestion that Ignatius of Antioch, in his own Letter to the Ephesians (perhaps about A.D. 115), utilises the canonical Epistle to the Ephesians in a way which would be characteristic of him if he regarded the Epistle as a document held in particular esteem by those to whom his own Letter was addressed.

other as such, actually collaborating in a single common task of worship and proclamation of the gospel, and continuous with Christian origins by its concrete relationship to the apostolic college and the first believers.

There is no evidence that this writer's mind was in any way occupied with the problems that might have been raised by the existence, within the sphere of his knowledge, of a considerable body or bodies of Christians existing outside the visible unity of the religious fellowship to which he himself belonged. Just for this reason, it may be argued that he never explicitly faced *our* question: whether the Church was only *de facto*, or is also, essentially, a single historical communion. But we have suggested that, in any case, the deepest implications of his teaching about the Church would seem to lead to the view that 'Christianity itself', to use Robinson's phrase, is bound up with the visible unity of the Church.

Schism, unfortunately, would not be slow to show itself (as we shall see, there is evidence of it within the limits of the New Testament). But when it did appear it was met by the explicit conviction that the Church was essentially and visibly one society or communion. And there is no sort of evidence that the Catholic Church or its spokesmen were aware that, in taking this as a principle, they were diverging from, or even improving on, the teaching of St Paul and the other New Testament writers.

Chapter 11

THE NEW TESTAMENT (2)

FOR the interpretation of the Epistle to the Ephesians we sought the help of the Anglican Dean Robinson. We may similarly turn to the late Anglican Dean Selwyn for some account of the doctrine of the Church in the First Epistle of St Peter.[1] Selwyn reminds his readers that the word 'Church' (*ecclesia*) does not occur in the Epistle, which, however, brings the Church before us as 'a race, a people, a temple, a flock; and the element of order involved in these is not without emphasis in each case. But organisation, as distinct from order, figures very slightly in the total picture. It is as though for St Peter the Church had no outside edges, no external boundaries: it is a flock, not a fold':

> And yet, though the word 'church' is absent, the thing itself permeates the Epistle. It is the meeting-place of the Epistle's theology and ethics. 'From God—in relation to God—unto God'; that is one of the trumpet-notes of the letter, and the Church is the subject of it. The supreme *differentia* of the Church is its faith and holiness. At the same time this faith and holiness are embodied and visible, constituting a challenge to the world around them and exposing Christians to persecution. . . . The line of demarcation between the Church and the world is not inward and invisible alone; it is also outward and concrete, marked by the tears and sometimes the blood of the persecuted. . . . Conversion to Christ led to baptism, which was the door of admission to the Church; conversion to the Church was sealed in the same sacrament, and led to faith in Christ, and through him in God. And the step was a crucial one, involving divine Judg-

---

[1] *The First Epistle of St Peter* (1949). Selwyn defends the apostolic authorship of the Epistle, which he would date in consequence to about A.D. 64. In 1947 F. W. Beare's commentary had been published, placing the date of the Epistle in the second century; this work was apparently unknown to Selwyn when he reached his very different conclusions. As in the case of *Ephesians*, the date is less important to us than the fact that *I Peter* has the authority belonging to a canonical book.

ment. Strictly speaking, it was not the convert who accepted or rejected Christ or the Church, but God who accepted or rejected the convert. To refuse to take the step when opportunity is offered is to continue under the condemnation in which the whole unbelieving world is lying; to take it is to enter the sphere of salvation. That is why . . . we must say of St Peter that he teaches the doctrine expressed later in the phrase, *extra ecclesiam nulla salus.* . . . The Church's ultimate basis, according to I Peter, is 'the causeless, sovereign, free, eternally unchangeable Will of Love of the Father, of the God of grace and Lord of the Church, ever worthy to be worshipped' (cf. 1, 3; 4, 11; 5, 11); and his work is the reconciled Church. . . . The close-knit unity of the Church, and its dependence upon Christ are brought out with special force in the image of the Church as God's true Temple, fulfilling the highest prophetic ideals of the Temple of Israel. . . . Christians are not only the stones of which the house is built, deriving their unity from their relationship to the whole design: they are also the body of priests who serve in this temple and offer the spiritual sacrifices which are its primary purpose. . . . The resultant picture of the Church is of a divinely established institution, at once priestly and sacrificial.[2]

Selwyn's language is not altogether clear, but he appears to find in I Peter the notion of the Church as a visible entity, a reality whose maker is not man but God, and the ark of salvation.[3] He sees in the image of the temple an implication of the Church's unity—whether simply as a fact, or as a condition of her existence, is not made explicit. It hardly needs to be emphasised that, once again, we here find the New Testament witnessing against the idea of the Church as a merely invisible entity. That it is something more than that comes out with particular clarity in Chapter 5, where the author, addressing officials in the local Christian communities, whom he calls 'elders', and with whom he associates himself as their 'fellow-elder', urges them to

[2] *Op. cit.* pp. 81-84. One comment seems called for: though it is God Who accepts the convert, it is surely the potential convert who in the first instance rejects Christ.

[3] Cf. 1 Pet. 1, 20 f., which finds in the ark of Noe, the only refuge from the deluge of divine judgment, a type of baptism. But baptism, for primitive Christianity, is the gateway to the Church, which consists of baptised persons, and Selwyn feels able to write that the author of I Pet. 3, 18-22, 'thinks of the Christian Church as the "antitype" of the ark, and of the waters of Christian baptism as prefigured by those of the Flood' (*op. cit.* p. 334). The comparison of the Church to Noe's ark, with the implication that 'outside her there is no salvation' became classical in Christian antiquity. According to a recent theory, I Peter embodies or reflects a 'baptismal liturgy'.

'shepherd the flock of God' in its local branches in which they, the elders, are functioning. The flock of God is the Church, the heir of that Old Testament People of whom God was the shepherd (Ezech. 34, 31, referred to by Selwyn *ad loc.*); and this Church is, it seems, identified with the concrete visible Christian body of which the local communities were several representatives. In its universal or catholic aspect, the epistle refers to it as 'your fraternity in the world at large' (I Pet. 5, 10, with Selwyn's note *ad loc.*). Thus we can conclude that, in the mind of this author, the Church is a visible, supralocal, entity whose members recognise each other as 'brothers', and which, in its local embodiments, is equipped with officials who have a pastoral task. Whether the intercommunion of these local communities is essential to their status as 'parts' of the whole is not clearly indicated; one can only say that the idea would be entirely consistent with the epistle's teaching, and with the comparison of the Church to a *structure* of 'living stones' built up on the incarnate Christ.

The last chapter of the Epistle to the Hebrews, like I Peter 5, presents us with the picture of a local community, or several such, with officials (here called 'leaders'): 'Greet your leaders and all the saints' (13, 24). It would seem that, as in Ephesians, the 'saints' are not 'good' Christians, but just Christians, members of the local community. And it can hardly be doubted that these communities, or their members, together make up the People, to 'sanctify' which 'Jesus died outside the gate' (13, 12). This Christian People is the Church (the word is not used in this sense in Hebrews), identified by the author with the Old Testament People of God, and living under the charter of the 'new covenant' in the blood of Christ. For this author, the Christian People is the very embodiment of God's final redeeming purpose for mankind. With its local officers and its concrete baptised membership, it is anything but a purely invisible entity. It would perhaps be true to say that its essential unity as a visible whole is not an issue of which the author is conscious; he does not face the question of schismatical communities, though he does urge his readers 'not to give up (attendance at) their common meetings, as is the custom with some' (10, 25).

In contrast, the author of the First Epistle of St John has to face the question of schism, and in doing so gives us perhaps the clearest inspired teaching on the visible unity of the Church; though he never uses the word 'church' itself.

The epistle opens with a tremendously emphatic assertion of the origin of the Church's preaching in direct sense-contact with a flesh-and-blood Christ:

> Our message concerns that Word who is life; what he was from the first, what we have heard about him, what our own eyes have seen of him; what it was that met our gaze, and the touch of our hands. Yes, life dawned; and it is as eye-witnesses that we give you news of that life, which ever abode with the Father and has dawned, now, on us.[4]

Here the Word of God is not merely the teaching which came from the lips of Jesus (though it includes this); it is Christ himself, in the fullness of his incarnation and its implication of a supra-temporal existence; the 'historical Jesus' whom his disciples had known, with whom they had been familiar. His life on earth was the manifestation of a life whose ultimate home is 'with the (or His) Father'. The disciples' contact with him was not intended as a privilege to set them apart from all others, but a condition making possible their function, which was 'to give news' to others who had not been eyewitnesses, to bear witness of the 'life with the Father' as it had been manifested to them: 'What we have seen and heard we announce to you in your turn, so that you too may have communion with us. And the communion which is ours is a communion with the Father and with his son Jesus Christ.[5] What Christianity offers, then, to mankind is communion with God. Communion with God the Father is something that belongs to the Word in eternity (the 'life' was 'with the Father'). When the Word became incarnate ('was manifested'), it was as though the 'communion' had been incarnated also. The disciples were drawn into that communion by their association with Christ in the flesh. And this was the source of a further expansion of the communion, in which the actual historical presence of Jesus has its place supplied by the presence and witness of the disciples.

[4] I, 1-3 (Knox). 'What we have heard of him' is surely a mistranslation; the context demands the rendering (to follow Knox's general scheme of rendering, which I confess I find unsatisfactory) 'what we heard (him saying)'.

[5] I, 3.

Thus others, who had not seen or heard Christ, were brought into communion with his disciples, and in that communion were at the same time in communion with Christ and with the Father. If the whole point of Christianity is to bring men into union with God, it is also true that union with God is identical with union with Christ, and this again is identical with union with the eye-witness disciples. The flesh-and-blood manifestation of life in Jesus has, so to speak, an extension in the flesh-and-blood fellowship of the Christians, linked to the incarnate source of life by their union with the disciples.

It is primarily within this fellowship (a word which we are using for the moment without accurate determination of its implications) that the great divine and Christian virtue of charity is to be practised. It is he who 'loves his brother' (in the Christian terminology of the New Testament the 'brethren' are the Christians) who abides in the light of God (2, 10).

This fraternity of concrete fellowship is, in the author's mind, set sharply over against 'the world' outside it. So much so that 'the world' is not to be loved. This, however, does not mean that non-Christians are not to be loved; indeed, the disciples had gone forth precisely to convert the non-Christians and to bring them into the orbit of incarnate love.

But not only is there the Christian fraternity on the one hand and the world on the other; there is a *tertium quid*, and its representative figures are called by our author 'antichrists'. His readers had been taught that *the* Antichrist was to be expected, and the appearance of these anticipatory types of that eschatological figure is a proof that they are already living in the 'last hour'. Who are these portents? It emerges eventually that they are such as maintain the lie that Jesus was not the Christ. Such, indeed, was the position of the unconverted synagogue. But these antichrists are not unconverted Jews; they are what a later age would call 'heretics'. Their origin had been in the Christian fellowship itself, but they have left it: 'they went out from us' (2, 19). The very fact that they could do this is a proof, quite apart from their false belief, that the fellowship does not consist exclusively of 'saints' in the modern sense of the word, despite the fact that it is the abode of sanctity: 'had they been of us, they would have remained with us' (2, 19). Thus the outward guise of Christian membership may conceal a heart alienated from charity, darkened by sin. And the external break with the fellowship is by itself a proof of such alienation. We can almost hear Cyprian saying that 'good men do not leave the Church'. It is surely very remarkable that the epistle offers, as a complete refutation of the pretentions of these heretics, not the fact that their belief is heterodox, but simply the external fact that they have left the visible fellowship to which the author and his readers belong. Latent within this argument is the conviction of the indivisible unity of the visible Church. It anticipates Cyprian's 'short way with heretics': it is superfluous to ask what the Novatianists teach; it is enough to know that they teach outside the Church. It is taken for granted that any teaching thus given, and contradicting the Church's teaching, is false.[6]

Did the author of I John, when he wrote of the heretics who 'went out from us but were not of us', have in mind the scene in the fourth gospel, where the disciples are grouped in fellowship around Jesus, 'the light of the world', and Judas 'goes out' to betray his master, and 'it was night'?[7]

It is after the exit of this 'son of perdition' that the fourth Gospel puts upon Christ's lips the great prayer:

> . . . I have made thy name known to the men whom thou hast entrusted to me, chosen out of the world. . . . Now they have learned to recognise all the gifts thou gavest me as coming from thee; . . . I am remaining in the world no longer, but they remain in the world. . . . Holy Father, keep them true to thy name, thy gift to me, that they may be one (thing), as we are one (thing). . . . I have watched over them, so that only one has been lost. . . . The world has nothing but hatred for them,

[6] The absence, in this passage of the epistle, of any attempt to distinguish between the objective status of schism and the possible good faith of the schismatics is characteristic of the New Testament with its 'apocalyptic' objectivity. It is also, I suspect, a personal characteristic of this author, whose profound Christian charity is built up on a nature of extreme vehemence and is coloured by an intellect which sees all issues in clear-cut black and white. The epistle, it might be suggested, echoes the accents of the Sons of Thunder, eager to call down fire on the inhospitable Samaritans.

[7] This is not the place, nor have I the competence, for a full discussion of the problems of authorship raised by the 'Johannine' books. I take it that the first epistle is from the same mind as the substance of the fourth Gospel, or at least that it has a relationship with that Gospel that may be compared with the relation of Ephesians to the rest of the Pauline *corpus* (leaving the Pastorals out of account). And, despite all difficulties, it seems to me that the intense insistence on sense-contact with Jesus in the opening verses of the epistle can hardly not come from an eye-witness.

because they do not belong to the world, as I too, do not belong to the world. . . . It is not only for them that I pray; I pray for those who are to find faith in me through their word; that they may all be one (thing) . . . in us; so that the world may come to believe that it is thou who has sent me. And I have given them the privilege (glory) which thou hast given me, that they should all be one (thing), as we are one (thing); that while thou art in me, I may be in them, and so they may be perfectly made one (thing). So let the world know that it is thou who hast sent me, and that thou hast bestowed thy love upon them, as thou hast bestowed it upon me.[8]

The unity of which this prayer speaks is not a merely invisible unity; it is a unity which will serve as a motive to induce 'the world' to believe in the divine mission of Jesus, and is therefore a visible unity. But is it a unity that belongs to the Church essentially, or is this visible unity only of her *bene esse*? We are not here assuming that John 17 is a verbatim record of words actually spoken by Jesus. Our question is, whether so spoken or not, what did these sayings represent in the mind of the inspired author of the Gospel? And it appears very probable, if we believe that this author's mind is also the mind from which I John originated, that one who held that schism is self-condemnatory would also hold that the prayer of John 17 implied that visible unity is of the Church's *esse*. We may observe, not only that this unity is immediately linked with 'abiding in the name' of the Father: 'Keep them true to thy name . . . that they may be one thing', but that it is immediately linked with the 'glory' of God, given by the Father to Jesus and by him to the disciples: 'I have given them the glory which thou hast given me, that they should all be one thing'. For a primitive Christian there could be no doubt of the permanence in history of the essential results of Christ's redemptive work ('I have overcome the world', Jn. 16, 33), and among these results he would count fidelity to 'the name' of the Father of Jesus Christ, and the 'incarnation' in some abiding form of 'the glory'.

[8] 17, 6-23 (Knox). I have several times inserted the clumsy addition 'thing', to make clear that the Greek for 'one' is neuter. Ephesians speaks of the Christians as 'one man'; the Johannine expression perhaps brings the concrete character of Christian unity more emphatically into view. In verse 22, Knox's rendering 'privilege' seems to me a paraphrase rather than a translation.

The same Gospel gives us another saying about unity (ch. 10).
Jesus is 'the good shepherd', the shepherd, it would seem, of the
flock of God, with an implicit reference to the Old Testament
doctrine of God as the shepherd of Israel. But he does not look
only to the confines of the race of Israel for the sheep of his
future flock. He has 'other sheep which do not belong to this
fold'. They, too, have to be brought in. They will 'hear the
voice' of the shepherd calling them, and so there will be 'one
flock,[9] one shepherd'. Here the unity of the flock seems as
integral to the new religious dispensation as the one shepherd.
The presumption may be thought to be that the flock will be
visible, as its shepherd had been, and that its unity will similarly
be visible. Such certainly seems to be the implication of Jn. 21,
15-9. Here the good shepherd, whose visible presence will no
longer be with his flock, gives the care of his sheep to Peter;
doubtless so that the unity of the flock may still be polarised
in a single visible shepherd.[10]

The author of the fourth Gospel and the three Johannine
epistles has often been described as a 'mystic', and it has sometimes been implied that he was not the sort of man who would
have been interested in sacraments or in a visible Church and
its unity. But the existence of a positive sacramental interest and
of a positive view of the Church is fairly widely recognised in
Anglican and Protestant scholarship today. Dr Howard provides an example of this. But he writes:

It is unfortunate that the prayer for unity (ch. 17) is so often
quoted as though it referred to a uniform polity or to a centralised
ecclesiastical bureaucracy (!). This thought is quite foreign to the
context. As Titius has said: ' . . . The perfect unity of the

[9] Knox, following the Vulgate, reads here 'one fold'. It has often been pointed
out that the better reading is 'one flock'. I do not myself think that this makes
much difference to the argument.
[10] On the Vulgate reading in 10, 16 ('one fold'), C. K. Barriett (*The Gospel
according to St John*, p. 313) writes: 'This is a mistranslation, but not so misleading as is sometimes supposed; there is nothing to suggest that John thought
of one flock lodged in a number of different folds.' The same scholar (p. 422),
commenting on the words 'I am not praying for the world' (17, 9), points out
that John teaches that God 'loves the world' (3, 16), and that there is here no
withdrawal from that position 'in favour of a narrow affection for the pious';
but to pray for the world *as such* 'would be almost an absurdity' since the only
hope for the world is that it should cease to be 'the world'. He is inclined to see
in the designation of Judas as the 'son of perdition' a reference to the figure of
'the man of sin' or Antichrist; if so, our suggested comparison of the heretics
of I John with Judas is somewhat strengthened

faithful is . . . traced to the community of their life with Christ in all its relationships. It is thought of . . . as producing a community binding individuals together into complete union.'[11]

It is hardly disputable that there is no thought of 'a centralized ecclesiastical bureaucracy' in John 17. The Roman *curia* was not born for several centuries after Christ. This chapter has nothing to say even about a central *focus* of the life of the Church on earth. Nor does it teach a *uniform* polity. But it must not be inferred that John did not accept the idea of a *single* Christian polity. On the contrary there is every reason to suppose that the success of the Church's mission to the world is linked up in this chapter with her self-manifestation as a single body-and-soul community. A community does not exist without some organisational elements, and the author of the Johannine epistles had no hestitation in exercising what can only, in modern terms, be described as an authority of discipline or jurisdiction over the churches which he regarded as within his sphere. Such authority is also implicitly claimed for Peter when, in the last chapter of the Gospel, he is put in charge of the 'sheep' of Christ's one flock.

As an illustration of Anglican exegesis of the fourth Gospel, the following from E. C. Hoskyns is not without interest; it is from his commentary on chapter 17:

> Christian unity is not merely a unity of purpose and a unity of means employed to effect this purpose. It is, rather, a vital organic union, not only similar to, but veritably identical with, the union of the Father and the incarnate Son, *that they may be one, even as we are one; I in them and thou in me.* This peace of the Church does most surely draw to God His scattered children, for it is the concrete expression of His love. It must not therefore be supposed that the unity of the Church is to be attained by a long history of human endeavour. The believers are wrought into one concrete organic union of charity by an act of God, since to *perfect* is an almost technical term for a mighty act of the Father or the Son. . . . In this sense the Lord prays *that they may be perfected into one.* Nor must it be supposed that this exaltation of the Church results simply in the substitution of the Church for the Christ as the object of belief. Faith remains faith

---

[11] *Christianity according to St John*, p. 137. Again (p. 133) this author, commenting on the teaching on the unity of the Church in the allegory of the True Vine (ch. 15), says that this unity 'is not of organization but of organic life'.

in Jesus as The Apostle of God . . . the purpose of the glory and
unity of the Church is that the world may believe in Jesus.[12]

It is worthy of note that this passage affirms that, in the idea of
John, the unity of the Church is something deeper than a unity
of function and of means (may we include sacraments and
ministry among the 'means'?). It is also a *concrete* unity, a
visible expression of God's love (thus, as for Augustine, the
Church is charity in concrete historical embodiment). It is not
the result of human effort (not therefore a so-far unrealised
ideal), but an effect of an act of God. And the purpose of this
unity, concrete and visible and not depending primarily on
human co-operation but on God, is the mission to the world
which the Church has received from Christ, and Christ has
received from his Father.

[12] *The Fourth Gospel*, p. 505.

Chapter 12

THE NEW TESTAMENT (3)

As was suggested earlier in these pages (ch. 4), the progress of modern scholarship, in its 'quest of the historical Jesus', has shown that the beliefs and interests, the experience, of the primitive Church, lie across our path and at first sight seem to shut Jesus himself, as he really was in the actuality of his earthly life, from our view. We might wish that we had access to the reports of an able and independent newspaper correspondent for the events from the baptism of Jesus to the finding of the empty tomb; or to the *procès verbal* of a commission of impartial judges sitting on the evidence of the original disciples within a few months of the resurrection of Christ. But in fact we have neither. Nor have we the signed dispositions of contemporary Jews or others who had remained unconvinced by and hostile to the 'good news from God'. Our sources of information are, almost exclusively, such as emanate from a society of believers and its members. Written by believers, incorporating oral traditions compiled, if not created, by and for believers, our documents are written from faith to faith. This does not mean that they are of necessity unreliable in substance; indeed, if Jesus was what the primitive Church believed him to be, only faith could have had historical insight into his life and death and resurrection. But it does make the task of the independent historian of Christian origins a peculiarly difficult one. The reply of the best and most circumspect scholars today, to a request for a reconstruction of the history and 'message' of Jesus, would probably be that the time is not ripe for such definitive work.[1]

---

[1] Professor D. E. Nineham, in 'Eye-witness Testimony and the Gospel Tradition, III' (*Journal of Theological Studies*, October 1960, pp. 253 ff.), writes: 'The gospels must be treated in the first instance as so many formulations of the early Church's growing tradition about the ministry of Jesus; the only thing for which they certainly provide *direct* evidence is the beliefs about, and understanding of, that ministry in various parts of the early Church between the middle of the first and the early part of the second centuries . . . the *coup de grâce* is

What we can say, and what in effect was said thirty years ago
in *The Riddle of the New Testament* (Hoskyns and Davey), is
that the fact and the faith of the primitive Church together
constitute a phenomenon of such magnitude and such special
characteristics as to demand a historical cause of proportionate
size and quality.[2] And it is probable that, among believers today
who are competent to judge, something like the following reconstruction would be accepted, at least provisionally, as not far
from the mark.

Jesus of Nazareth was, in one aspect, a man who belonged to
a particular age and environment. He spoke to the men of a
particular social and religious culture—to the Jews of the great
tradition in Palestine in the first half of the first century A.D.
His public utterances were ordinarily in the Aramaic language
current in that culture. His teaching expressed itself through
the concepts and in the mental outlook with which they were
familiar.

In this teaching, and in all his public work, Jesus presupposed
the validity of the central Jewish religious tradition as it had
been crystallised in the Old Testament literature. For this
tradition a typical Jew, whatever else he was, was a member of
a holy community, the community which had been fashioned,
adopted as his own, and 'educated', by the one, divine, righteous
Creator of all things. The holy community had a strong racial
colouring, and members of it were glad to describe themselves
as the children of Abraham. But in fact the community included converts, and descendants of converts, of other racial

finally given to the attempt to write a "Life" of Jesus in the modern sense.' One
might wish to question the implication that the four Gospels were not all written
by the end of the first century. And it is fair to mention that H. Riesenfeld
('The Gospel Tradition and its Beginnings', in *Studia Evangelica*, 1957) has
reacted with some vigour against the agnosticism, to call it such, of some
modern critics as regards the possibility of 'discovering' Jesus through the
primitive Christian tradition.

[2] It hardly needs to be said that Christian faith need not pre-suppose, has
probably never rested simply upon, a reconstruction of 'the historical Jesus'.
It is not less 'rational' on that account. On the historical cause of Christianity,
cf. P. Benoit (*Exégèse et Théologie*, p. 98, in a review of 'Le Problème de
Jésus', by Jean Guitton; the passage quoted is a statement of a position
put forward in the book reviewed): 'The magnitude of the spiritual
upheaval which overthrew two earlier religions (Judaism and paganism) and
conquered the world so suddenly, so profoundly, and so permanently, cannot
be explained simply by the activity of the twelve Apostles; behind them we
perceive a higher and more adequate cause: the personality of Jesus, whatever
may be the truth about the mystery of Jesus.'

origins. The formal basis of membership was, therefore, not exclusively racial. Rather, it was the practical acceptance of the religious tradition of the Jews as being the divinely revealed way of life for men. The name given to this tradition was *torah* (inadequately translated into Greek as *nomos,* and into English as Law). If the tradition was often referred to as the Torah of Moses, this need not mean that every detail of it was thought to have been articulated by the great prophet of the Exodus. There had been other prophets after Moses. It is true, however, that there was a tendency to regard not only their teaching but that of the Wise Men and the priests as in some sense all pre-contained in the revelation through Moses, as development, or at least application of, that revelation. It is important to remember, too, that Moses' teaching was not regarded as his own invention; it was given by God, and the function of Moses had been to be God's mouthpiece, the mediator of the divine revelation. All this enables us to measure, in some degree, the implications of the New Testament teaching that Christ was greater than Moses, his gift to mankind something greater than the Torah.

It has often been remarked, and it is important, that the 'pivot' (to use a picturesque word of Leon Roth in *Judaism; a Portrait*) of Judaism was not faith, not even faith in God, but obedience, a practical conformity to a programme of practical living.

But of course Judaism implied a faith. You would not submit to 'the yoke of the Torah' unless you believed in the one righteous Creator, in the Torah as his manifestation of his will and indirectly of his nature, and in the divine vocation of the holy community.

Along with the faith there went a hope, sprung from belief in the community's divine vocation. This was the hope of what we have learnt to call the Messianic age, when a fresh intervention of divine power and mercy would enable the community to rise to the height of its destiny and to enjoy the blessings foretold to the fathers of old. There was a widespread expectation that this age would be inaugurated by a personal Messiah, a scion of the old royal House of David.

The Torah made provision for corporate sacrificial worship. This worship had long been concentrated in the Temple on

Mount Sion, and its ministers were the priests of the line of Levi. For although Judaism was not formally a racial religion, yet race in fact played a great part in it, and just as the Messiah was expected to come from the line of David, so—and more generally—it was recognised that priestly legitimacy supposed physical descent from the patriarch Levi. The Torah, in fact, was not only a religious code; in many of its features it expressed a national culture, and full conversion to Judaism practically involved taking upon oneself the 'nationality' of a Jew.

While the community's cultus was thus in the hands of the Levitical priesthood, the Torah in its wider aspects was largely cared for by the scribes, members of the schools of religious wisdom and interpretation that had grown to power in post-exilic Judaism. The priests, we gather from the New Testament, gravitated to the more conservative religious ideas of the Sadducean party, which frowned upon 'modern' developments of belief like that in the personal resurrection of the just; whereas many of the scribes belonged to the advance-guard, the Pharisees. It is most interesting to observe that, despite the vehement invective against the Pharisees in the New Testament, primitive Christianity accepted the 'doctrinal developments' which were characteristic of that party.

The Dead Sea Scrolls have reminded us that, alongside the great central tradition of Judaism, there could exist what was virtually a schismatical sect. The members of this dissenting body held that the true holy community, with legitimate continuity, was their own society, and they regarded the Jerusalem priesthood as intruders. And they had their own version of the Messianic hope. While in some respects they offer a fascinating parallel to the primitive Christian Church, they differ basically from it in one respect which will be pointed out below.

Jesus, however, addressed himself, as has been said, to the adherents of the central tradition. He gave full acceptance to their implicit claim to be the true inheritors of the Covenant and the Torah. His whole life work presupposes the validity of the concept of the holy community and the identification of this community with the religious society which recognised the reigning Jerusalem priesthood. If he may be described as a reformer and a critic of the contemporary establishment, he initiated his protest from within.

His public life was one of word, of action, and in the end, of suffering, culminating in the death of a criminal. At the heart of his public teaching was a 'message', a 'good news from God', delivered as a 'proclamation', and as with the authority of one commissioned for that purpose by God.[3] Our sources sum up this message in the formula: The Reign of God is at hand. There can be no doubt that such a proclamation meant that the Messianic age was about to dawn. Already implicit in the message was a claim, on the part of Jesus, to prophetical status. He did not pretend to have worked out from the Torah the date at which the Reign might be expected; or, if he did, this was only by way of confirmation. He claimed to know its proximity by prophetical intimacy with the divine purpose.

However, the content of the proclamation, with its reaffirmation of the Messianic hope, was also by implication a reaffirmation of the divine vocation of the holy community. God would visit and redeem his people.

Alike by his teaching and by his 'wonderful works', Jesus implied that the coming of the Reign was intimately allied with his own ministry and his own person. In fact, he claimed that, in a mysterious and anticipatory sense, the Reign was already operative in that work, in his personal history and ministry. If, on the whole, he avoided, almost if not quite to the end, any public assumption of the title of Messiah, this was probably due to two reasons. His own conception of the Messianic role stood in sharp contrast with that which was popularly held.[4] And secondly, there was the fact that till his ministry had been accomplished he was still, from one point of view, only on the way to becoming Messiah. He was, indeed, 'he that should come'; there was none other to look for. But in his historical manifestation he came not to assume, there and then, the pomp of kingship but the vocation of a servant; a servant of the

---

[3] The noun *kerygma* (proclamation) happens not to be used in the Gospels of the preaching of Jesus. The corresponding verb is frequent in the Synoptic Gospels.

[4] A modern Christian theologian might accept for himself the hypothesis of the evolution of species. At the same time, he might seek to avoid the word 'evolution' in his teaching because the scientific hypothesis has become coloured in the popular mind with a false philosophy.

members of the holy community, and, probably, in a still deeper sense, the Isaianic Servant of the Lord.[5]

If we can trust our documents, and on this point they appear to be trustworthy, the latter part of the ministry of Jesus was clouded over by the accumulating evidence that Jewish official-dom would reject his preaching and his claim. He will, then, have given private warning to his intimate disciples that the historical outcome of his work—since all the effective cards were in the hands of his enemies, except indeed that miraculous power which he would not exercise on his own behalf—must be catastrophic 'failure' (our sources are more explicit: he fore-told his own death through the contriving of those who held authority among the people). He had come to the people of the Messianic hope. He had come, their hoped-for Messiah, though not in the role of a Messiah already in the full public exercise of his authority. But the people of that hope, so far as their leaders could speak for them, and to the extent that they were willing to aquiesce in their leaders' decisions, had not received him. They had not accepted him at his own valuation of his person and his function. Another pseudo-Messiah?

Jesus was executed because he would not admit that his claim was false. But before the end he had not only, we are told, directed the minds of his followers forward to some strange reversal of affairs which would be the divine answer to his death, but had taken concrete steps to ensure that what he had initiated should survive him even in the historical order. He had summoned to him certain of his followers, men who were pre-pared to accept his teaching as from God and his claim as valid. From among these followers, then, 'he appointed twelve to be his companions, and to go out preaching at his command, with power . . . to cast out devils.'[6] The evangelist goes on to give

[5] Doubts are still expressed whether the New Testament identification of Christ with the Servant of the Lord goes back to the teaching of Jesus himself. If, however, he was, as Christians believe, the Envoy of God, and if, as there is every reason to believe, he read his own destiny in the pages of the Old Testament, it seems to me most probable that, at least as the clouds gathered about him, he would have turned to those same pages for some prefiguring of a rejected and suffering Messiah. Where could he have found so clear a pre-figurement as in the Servant passages of Isaiah and in some of the Psalms? In other words, the theological problem which, it is suggested, led the early Church to turn to the Servant Songs, must have been present already to the mind of Jesus.

[6] Mk. 3, 14 f. (Knox). For *appointed* the Greek has a word which means created. The 'preaching' was to be the proclamation of the coming Reign of God.

a list of twelve names, not forgetting 'Judas Iscariot, the traitor'. This mention of Judas among the Twelve is important, as evidence that the apostolic college was in fact instituted by Jesus. It seems unlikely that a later inventor of such an institution would have included the betrayer among those alleged to have been chosen by the Christ himself.

Jesus had done something else that was to be important for Christian institutions. On the night of his betrayal he had given his disciples to eat of what he called his 'body', and to drink a cup which was 'the new covenant in his blood'. He thus provided the prototype of what became the central liturgical rite of the Church at its weekly meetings for prayer and worship. Thus 'those who believed in his name' would have not only a new officialdom but a new corporate worship.

The crux of the matter was precisely—believing in his name. If, under the old covenant, the holy community existed for the realisation of a future divine purpose, if it looked forward with the whole of its being to the Messianic accomplishment, then obviously—granted that the Reign of God was anticipated in the mysterious historical lowliness of Jesus and his ministry— everything must depend on the response to Jesus' message and to his claim. The holy community, and that is to say its members, must make an act of faith in him. Unless that faith was forthcoming, not only would Jesus' mission be a failure, but the holy community would have lost the reason for its existence in rejecting its Messiah. Yet if Jesus was what he claimed to be, the failure of the mission was impossible: for the mission was the break-through into history of the eschatological Act of God.

The official rejection of him was therefore paradox and irony at their extreme development. This was the greatest 'refusal' that could be conceived. The persecution of the Old Testament prophets bore no comparison to this, precisely because this was the rejection of the 'final' Act of God. It is the recognition of this refusal that underlies the tremendous prophecy of the downfall of Jerusalem and the destruction of the Temple. The rejection of Jesus must spell not only his own death but, necessarily and as part and parcel of his own passion, the 'death' of the holy community.

Yet once again, since his claim was true, neither his own

death (the death of the Messiah) nor that of the holy community could possibly be the last word. There must be a 'resurrection from the dead'. And in fact Christ rose in his own body, glorified. And in and through his resurrection the holy community also rose to a new life in the 'little flock' of those who had believed in him. Henceforth there would be two so-called Israels. There would be 'Israel according to the flesh', surviving as a mere historical phenomenon (till it should recognise its Messiah), but not surviving any longer as God's holy community.[7] And there would be the true, old but regenerated, holy community, an Israel according to the spirit of the gospel and the resurrection.

To this true Israel, complete with its new hierarchy and its new rites, there was applied, for purposes of distinction, an old name: it was the Church, the *ecclesia* of God, the sacred con-vocation of the People of God gathered together as in the wilderness, in the crisis of a new and greater Exodus; in a new beginning which would remain for ever new.

If the broad lines of this reconstruction of Christian origins can be trusted, the old question whether Jesus 'founded' the Church is already answered. The claim to be 'he that should come' was a claim that the Messianic age was bound up with his work and person (the Isaianic 'signs of the Reign' are already being fulfilled in Jesus' ministry). But the Messianic age was *ex hypothesi* to be essentially a realisation of the potentialities and the destiny of the holy community. Indeed, it might be urged that the idea of a perfected and transfigured holy com-munity was actually more basic to the Messianic hope than was a personal Messiah appearing in the flesh. It was universally conceded that the inauguration of the Messianic age would be an Act of God. It was not universally, even if it was very

[7] This, curiously enough, is the first 'Christian' schism. To the unbelieving eye, the primitive Christian Church was 'in schism' from Judaism. But to the believer in Jesus, the roles are reversed. What the Samaritan community is to the main stream of Judaism, that Judaism is to the Christian Church: a monu-ment to arrested development. And here it may be observed that, whatever the consequences to the schismatic, every schism has deplorable repercussions on the holy community. Urs von Balthasar writes (*Martin Buber and Christianity*, pp. 98 f.): 'The scriptures of Israel rightly belong to the Church—but its books are not the whole living revelation: the heart of Israel is wanting. . . . Certain aspects of Christ . . . are only intelligible from within, to the Jew, and the faculty of understanding "from within", that "inside knowledge", ought by rights to be communicated to the Church from within.' I should wish to deny that the Church has lost any part of the *revelation* to Israel; what has been lost is a contemporary Jewish insight into that revelation.

generally, held that the agent of this inauguration would be an Anointed One. Of the two texts from the Book of Isaias to which Jesus alludes in his answer to the question 'Art thou he that should come?' (Mat. 11, 5), one is from a passage (Is. 35, 5) in which no agent other than God himself is mentioned.[8] The one thing that Jesus is never represented as doing is to cast doubt on the idea of the holy community. To have done so would have been to bring into question his own claim and message, which were essentially Messianic.

The preformation of the Church in the 'little flock' of the disciples was therefore only to be expected, at least from the moment when it became clear that official Judaism would reject the proffered message. And the survival of the Church was assured from the moment when the disciples believed in the resurrection of Jesus.

It has, of course, been objected that Jesus cannot have intended to found the Church, least of all to launch it on a career of millennial duration, because he held a foreshortened apocalyptic view, in which the end of history would follow almost simultaneously upon the termination of his own ministry. What must be the Christian reaction to this objection?

It may readily be granted that we are face to face, here, with one of the still disputed questions in the critical history of Christian origins. But it is also a question to which the Christian need not wait in suspense for an agreed critical answer. A Christian is one who believes that Jesus was the Word of God incarnate, the divine salvation of mankind in act. He cannot fail to infer that, in some sense and with whatever qualifications and discriminations, the subsequent history of Christianity is the divinely intended outcome of the work of Christ. The world and Christianity have in fact survived that work by nearly two thousand years. The question for us then is: what was *God's* plan for a mankind which was actually thus to endure? We shall naturally seek an answer to this question in what it appears that the incarnate Word actually said and did. Historically, it is more probable that he established the college of the Twelve and instituted the Eucharist, than that he committed himself, in official utterances, to an apocalyptic chronology that was

---

[8] A Christian will of course reflect that the *legatus Dei*, the Anointed of the Father, was himself God.

irreconcilable with subsequent events. And it is overwhelmingly probable that he worked within the framework of ideas within which the notion of a redeemed world without a holy community would have been inconceivable.

But in fact, the case against the extreme apocalyptic school of criticism does not rest solely on *a priori* considerations coupled with the evidence for the institution of the Twelve and of the Eucharist by Jesus. It rests also on sayings of his which there is good reason to accept as substantially authentic. One of these is the prediction of the destruction of Jerusalem and the Temple within the lifetime of some of those contemporary with himself. This implies a historical occurrence (seen, be it granted, within a context of eschatological interpretation) which it appears to envisage as considerably later in date than the termination of the mission of Jesus himself. In the same prophetical discourse there is the vista of 'wars and rumours of war'—which are not to be taken as signs that the end is at hand—not to speak of what is probably a spiritual decadence within the Christian fellowship itself ('the charity of most men will grow cold'). None of this seems consistent with an immediate end of history. Moreover the (probably authentic) saying 'thou art Peter, and on this Rock I will build my Church; and the gates of hell shall not prevail against it' seems to imply a Church built so as to withstand a prolonged warfare on the parts of the forces of disintegration. The evidence, in other words, is by no means all on the side of the extreme apocalyptic school of biblical critics.

On the other hand, the older school of Liberal Protestant exegesis had its own, quite different, reasons for questioning the idea that Jesus could have founded the Church. These critics held that any such interest in ecclesiastical institutionalism was inconceivable in one who was a teacher of pure religious ethics in the line of the Old Testament prophets. On this view, the Gospel proclaimed little more than the universal fatherhood of God, the universal brotherhood of man, and the charity—as variable in its expression as the varieties of human situations—which would fit these two sets of relationships. But the rise of the apocalyptic school of exegesis in reaction to this liberal Protestant view is itself an indication that the liberal Jesus is not a reconstruction dictated necessarily by the evidence of the historical sources, but is rather a product of the liberal mentality.

Modern scholarship is not now so confident in pointing the contrast between prophetism and sacerdotalism. The prophets were certainly ready enough to denounce the priests and the magical attitude which was so often engendered by sacerdotalism. It is not, however, quite clear that the essential trend of prophetism was towards a radical rejection of institutional religion. Sacerdotalism and prophetism in the pre-Exilic period were a sort of thesis and antithesis in the dialectic of Israelite religious evolution. In the post-Exilic period (already in the Book of Ezekiel) we see a movement towards synthesis, and this had been accomplished well before New Testament times.

Modern Judaism, it is true, being destitute of an actual system of sacerdotal sacrificial worship, may be inclined to 'play down' the sacerdotal element. Leon Roth (in *Judaism; a Portrait*) hazards the suggestion that the sacrificial part of the Torah was, from the first, a concession to the residuary paganism of the primitive generations of Israel. Without going so far as this, it is possible to think that a certain interior detachment from the cultus was already beginning to take place in the minds of the Pharisees, fostered perhaps by their antagonism to the Sadducean priests. And it may be that, in fact, the growth of civilisation and the unescapable atmosphere of philosophic criticism had made the system of animal sacrifices seem somewhat crude and out of date. St Paul may even have experienced a certain relief in finding that his new faith emancipated him from this aspect of the Torah.

But it must be said that Jesus, so far as our evidence goes, never criticised the Temple cultus as such, though, like the prophets before him, he was emphatic in his criticism of the corruptions to which all institutional religion is only too prone. He is represented as taking part in the Temple festivals, and as sending healed lepers to report themselves to the priests. There is, no doubt, a striking passage in St Matthew's Gospel where he claims to be immune from the Temple tax. But the basis of the claim was not that the tax was not of general obligation but the fact that he is the Son of God. This is an exception which proves the rule. The prophetic-sacerdotal synthesis is epitomised in the saying: 'Be reconciled with thy brother first, and then come back to offer thy gift' (Mt. 5, 24).

It is true that he foretold the downfall of the Temple and, by implication, of the whole Jewish cultic system. But the grounds for this, I have suggested, were not that the cult had always been invalid, but that official Judaism had 'committed suicide' by rejecting the Messiah and the new dispensation which he was inaugurating.

The infant Church, driven on by the dynamism of events, and in particular by the logic of St Paul, soon detached itself in principle from the Jewish cultus. Circumcision, it was decided, was no longer necessary for converts from paganism. This decision was one that went to the roots of the whole issue. The old and the new Israel were no longer concentric. When the Temple was destroyed, the Church could accept the obliteration of the Jewish sacrificial system and Temple worship without any shock to its own essential life.

But if circumcision had been discarded, baptism had replaced it. If the Temple sacrifices were no more, there was the Christian Eucharist, and the Fathers were quick to realise that this fulfilled the words of Malachias: 'No corner of the world, from sun's rise to sun's setting, where the renown of me is not heard among the Gentiles, where sacrifice is not done, and pure offering made in my honour.'[9] If the High Priest had lost his jurisdiction over those who believed that Jesus was the Messiah, there was the apostolic ministry. And if the believers were 'cast out of the synagogues' by their former brethren, what did this matter, since they were incorporated in the brotherhood of the new believers, and were in fact the new and true Israel, citizens of that Jerusalem that is from above, members of the regenerated holy community?

As we have seen, the New Testament attributes the institution of the college of the Twelve to Jesus himself, and derives the Eucharistic rite from what he had done and said at the Last Supper. Only the last chapter of St Matthew's Gospel (and cf. Mk. 16, 16) directly affirms that Jesus had told his disciples to baptise their converts, though the fourth Gospel may be taken to imply as much. In any case, the evidence suggests that the practice was universal from the first Christian Pentecost onwards, and this, together with Jesus' recorded attitude to John the Baptist and his personal reception of John's baptism, may

[9] I, 11.

indicate that Christian baptism was the carrying out of what he had himself commanded.

To repeat, there is no evidence that Jesus ever cast any doubt upon the principle of the holy community, a principle which entailed that, despite repeated backsliding and rebellion and the falling away of individual members, the community itself would never fail (cf. Leon Roth, *op. cit.*); there is overwhelming reason to suppose that he took it for granted. And we have argued that the Christian 'hierarchy' and cultus, which superseded those of the old Israel, and which in themselves suggest the existence of a religious society, appear to have starting-points, at least for their major elements (the apostolic ministry, baptism, and the Eucharist), in arrangements made by Jesus himself.

Thus once again, we seem driven to reject the hypothesis that the Christian Church is essentially an invisible entity. The only question that could arise is whether, in the intention of Jesus, and so far as his actual institutions go, the regenerated Israel was, for Jesus, essentially a society, or only a social tendency and ideal. We may approach an answer to this question by observing that the active nucleus of the new 'cell' of life, into which he breathed his own life, was the college of the Twelve. And this was a body of men who, in the words of the fourth Gospel, had not chosen Jesus, but had been chosen by him; 'and one of them was a devil' (Jn. 15, 16; 6, 71). The 'holiness' and the unity of the apostolic college were thus not dependent on the contingent co-operation of its members, but on the Act of Christ, himself the 'apostle' of God. Similarly, the figure of the Church built upon a rock, which the gates of hell would not prevail against, is hardly congruous with the notion that the Church is but a social tendency.[10] But thirdly, it must be remembered that the old Israel was not merely a race, and not merely a tendency towards community, but an actual community. It was, to use the word of the Epistle to the Ephesians, a *politeia*, a living together; or, as Josephus expressed the matter for his Gentile readers, it was a *theocrateia*, a form of organised human life in which God held the reins as sovereign authority. It was this Israel that Jesus took for granted, and it was in order to

---

[10] On the social tendency hypothesis, the words of the famous saying could be re-expressed thus. 'Thou art Peter, and upon this Rock I will build my social tendency, and the gates of hell shall not prevail against it.'

replace the existing institutional framework of this society that he seems to have established the Twelve and certain elements of cultus. Just such a society in fact resulted in the religious movement of which his own ministry was the origin. The burden of proof is on those who would deny that to be such a society was part of Christ's intention for his Church. But if it was part of his intention, then the survival of the Church, which is guaranteed by God, is bound up with its remaining what he made it.[11]

So far in this chapter I have tried to offer a reconstruction of Christian origins which would win a fair measure of support from believing Christian scholars.[12] Perhaps it will not be entirely out of place now to suggest with somewhat fuller precision what, as it seems to me, may have been the actual facts of the case. It will be observed that my presupposition, in what follows, is that it is agreed that Jesus was God incarnate.

[11] That the Judaism of the great tradition in which Jesus worked was essentially a society may be suggested from what we know of the sect of the Dead Sea Scrolls. It seems that the sectaries denied the legitimacy of the existing priestly hierarchy at Jerusalem, and held it unlawful to participate in the liturgy for which this hierarchy had made itself responsible. They had, however, no intention of rejecting the ideas of hierarchy and liturgical worship. Their position, so far, was analogous to that of English or Scottish Jacobites in the early eighteenth century—royalist, yet denying the right of the ruling House to their allegiance, which they reserved for a Pretender. But the Dead Sea sectaries pursued their views to a logical conclusion, and held that their own body, to the exclusion of the community of the great tradition, was the People of the Covenant, the true holy community, to whom the Messiah had been promised. The same pattern of thought and claim reappears with Christian schismatic bodies of the pre-Reformation centuries, each claiming to be exclusively the whole Church. In making such a claim the Dead Sea sectaries were in all probability reflecting the 'ecclesiology' of the tradition from which they sprang; they differed from other Jews, not in their idea of the holy community as essentially a society, but in their identification of the body in which the idea of the holy community was actualised.

So far, the Dead Sea sect seems closely to resemble the primitive Christian Church, if our reconstruction of the latter is substantially correct. But the sectaries differed from the Christians in so far as the former did not, it seems, make any claim to have been the recipients of a fresh and transforming revelation beyond that which, like the Jews of the great tradition, they claimed to have inherited from Moses and the prophets. They did not claim to be living already in the Messianic Age. Their dispute with the great tradition lay within the limits of the Mosaic dispensation; it was essentially one of legitimacy, and of the correct interpretation of the Torah. But Christianity from the first made the far more audacious claim to have already witnessed what the prophets and ancient sages had foretold. The theological basis of Christianity was thus profoundly and excitingly different from that of the Dead Sea sect. But its attitude to the idea of the holy community as essentially a society was, if I am not mistaken, identical.

[12] An exception should probably be made for the bodily resurrection of Jesus. This was undoubtedly the faith of primitive Christianity, and is unquestionably the teaching of the New Testament. But a good many scholars who believe that Jesus is God would yet feel some hesitation in affirming his *bodily* resurrection.

The Jesus of Liberal Protestantism is, in my opinion, a product of the *Zeitgeist* of the nineteenth century.[13] The 'apocalyptic Jesus' is in the nature of a corrective to the Liberal Protestant Jesus, but is itself an extravagant overstatement of one part of the evidence at our disposal. That these two strongly contrasted interpretations should each have gathered such wide support may be an indication that Jesus was a far more complex person than either school of thought imagined.

What we know about him before we start to 'reconstruct' him is that he stands at the source of one of the greatest historical phenomena of all time: Christianity. To him Christianity looks back, as to one who is not only its Lord but its founder. And Christianity, at least up to the time of the Reformation, was essentially an institutional reality, not merely a social aspiration. It was a historical 'body', with its own 'ethos' and influence, and it was as such that it worked on and within human personalities as well as on the wider stage of history. It may be compared with something much less great than itself: the Roman Empire.

At the origin of the Roman Empire there stands Augustus. Even if we knew nothing more than this about Augustus, namely that the Empire dates from his principate, few of us would be tempted, as we contemplated the majestic story of that long-enduring polity, to doubt that its originator was a man of very great intelligence and practical prudence, who put himself into what he created, and is to be estimated at the value of what he founded.[14] *Si monumentum requiris, circumspice.* Similarly, it appears to me that one may reasonably presume that the Founder of the Christian religion was endowed, in his human nature, with great intelligence and great practical prudence.

It is necessary to react deliberately against the aftermath of the circumstances in which each of us came to his first and almost ineradicable 'idea' of Jesus. Most of us learned about him, long before we had to bother our heads with Augustus and the Roman Empire, at the nursery age. He was presented

---

[13] Doubtless my own belief in the orthodox Christology plays, in my own reconstruction, a role analogous to that of the *Zeitgeist* in Liberal Protestantism. But then, I happen to think that the traditional Christology is true, and the nineteenth-century *Zeitgeist* relatively untrue. And I am writing primarily for Christian readers.

[14] Augustus's moral qualities are not here in question.

to us in an anaemic portrait, by means of a carefully selected choice of attributes, from which few of us ever shake our imagination completely free. Not many of us have ever experienced the shock which an adult but quite fresh mind would receive from a first reading of the Gospels.

And when we do turn to the Gospels for enlightenment, we are again led astray by the popular and Semitic imagery and the particular pedagogic colouring, of the reported sayings of Jesus. Jewish pedagoguy was practical in its aims and very concrete and pictorial in its methods. A marked sense of humour also impregnates the teaching of the Rabbis—and humour varies with the culture in which it is expressed. Jesus was a Jewish teacher of Jews, not so much (directly) the learned and cultured Jews but the crowds who 'knew not the Torah' and the group of semi-educated disciples. All this, and (in the case of those of us who are Christians or post-Christians) a sort of mistaken reverence which shrinks from looking the facts in the face, can result in our viewing Jesus as a somewhat romantic, not quite masculine, not entirely real, person; someone whose feet are not firmly planted on the earth; someone to whom we would not think of attributing intellectual brilliance, or far-seeing strategy, or an audacity both dazzling and realistic. I believe that the net result of all this is something that is remote from the truth.

To illustrate the wealth of meaning latent in sayings that are sometimes dismissed as little more than poetry, we could take the more celebrated of the two mentions (by name) of 'the Church' in St Matthew's Gospel:

(Simon Peter, on behalf of the disciples, has just professed the belief which was the differentia of Christianity as compared with Judaism, that Jesus is 'the Christ, the Son of the living God'. Jesus replies:) Blessed art thou, Simon son of Jona; it is not flesh and blood, it is my Father in heaven that has revealed this to thee. And I tell thee this in my turn, that thou art Peter, and it is upon this Rock that I will build my Church; and the gates of hell shall not prevail against it; and I will give to thee the keys of the kingdom of heaven; and whatever thou shalt bind on earth shall be bound in heaven, and whatever thou shalt loose on earth shall be loosed in heaven (16, 17-19).[15]

[15] I shall assume here that the sayings that make up this passage are authentic. The language of the passage, beneath its Greek dress, is so steeped in 'Aramaism'

It should be noted that, although the evangelist has not shrunk from giving the name Peter to the first apostle long before this section of his Gospel (and indeed in this very pericope he calls him Simon Peter), yet neither here nor elsewhere does he ever represent Jesus as addressing his as 'Peter': 'Blessed art thou, *Simon bar Jona,* for not flesh and blood', that is human perspicacity, 'but my Father in heaven has revealed this to thee'. We are reminded of the earlier passage: '*Father,* I give thee praise that thou hast hidden all this from the wise and prudent, and *revealed* it to little children' (11, 25). Simon, then, has recognised the function and status of Jesus with the help of a supernatural illumination. 'And I in my turn (in response, that is, to Simon's designation of Jesus as "the Christ, the Son of the living God")[16] say to thee, Thou art Peter.' As we know, 'Peter' is the translation into Greek of the Aramaic Kepha. The parallelism with Simon's profession of faith indicates that the term 'Kepha' here is not a proper name but the designation of a function or status. This is confirmed by the continuation: 'And on this Rock (*kepha,* no doubt, in the original Aramaic) I will build my Church, and the gates of hell will not prevail against it.'[17] The function of Jesus, as the Messiah, was the inalienable one of

that it must be supposed to be a translation. C. F. Burney (*The Poetry of our Lord,* p. 117) finds that the passage is cast in the four-beat rhythm which he also discovers in the Matthaean form of the Lord's Prayer, and that it falls into tristichs. He offers a rendering back into Aramaic, in which the rhythmical beats are indicated.

[16] However, the possibility must be granted, that 'the Son of the living God' was not part of Simon's original profession of faith.

[17] The Church will not be built on Simon's profession of faith, but on Simon; and not on Simon as 'flesh and blood' simply, but on Simon *in his official role as Rock.* We are not at the moment directly concerned with the question whether the Rock function was transmissible from Simon to a successor or successors. It may, however, be remarked that the possibility has been denied on two grounds. (1) The Church is founded on the *person* of Simon; and a human personality is not transmissible. (2) The Church is founded on the *apostleship* of Simon; and apostleship, involving eye-witness, is not transmissible to anyone who has not actually seen the historical Jesus. Neither argument can find any support in the Matthaean passage. (1) The Church is not to be built simply on 'Simon' but on Simon *qua* Rock; not on his person but on his function or office. A function or office can be transmissible. (2) The fact that the apostles were eye-witnesses *qualified* them for their function as the original officials of the kerygmatic Church. They could not transmit this qualification; nor could they transmit their unique standing as *original* officials. But there is nothing to show that they could not transmit their function as *officials.* Moreover, Simon shared with the Eleven his status as an apostle; his status as Rock is not said to have been shared by them. Elsewhere in the New Testament, the apostles are described as the foundations of the Church; but the Rock is more than a foundation—it is the substructure on which the foundations are established.

being the one Lord of the Messianic Age, and therefore of the holy community in the Messianic Age. The function of Simon, as the Rock, will be to give an unshakeable stability and permanence to the holy community; this is, of course, a supernatural function, deriving not from his natural powers but from his investiture by the Messiah.[18] Our passage goes on: 'I will give to thee the keys of the kingdom of heaven.' Peter, then, is to be God's grand-vizier in the realm of Messianic accomplishment. 'And whatever thou shalt bind on earth etc.'; binding and loosing is a rabbinic figure for the exercise of a juridical function. The promise that what Peter binds on earth will be bound in heaven is a promise that his juridical decisions will represent those of God. Thus the official action of God's grand-vizier in the sphere of the holy community's historical life is taken up into the sphere of the divine, and an unbreakable link is forged between history and heaven; a link which Christians can only see as flowing from the original link of humanity with God in the incarnation.

This group of sayings has been the subject of unending controversy in the argument about the Petrine claims of the Roman See. But whatever position one adopts in that controversy, it cannot be denied that there is a wealth of intellectual meaning latent in the sayings, or that they express a mind that is directed to the problem of the survival and organisation of the holy community. I have assumed that they are genuine sayings of Jesus. When all allowance has been made for a process of development which, as it has gone on ever since New Testament times, so also is discernible within the limits of the New Testament itself, it nevertheless appears to me that, lying behind the data of the Gospels and the other New Testament literature, there is the working of a single human mind, integrated, immensely balanced and lucid and rich. If this mind is not the mind of Jesus, then two consequences must follow. Firstly, that the real Founder of Christianity was not Jesus, but some pre-Pauline, Palestinian, Great Unknown. Secondly, that this unknown genius so imposed his mind upon the evangelical tradition (at a stage before the earliest form in which we can

[18] Similarly, the Christian believer ('the man who hears these commandments (words) of mine and carries them out') had been described (Mt. 7, 24 f.) as 'building his house upon a rock', where no earthly vicissitudes would shake it.

reconstruct it) as to obliterate the real Jesus from that tradition, and from the minds and memories of the original disciples.[19]

According to St Luke (2, 52), the child Jesus 'advanced in wisdom with the years'. Christians, believing that the child of Mary was God the Son, realise that there is a sense in which Jesus began his historical life at the point to which each of us hopes in the end to attain.[20] From the first he was what theology calls a *comprehensor*. But he was also, as we are, *en route*; he was a *viator*. And as a traveller on life's journey he shared with us the experience of a growing apprehension, through acquired knowledge, of the human and divine *milieu* in which he lived, and of its implications for himself.

It must be doubtful whether we shall ever, through historical investigation, be led to reconstruct a real development in the Messianic ideas of Jesus. What I think we may be able to do is to discover a development in his evangelical, Messianic, strategy.

This strategy seems to have comprised a first stage, a *thesis*, in which he made his appeal to contemporary Judaism, as though in the hope that there would be a collective, nation-wide, acceptance of his message and his claim. Judaism may be said to have come to birth when the people of the Exodus accepted the Mosaic covenant and its conditions. Now the time had come for its rebirth to the further, final, revelation, the new covenant, of the mysteriously anticipated Messianic Age. Our human

[19] I am entirely sceptical about the 'creative' consciousness of the primitive Christian collectivity, as the source of the religious system behind the New Testament, and of the New Testament figure of Jesus. I agree that the collective mind can develop an idea deposited within it, and the possibility of such developments has to be reckoned with by critical historians. It can also contaminate a received idea by combining with it incongruous elements from other sources. I do not believe that it is apt to *create* an organic system of insights, concepts, and practical embodiments together with the implied personality which they seem to express. It might invent a mythical 'lay figure', but the figure would not be spiritually 'alive'; nor would it be likely to cohere with its supposed historical situation. *A priori*, it is much less likely that the collective consciousness of the primitive Christian community created the New Testament Jesus and the Christian religion, than that it failed, in its tradition of the facts, to do justice to his greatness and the brilliance of his thought. The real historical Jesus may have been more 'Johannine' than the Synoptic tradition represents him as being. And it is possible that the evangelists and their predecessors saw less in what they have transmitted than later ages have been able to see.

[20] According to the Greek patristic tradition, God became man in order that man might be 'divinised'. We, too, are already, by grace, 'sharers of the divine nature' (II Pet. 1, 4). But for us the consummation of our human nature in the divine is a hoped-for development. The human nature of Jesus had no subsistence except in the person of God the Son.

imagination delights to play with the questions that begin
'What would have happened *if*'. What 'would have happened'
if this first phase of the Messianic strategy had attained its
apparent goal? There would have been no contrast to draw
between an 'Israel after the flesh' and a 'Jerusalem from above'.
Church and Synagogue would have been identical. The Gospel
would have been carried forth with all the massive means of
propaganda afforded by Jewish institutions not only in the
homeland but throughout the Dispersion. In a very literal sense,
the nations would have brought their tribute of faith and culture
to a regenerated Sion. The High Priest of the old Jewish hierarchy would presumably have been the Pontifex Maximus of
the renovated religion; there would have been no room for a
Peter or for his alleged successors. That we are in the world of
fantasy is disclosed by the consideration that there would also,
presumably, have been no redemption by the death of Christ.

The *antithesis,* or second stage in the Messianic strategy, is
the controversy with the governing powers and influences in
Palestinian Judaism. Aspects of it are recorded in the Synoptic
Gospels, and it is of course a dominant theme of the fourth
Gospel. It culminates in the prediction of the destruction of the
Temple, itself a consequence of the 'failure' of the strategy of
the *thesis.*

Concurrently with the development of the *antithesis,* there is
the strategy of *synthesis,* a race against time. As we have already
reflected, it was inconceivable that the mission of Jesus should
really fail. It must succeed, even through the jaws of death; and
it could only succeed because it was God's purpose and his
omnipotence was engaged in it. The strategy of synthesis is
expressed in the preformation of the regenerated holy community: the giving of a structural pattern to the 'little flock',
the training of its future leaders, and the institution of appropriate sacred rites. That the full genius of Jesus was exerted in
this synthetic stage of his strategy may be inferred from the fact
that what he thereby created has survived to the present day,
still the only hope of mankind because it still bears witness to
the new Messianic Torah and to the one name 'by which we
must needs be saved' (Ac. 4, 12).

It is not given to mere man to create anything absolutely
permanent on earth. That Christianity has in fact survived to

8

the present day may, to a reasonable mind, already amount to a sort of moral miracle. That it will survive till the end of history is, of course, a matter only of faith, and of faith in 'the heavenly Father' of Jesus, who raised him from the dead. History can, however, tell us two things. It can tell us that the survival of Christianity has been associated with, and apparently dependent upon, the continuing existence of the Church as a real historical and unique community. And it can tell us that the view that the Church is a refoundation, by Jesus himself, of the holy community of the Old Testament is a view that is consistent with the historical evidence that has come down to us.

The scope of our argument has limited our attention, in this chapter, to only one aspect of Jesus' thought and work and teaching. It would be ridiculous to suggest that his significance is limited to this aspect. He was more than the originator of an ecclesiastical polity. He was also one of those great witnesses to the invisible and preachers of righteousness whom the Jews called prophets. He was a martyr in the cause of God the revealer. He was God's redeeming Word to mankind, speaking to the heart of humanity and to every individual human heart: 'Come to me, all you that labour and are burdened; I will give you rest. Take my yoke upon yourselves, and learn of me; I am gentle and humble of heart; and you shall find rest for your souls. For my yoke is easy, and my burden is light' (Mt. 11, 28-30). It may be said that these are far more important truths about him than the alleged fact that he founded the Christian Church. The point need not be argued. All that matters here is that he was *also* the founder of an institution, and that this was an essential part of his work and mission; just as it is true that he was indeed God the eternal, but *also* a historical man.

Chapter 13

ESCHATOLOGY AND INCARNATION

While it can hardly be denied that the theory that the Church is a merely invisible entity is contradicted by the New Testament evidence, and while the theory that she is essentially a unique historical communion, visible as such, can adduce much from the New Testament that appears to support it, it will probably be felt by many that the New Testament does not positively exclude the hypothesis that the Church's visible unity on earth is not of her essence, but rather in the nature of an ideal whose realisation is set before Christians as a goal. We have indeed been able to point to at least one text (I Jn. 2, 19) as being quite irreconcilable with this view. But there will doubtless be those who are impressed by the lateness of this text, or who will offer a different interpretation of its implications, or who—in the last resort—will remind themselves that the devil can quote individual texts to his purpose.

As far as the New Testament evidence in general is concerned, the defenders of the 'potential society' view of the Church might argue somewhat as follows:

'The Church is, indeed, in the divine intention, a complete society such that schism between its parts or members would be inconceivable. And as such a society was the intention of divine Providence, so also was it the intention of the incarnate Word. He gave it the endowments which might enable it to realise this intention, and he prayed that his intention might be realised.

'However, the divine intentions, though ultimately assured of realisation, are in fact realised perfectly only in the world to come. It is therefore certain that, after the Second Coming and the Last Judgment, the Church, in the glory of heaven, will be both perfectly one and perfectly holy. And, insofar as her title "apostolic" means "faithful to the truth committed to the

Apostles", she will then be also perfectly apostolic. Moreover, she will be perfectly "catholic", both as holding within her glorified fellowship all the predestined from every age and area of the world's history, and as resuming and consummating every value of human history. All this will be true of the Church after the Second Coming; thus the divine intention will be realised and the divine promises fulfilled.

'But on earth, in this interim between the resurrection of Christ and his Second Coming, the Church exists only in an imperfect phase and state. When we confess our faith in "one holy catholic and apostolic Church" we are speaking with a future reference, of the Church as she should be and "in that day" will be. That this is so is proved, as was said previously, by the fact that on earth she is composed not of saints only but of saints and sinners. Even her saints are not completely holy on earth: "If we say that we have no sin, we are cheating ourselves" (cf. I Jn. 1, 8). The "holy" Church is thus, on earth, far from being simply holy; at best she is imperfectly holy. So, too, the "catholic" Church is far, at present, from being really universal either in extent or in depth of penetration. Then, also, her "apostolicity" is a varying quantity, as she progresses or recedes in her assimilation of the deposit of faith.

'In the same way, we must hold that the "one" Church is not on earth actually and completely one. The imperfection of her unity is disclosed, in part, in the divisions which exist between numerous societies of baptised Christians. This is a fact, and it is no good shutting one's eyes to facts. Certainly, Christ prayed that "they may all be one, that the world may know that thou hast sent me". But these divisions exist, and they do in fact, and in their measure, hide from the world the truth of Christ's claims.

'All this, however, does not mean that unity, holiness, apostolicity, and catholicity are not operative in the Church on earth. They are present as dynamic factors. The Church is, in consequence, tending towards the perfection of these four qualities. In particular, her unity is manifest not only in the large areas of Christian truth and sacramental endowment that are shared by the divided communions, but also, at least today, in the aspirations and efforts towards a greater unity which are taking shape in the ecumenical movement. On the other hand, to claim that the Church's unity is already actualised, and necessarily so, in her existence as a single one of the Christian communions, amounts to an illegitimate transference to the historical order of truths which refer really to the Church's post-historic goal.'

An attempt will here be made to meet this argument. It will be observed at once that it is not based on Scripture. It is an attempt to show that a certain view of the Church, while not vouched for by the New Testament, is recommended by the facts of post-biblical Christianity and is not irreconcilable with biblical authority. In other words, it maintains that the evidence of Scripture is not peremptorily in favour of the belief that the Church must be a single communion; it does not embark on the hopeless task of proving that Scripture has any other positive view of the Church.

The extreme apocalyptic school of biblical criticism performed one signal service to scholarship: it reminded us that the Gospels and the other books of the New Testament are to be read not in the context of modern European thought but in that of the ideas current in the places and times when these books were being written. In particular, the sayings and mission of Jesus are wonderfully illuminated when they are seen against the background of the apocalyptic imagery and thought of Palestine in the first century A.D. If to be an apocalyptist is to use the language and ideas of this *milieu*, then Jesus was an apocalyptist.

Apocalyptic, though it may reflect the influence of Persia, is yet genuinely a development from Old Testament prophetism. But the writers of apocalyptic books did not, as a rule, claim to be the immediate recipients of revelation. By the device of pseudonymity they attributed their alleged revelations to worthies of ancient times. They differ from the classical prophets also, as having a horizon that extends beyond Palestine and its history to the great world empires; indeed, they sometimes break through the time-barrier to deal with a post-historic dénouement of a super-Messianic kind, which they sometimes find difficult to harmonise with the traditional Messianism of fulfilment in this world.

But they agree with the prophets in finding the clue to human life and the norms of human behaviour not in a philosophical investigation of nature and human nature, but in the revealed will of God. And, like the prophets, their outlook is profoundly historical. This statement may sound strange to one who knows how fantastic some of these books are. These writers, it is true, did not have the sort of concern for historical truth that is characteristic of a modern scientific historian. What they had, and in this they agreed with the prophets and stand in marked contrast with the Greek philosophers, was a conviction that the actual historical process is a stage on which a single divine purpose is being worked out; the will of God is discernible—to the enlightened eye—in a particular stream of historical events. To state the difference at, perhaps, an even deeper level, they *believed in time*. Greek philosophy, on the other hand, at least the Platonism that held sway in the Greek world when Christianity was born, must seem to us who have been brought up in the Jewish-Christian tradition, ultimately frivolous in its attitude to time. For Plato, time was the moving shadow of eternity, a shadow without intrinsic meaning, a process, or rather a succession, of moments that returned upon itself; not a straight line moving from its beginning to its end, but a circle that will for ever be repeating itself. This idea has given rise to great poetry; but it remains frivolous because it deprives human action in history of any abiding fruit or consequence. Whatever we do, however we try to ameliorate man's lot, it will all, most literally, come to the same thing in the end; or rather, there is no end for it to come to. Plato sought refuge in a turning away from history to the contemplation of the eternal ideas. The soul, he held, was held a temporary prisoner in its body, and its task was to 'practise immortality'.[1]

The Jewish belief in the value of history is closely connected with the conviction that the Jewish religious community was a holy community, chosen by God, protected, preserved, and educated by him, and called to a destiny and a task in the divine purposes. This holy community was, it was held, identical with the actual historical Jewish collectivity. This actual people

---

[1] Aristotle, it must be allowed, was convinced that there was in every material thing an intrinsic 'purpose', a tendency towards its own perfection. And he had some idea of development in history, at least in such a limited department as the evolution of philosophy from Thales to himself. But he does not appear to have generalised his outlook, so as to find a purpose in human life collectively and universally.

had been rescued from Egypt by a tremendous manifestation of divine power. It had received its vocation in an actual historical event, the revelation at Sinai. Its priests (and its kings in the days of the Davidic monarchy) received a divine consecration for their actual historical functions. And although the great prophets were unsparing in their condemnations of the actual Israel, its rulers and its priesthood, and threatened that the divine favour would henceforward be concentrated upon a holy 'remnant' of the people, yet this remnant in its turn was always regarded as a historical collectivity, and as the true inheritor of the status and vocation of the *ecclesia* of the desert, with which it was continuous as being a remnant fashioned out of the élite of the condemned Israel.

This belief in the meaning and worth of history is further closely linked with the profoundly moral outlook of the creators and propagators of the Jewish tradition. Even pagan 'gods' are, of course, 'holy'; they transcend the status and nature of ordinary things and human persons. But they are not necessarily morally good. In contrast, the holiness of the Lord of Israel, while it lacked nothing of the quality of transcendence, was also a moral holiness. He was, in a transcendent sense, the perfection of what human moral ideals and standards pointed towards; indeed, by his Torah, he was himself the author and source of man's moral ideals. Having made Israel his holy community, he demanded of this community and its members a holiness that should resemble his own.

Moral holiness is a perfection of the will, and human history is the product of the human will reacting creatively to its total environment. God, then, was interested in the very fabric of the concrete history of Israel, and required that his will should be incorporated in that history and in the actual events that were its texture.

This deeply historical attitude to history bore fruit in two different directions. Looking outwards and backwards, it led to, or reinforced, the notion of God as the Creator both of man (history's agent) and of the natural environment in which man lives and labours. This belief reached its apogee in the realisation that God created the universe 'out of nothing'; God had only to speak, and the world came into existence. Thus not only is man's will subject to the law of God, but the very fabric of material things and the very 'flesh' of man's being was wholly and without remainder an expression of the divine will. It is to be noted that the Creator who was the Lord of Israel must be the master not only of Israelite history but of all history, at least so far as it is relevant to the story and destinies of Israel itself. So Isaias sees the Assyrians as the scourge raised by God to punish Israel, and deutero-Isaiah sees Cyrus as an anointed servant of the Lord. Thus the first step towards the world-wide horizons of apocalyptic were already taken by the prophets.

Looking forwards, this attitude to history created or supported the Messianic hope. Seen in the light of the Davidic monarchy, the supreme dominion of the Lord was depicted as a kingship. The Lord was the heavenly king of the whole world, but more especially of Israel. But it seemed obvious to the prophets that even in Israel his writ did not run. The people and its rulers were not carrying out God's revealed will; they were obstructing and flouting his purposes. Hence, on the one hand, the threats of punishment. But hence also the almost inevitable looking forward to a period beyond punishment, when a purified remnant would pay the divine King due allegiance; when the Lord would write his Torah in the hearts of his people, so that obedience would become their second nature, and they would carry out God's precepts with a loyal will and with joy. That would be the age in which the Reign of God would have 'come' in a new sense, when the Lord would be King not only *de jure* but *de facto*.

All this lies behind and is contained within Apocalyptic. But if, on the one hand, there is a certain lowering of tone in the apocalyptic literature, due to the fact that the apocalyptists no longer dare to claim immediate revelation from God, there is, on the other hand, an expansion of the horizon, brought about by the new interest in the life beyond the grave and the resurrection of the holy dead. The result was that the 'last things' (in Greek, *ta eshata*, hence 'eschatology') now tended to be located beyond history altogether. This, however, did not entail a complete dissociation from history. Apocalyptic did not so much look 'up' above the temporal to the eternal sphere, as 'forward' to a post-historical realisation of the will and purpose of God, a realisation that would grow out of, while at the same time transcending, history. If Greek philosophy was driven on by its own immanent dialect beyond physics to metaphysics, the meditation of the Jews was drawn on not to metaphysics but to what we may venture to nickname *metachronics*. Thus history was not volatilised and its values lost in a supernatural plane of Platonic Ideas. It was given a more momentous value than ever as leading on, by its subservience to the divine purpose, to a goal which would be beyond history and would nevertheless be a 'regeneration' of all with which history had been pregnant. It must, however, be added that there was a pessimistic strain in Apocalyptic, whereby it was led to emphasise the infidelity of actual history to the divine purpose; so that the dénouement of the great Coming of God's Reign would at the same time be a great catastrophic manifestation of that punitive justice of God about which the prophets had had so much to say.

The extreme apocalyptic interpretation of the gospel was popularised in England by Schweitzer's *Quest of the Historical Jesus*. It was found that Jesus and his teaching fitted easily and excitingly into the general framework of ideas outlined above. The inference was drawn that Jesus had become possessed of the apocalyptic outlook, and had taken to himself the task of, so to say, forcing the hand of God by rushing upon a martyr's death, which would lead the heavenly King to bring the great dénouement immediately to pass. This apocalyptic vision and function, it was thought, completely dominated Jesus' ministry and teaching. Even the moral teaching of the Sermon on the Mount was only an *Interimsethik*, a provisional blue-print for living during the brief interval before the End. As was remarked earlier, this new picture of the historical Jesus, while in profound and glaring contrast with the liberal Protestant picture, still gave no room for the possibility that Jesus could have intended to found an enduring 'Church militant on earth'.

The debt of exegesis to the apocalyptic school of interpretation is immeasurable. We need not again go over the reasons for holding that this interpretation is not the final answer to the problem of Jesus. The truth seems to be that it fails to distinguish between the system of ideas, taken over by the Christian gospel from Apocalyptic, and the new 'insight' or meaning for which this system of ideas (in its pre-Christian form) was as inadequate as any such framework must be for the communication

8*

of a higher viewpoint.[2] It is easy to say that the apocalyptic teaching of primitive Christianity was doomed when the new religion entered into its mission to the Greeks, and especially when the 'Second Coming' did not occur. It may be more deeply true to say that it suffered from its own incapacity to convey adequately the reality of which it tried to be the expression.

What, then, was the new 'insight' or meaning that was poured into Apocalyptic by the Christian gospel, and ultimately burst its container? It was, to use the apocalyptic language, that the Reign of God which was yet to come when history should have come to an end, had already, in mysterious anticipation, arrived *within* history, in and as the Christian 'good news from God'. The metachronic was already present in time. This, precisely, was the 'new' factor with which men henceforth were faced. It is this, which is the very *differentia* of Christianity, that was overlooked by the extreme apocalyptic school of interpretation. Jesus was not merely the harbinger of the Reign of God; the powers of the kingdom were already operative in his ministry and in the paradox of a suffering Messiah and Son of God.

It is hardly necessary to argue at length here for the truth of this statement of the central Christian conviction and teaching, since it is widely conceded by modern scholars. It is the theme of Ac. 2, 17 ff.: 'In the last times, God says, I will pour out my spirit upon all mankind . . . (Jesus), exalted at God's right hand, . . . has poured out that Spirit'. It is the implication of St Paul's affirmation that, in the Christians, 'history has reached its fulfilment' (I Cor. 10, 11). We can see it straining at the fetters of traditional language, in St Paul's teaching that the Christian has *already* risen from the dead. It can be summed up by saying that, according to the New Testament, the Eschatological Hope, while remaining a hope for a glorious post-historic future, has become also a sacramental Reality because the Word of God has 'become flesh', and God has 'visited and redeemed his people'. Despite the cavils of the Arians, it was inevitable that the Church should eventually interpret this central affirmation

---

[2] Lonergan (*Insight*, p. 592) has an interesting paragraph on the problems that arise 'when new ideas have to be exteriorised through a gradual transformation of prior modes of expression'; 'The tension between meaning and expression will be at its maximum at the beginning of the movement: images and words that previously bore an established significance appear in strange collocations; they struggle under a burden of meaning that they do not succeed in conveying; quite suddenly they pass out of currency to be replaced by fresh efforts. . . .'

of the New Testament by explaining that he who was incarnate as the Son of Mary was consubstantial with God the Father. As I have written elsewhere, the New Testament writings are in large measure the deposit from a vast explosion of spiritual force, a sort of volcanic eruption, part cause and part effect, of the supreme event in human history, involving a transformation in the religious element of that history.[3] Set in a framework of apocalyptic concepts, this means that Christian eschatology is an *incarnate* eschatology; and, of course, that Christian incarnation is eschatological. Christianity in history means that we possess in sacramental actuality what was given to the world historically in Christ, and what we yet look forward to as the result of his Second Coming.[4]

It is important to realise that, radical as the Christian transformation of Apocalyptic is, the change that it entailed was not the substitution of some details for others in a complex of ideas, but a total elevation of the whole complex to a new and higher level. Thus the Christian gospel has room for a Messiah, a Reign of God, a covenant, a Torah. It takes up and applies its renovating spirit to such ideas as sacrifice and priesthood and Shekinah. It is not a deviation but an elevation.

In particular, the Christian gospel took over from Jewish Apocalyptic (which itself, of course, was faithful to the traditional Torah in this matter) the notion of the holy community as the beneficiary of the blessings of the End: 'Then assize shall be held on (the fourth beast), and all his power be taken away, crushed down and forgotten for ever. Then what royalty, what empire, what earth-embracing dominion shall be theirs, the people set apart for the most High! Sovereignty everlasting; no monarch but must bow to its yoke' (Dan. 7, 26 f.). As represented in the Synoptic tradition, Jesus had a predilection for the Book of Daniel, from which (directly or indirectly) came the title of 'the Son of Man'. Like everything else in the Torah, the Danielic figure of the Son of Man is profoundly transformed by the gospel, but there is no reason to suppose that it was dissociated from the notion of 'the people set apart for the most

---

[3] 'The Value of History', *Downside Review, Summer, 1950.*
[4] Cf. the antiphon of the feast of Corpus Christi, attributed to Thomas Aquinas. 'O sacred feast, in which Christ is received, the *memory* of his passion is celebrated, *the mind is filled with grace,* and *a pledge is given to us* of eternal glory.'

High'. The two notions are correlative, just as the general notion of the Messiah and the holy community are correlative.

But just as we have seen that, in biblical thought, a man was not a spirit inhabiting an alien body but rather an animated body, so also, in the same context of thought, a community will be an actual body-and-soul affair. It involves actual relations between its members through their bodies and their senses. It is essentially a *concrete* society.

There will be a wide measure of agreement on the point just made. Those who hold the view, outlined at the beginning of this chapter, that the Church has not yet become one single society and therefore is not, in its historical stage, essentially such a single society, nevertheless believe in 'the resurrection of the dead', and doubtless hold that, in the post-historic realisation of all Christian and human values, the blessed will enjoy, through their risen and glorified bodies, a real fellowship of a human kind: a body-and-soul relatedness, though of course a transformed one. The Church *in heaven*, then, will be a concrete society, but a glorified society. We do not look forward to a mere 'kingdom of souls' but to a fully human communion in 'a new heaven and a new earth'.

But a Christian cannot be content to postpone this real and complete human fellowship to the world to come, to as-yet-unrealised eschatological expectations, or even to some future historical time. The Church, the *ecclesia* of God, is an essential part of the eschatological Goal. Indeed, as the Body of Christ, it is the very *raison-d'être* of the whole historical and redemptive order—of what the Germans call the *Heilsgeschichte*. To deny that the Church *on earth* is essentially a real society is, in effect, to deny that there has been an adequate 'incarnation' of the post-historic Goal in the (Christian) temporal order. It is to say that the transformation of the holy community of the Old Covenant into the Messianic community of prophetic-apocalyptic expectation is not yet accomplished. And this—if one may speak bluntly—amounts to a partial relapse from Christianity into Judaism; since Christianity is differentiated from Judaism precisely by the claim of the former that the metachronic order is already present in time. In fact, this view that there is not on earth a real Messianic *community,* but only the prospect of one in the historical or the post-historic future, would leave

Christians worse off than the Jews under the former dispensation; since Judaism had its holy community, and Christianity would be left hoping for a future holy community but not enjoying the blessings of such a possession in the present.[5]

But we seem driven to ask a still more radical question. Before we come to it, let us consider an objection to our position which amounts to an *argumentum ad hominem*. 'You have yourself', it might be said, 'admitted that apocalyptic language, and the system of ideas which it represents, are inadequate for the expression of the truth of the gospel. But, surely, it is only by accepting such language at its face value that you are enabled to infer that an actual Messianic community, taking shape as a single Christian communion, is something that belongs to the gospel's unchanging core? "Fancies that break through language and escape" must not be held to be still fettered by the conditions of such language.'

Thus we are brought face to face with one of the most difficult problems that the preaching of a universal gospel has to face: how to 'translate' into concepts and language intelligible to its various audiences the Christian revelation, without diminishing or distorting its contents in the process.[6] The danger is that in abandoning the original language, we may inadvertently reject also the abiding content of the gospel. The process of translation is authorised by the fact that the Word of God adapted itself, in its New Testament expression, to the conceptual and linguistic habits of a particular environment. But the danger remains that the link may be broken between

---

[5] These consequences of the 'potential society' view of the Church are often concealed from view by the fact that those who hold this view nevertheless use the language of 'community' or 'society' about the Church, which they yet consider to be divided. As has been argued at length in Chapter 3 above, a society (or a community) is essentially an association of intercommunicating members; where there are two such associations, not intercommunicating with each other, there is not one community but two.

[6] Canon Phillips has given an amusing illustration of the problem of 'translation'. In the Apocalypse, Jesus says: 'Behold, I stand at the door and knock'. In a certain African language there was no word for 'door', and that for the simple reason that doors themselves were quite outside the experience of the tribe, which lived in dwellings with entrances that could not be closed. It would be consoling, if the translator's difficulties went no deeper than that. The Christian mission to the Graeco-Roman world found itself in an environment where the whole Jewish mode of approach to reality was alien and incomprehensible. The result can be seen in patristic scriptural exegesis, which so often misses what is present in the biblical text, and reads into it what the original author never dreamt of.

'the past fact of revelation and its actualisation in present time' (P. Evdokimov).[7] Meanwhile, the first presentation of the gospel retains a privileged position in virtue of the fact that, for Christians, the Bible is inspired literature. The criterion of all 'translations' is their fidelity to this primeval formulation of the 'deposit of faith'.

The question, then, that remains to be asked is: By what valid distinction would it be possible to reject the idea that the heavenly society of the blessed has been already 'incarnated' in history as a single historical communion, and yet to retain the idea that the Messiah, whose function is to be the Lord of the Messianic community, *has* been so incarnated? The notions of Messiah and Messianic community are bound up together; one might say that the two terms are correlative. If the Messianic community is only present in history in potency, how can we affirm with security that the Messiah has been there present in act? Thus, once again, we find that the choice between the traditional view of the Church and the Reformation view brings us face to face with the choice between the gospel and liberalism. To argue the case against liberalism would be beyond the scope of these pages, though this does not mean that it is unarguable. But our discussion of the meaning of the word 'Church' is a discussion between Christians; and while, on the one hand, the Roman Catholic and the Eastern Orthodox communions clearly stand for 'dogma' against 'liberalism', the World Council of Churches, as already mentioned, has itself declared against liberalism in its affirmation of the Godhead of Jesus Christ.

Certainly, the New Testament books are not the manifesto of liberalism. But their witness to the reality of the incarnation of the Word of God is, by implication, a witness to the reality of the 'incarnation' of the Messianic community as a genuine and unique historical society.

[7] Roman Catholics and Eastern Orthodox believe that the Church herself is the authorised interpreter of revelation, and that her interpretations are guaranteed by the Holy Spirit.

Chapter 14

CONCLUSION

WE have been engaged in an enquiry of a very limited scope within the general field of Christian theology. We have isolated one article of the Creed, that whereby we profess to believe 'the Church'. It can be misleading thus to isolate one article from the living whole of Christian thought. But we have not only concentrated our attention on the Church; we have deliberately neglected aspects of ecclesiology other than such as throw light upon the particular question: of what sort is the Church in her earthly pilgrimage; what kind of reality is she, and how can this kind of reality be described and distinguished from other kinds? Despite the disadvantages and even dangers of this twofold limitation, our procedure may be excused on two grounds. First, the question which we have been asking is one of fundamental relevance not only to the Ecumenical Movement but to the individual Christian who wishes to conform his living to the mind of Christ. And secondly, if an enquiry can be justified by the exhibition of some positive result, we seem to be able to plead such justification; we are in a position to give a definite answer to our question.

At an early stage of our enquiry we succeeded in distinguishing three different answers to our own question. The Church (militant here on earth) is either (1) a purely interior, invisible, 'mystical', entity, or (2) a visible entity which is not essentially a society or single communion, but is potentially such, or (3) essentially a single historical society or communion, visible with the visibility that appertains to such a historical society. We saw that *a posteriori* all existing theories of the Church which do not come either under heading (1) or under heading (3) fall fairly under our second heading. For our purposes, it is indifferent whether a given theory insists on episcopal ministry, apostolic succession, and a full endowment of the traditional seven sacraments, or (alternatively) is content to require of a body that claims to belong to the Church that it shall be a religious body of baptised persons who acknowledge the authority of the Bible. In either case, the theory holds that the Church is neither purely invisible nor necessarily a single communion. And in either case, this visible entity which is not essentially a single communion is capable of becoming such, if not in this world at least in the glory of heaven, where all divisions between the blessed ones will cease. And if our enumeration of possible answers to our questions thus covers all existing theories of the Church, it is further clear *a priori* that it covers all conceivable theories. Any theory which denies that the Church is essentially a single communion must either affirm that she is purely invisible, or affirm that she is potentially but not necessarily actually a single communion. This certainty that our enumeration of answers is *a priori* complete is important, because it means that it would be trifling with the truth to pretend to delay our decision between the three possibilities in the hope that some new sort of theory will emerge. There can be no theory of the Church other than these three.

We have turned to the Bible, as doctrinally authoritative, and also as a collection of historical documents, to see whether the New Testament writers, or the story of the Church in apostolic times, or what we can infer of the life and teaching of the historical Jesus, will provide any definite, even if only partial, answer to our question. Our hope has been in some measure justified. Neither the history of primitive Christianity, as it can be reconstructed from the New Testament documents, nor the theology of the New Testament writers seems to be reconcilable with the theory that the Church is a purely invisible entity. The history presents us with an actual body of believers, good and bad, who regarded themselves as, collectively, the Church. And the theology confirms this identification and definitely includes within the Church individuals who were far from holy in the moral sense of that word. Nor is there anything in the original teaching of the historical Jesus, so far as we can hope that we have distinguished it from the primitive Church's various re-presentations of the gospel, which can be taken as pointing to the view of the Church as essentially invisible. If the definitive appeal is to the Bible, it must be concluded that the upholders of the purely invisible Church have lost their case.

Thus we are reduced to choosing between the view that the Church is essentially a single communion, and the view that she is potentially such. It would appear probable that these are the two alternatives between which the strategists of the Ecumenical Movement will have to decide. Broadly speaking, the leaders of the Movement have assumed that the 'potential society' view is true, though they have tried hard not to prejudice the case in any official pronouncements.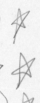

The witness of the New Testament to the Church in its own time is that the Church was a single communion. And the evidence of the history of that primitive age is that St Paul in particular worked hard and successfully to avert a breach between the Gentile and the Palestinian wings of the Church. These efforts, and the exhortations to preserve unity which are found in the Pauline literature might, at first sight, suggest that the unity of the visible Church was thought of as a precarious and contingent good, liable to be lost through human failures. But in fact such a conclusion is not necessary; the New Testament nowhere positively implied that schism would entail the Church in a loss of unity, though obviously it must at least mean that some are lost from the unity of the Church.

In fact it seems clear that the deepest implications of the New Testament point towards the conclusion that the Church is the 'Messianic community' mysteriously, but really, anticipated on earth and within history, just as Jesus was, in his historical life and ministry, the Messiah, but a hidden and humiliated Messiah. But if the Messianic community is, as its name implies, and as its religious values entail, essentially a body-and-soul unity of the blessed in heaven, then its real earthly anticipation must itself be an actual community—or, in Christian terminology, communion—of the baptised. We saw that there is nothing in the teaching of Jesus, so far as we can distinguish if from later developments, that would suggest any other conclusion. And when, towards the end of the New Testament period, the phenomenon of schism makes its appearance, we found the author of the First Epistle of St John reacting to it in the same way as the Great Church would react to similar movements later, and on the basis of the same conviction that schism as such stands self-condemned; the fact that the schism in question was also the result of Christological heterodoxy does not affect the argument here.

To expect that this evaluation of the New Testament evidence and teaching will meet with general acceptance would, undoubtedly, be extravagant optimism; though it is not optimistic to hope that there would be wide agreement that this teaching, or at least this evidence, seems to exclude the notion of a purely invisible Church and does not exclude the notion that the Church is essentially a single communion. There will, however, no doubt be many who are prepared to defend the notion of the Church as only potentially a single communion, as being one at least not contradicted by the New Testament evidence taken in its broad drift.

If, then, it is at present, and as things stand, impossible to get agreement on a notion of the Church as being the Scriptural notion, we are in a position, with regard to this disputed question of the Church's nature, similar to that in which Christians of the fourth century found themselves with regard to the question of the deity of Christ. As, in those days, Arians and 'orthodox' disagreed about the divine nature of Christ, and neither party would admit that its view was contrary to Scripture, so today there is disagreement about the nature of the Church militant, and neither party will admit that its view is excluded by Scripture or the implications of Scripture.

The orthodox party settled the Christological issue—for itself—by moving the debate from the Scriptural field and taking refuge in a conciliar definition; which, of course, it claimed (and, as we hold, rightly claimed) to be true to the meaning of Scripture.

This procedure is, for us, impracticable. There is no definition, on the point at issue between us, of an Ecumenical Council recognised by all parties to the dispute as authoritative. And since the large majority of those who reject the view that the Church is essentially a single communion also (and logically, from their point of view) reject the notion that conciliar definitions have an ultimate authority in the things of faith, the very notion of seeking a settlement of our disagreement in some future council that should command general acceptance is excluded.

Here it may be remarked that the question of the nature of

the Church is not one of those purely speculative questions which we can happily leave for solution in the world to come. On the contrary, it is bound to be of the most practical importance if the Ecumenical Movement is to find its fruition in a large-scale 'reunion' of Christians. And, it may be added, if to belong to the Church is, in the divine intention, a *sine qua non* of salvation (allowance being made here for the principle of 'good faith' outlined in a previous chapter of this book), then the question is of urgent practical importance for everyone who is not already certain that he does so belong.

To what tribunal, then, can we take our problem, since we disagree on the meaning of Scripture and any appeal to ecclesiastical definition is ruled out *a priori*? The suggestion of these pages is, that the one remaining Christian tribunal is the tribunal of Christian history. And the verdict of Christian history is not really doubtful. With no evidence of revolutionary innovation, the Church passed from biblical into post-biblical times, and to the explicit affirmation, in word and consequential practice, of the doctrine that the Church is essentially a single visible communion of baptised persons. We have been fortunate in being able to refer to first-rate scholars, who did not, or do not, themselves hold this doctrine as true, but who emphatically affirm that such was the conviction of post-biblical Christian antiquity, a conviction shared with the Great Church by the ordinary run of the 'schismatical bodies' of that age. And we have attempted, for ourselves, to illustrate the way in which this conviction underlay and underpinned the conciliar definitions to which the faith of modern Christians of all the great 'branches' of Christendom is tributary. The conviction in question did not pass away with the passage from antiquity to more modern times. It held the field, and was not seriously challenged, till the great Western upheaval known as the Reformation. It is among the architects and the heirs of the Reformation that the alternative ideas, that the Church is essentially invisible on earth, or that she is visible but only potentially a single communion, have found their champions. And while it is no doubt true that the problem of the nature of the Church seemed a very secondary one to the original Reformers, compared with the overwhelming character of the truths to which they felt impelled to bear witness (justification by faith, and the supreme majesty, rights, and transcendence, of God), it can also be maintained that the theories on the Church which they put forward are partly a rationalisation of the fact of the 'schismatical' situation in which they found themselves, and in any case lacked that definiteness and assurance which might be expected if they had been given a new and positive insight on this particular issue. Whatever may be thought of these suggestions, it can hardly be denied that, if history is appealed to as a *Christian* tribunal, and without *parti pris*, the verdict of its main body is, and has always been, in favour of the view that the Church is essentially a single communion. Protestantism has indeed put in a 'minority report', but the minority is a very small one compared with the authority behind the majority report; and it must be concluded that the majority report could only be rejected on grounds other than the appeal to history itself.

Such grounds have been adduced, as by Dr Greenslade in the book to which, earlier in these pages, we devoted a good deal of attention. It has been argued that there is some incoherence in the main tradition itself, at least in the form given to it by Augustine. It is also suggested that the notion of valid sacraments 'outside the Church', to which Western Catholicism has committed itself, leads to inacceptable consequences. And it has been urged that, since the fruits of the Spirit are found outside any one communion, and apparently associated with 'sacramental' ministrations which the adherents of the 'single communion' view of the Church regard as either invalid or at least illicit, the theory of the single communion breaks the indissoluble link between the Church and the fruits of grace.

Our reply to these arguments has been threefold. We have questioned the exegesis of Augustine which has given rise to the suggestion that he himself yielded, on occasion, to a leaning towards the theory of the 'invisible' Church. We have sought to find room for the existence of the fruits of grace, and indeed of high sanctity, 'outside' the visible Church, and this by a process of theological development which, we have argued, remains true to principles or beliefs already present and operative in Christian antiquity, and which is not inconsistent with the theory of the 'single communion'. And, thirdly, we have argued that to surrender this traditional belief is to commit oneself not to a new development of the faith and theology of the past, but to a revolution in thought, and one which cannot logically be contained within the limits of the problem which it seeks to answer. The traditional conviction that the Church is a single communion is intimately bound up, not in speculation only but in practice, with so much else in traditional Christianity, and in particular with our inherited dogmas, as the dogmas relating to the person and natures of the Redeemer, that to abandon it is to bring into the field of question and uncertainty much that is held, by Reformed and 'unreformed' Christians in common, as of the essence of Christianity. The *tertium gaudens,* once the belief that the Church is a single communion is rejected, is, logically speaking, not so much traditional evangelical Protestantism or any other version of doctrinal Christianity, but doctrinal liberalism of an extreme kind. It is a matter of thankful rejoicing to the present writer that the Ecumenical Movement has taken its stand against extreme liberalism. It has not therefore been necessary in these pages to embark on an attempted refutation of the latter, which is recognised so widely today as being not an alternative version of Christianity but the liquidation of the very core of our common faith that God has visited and redeemed his people. But it may have been not entirely irrelevant or useless to raise the question, how liberalism is to be answered in principle if the presuppositions of defined doctrine are removed.

There is, of course, a residual objection to the position which we have tried to recommend. It is the very simple and searching one: Where on earth at the present day can there be found a communion with the moral stature and record to sustain the role of the one Church of God?

Perhaps the first reaction to this question from one who believes that the communion to which he belongs is indeed that Bride which Christ would 'purify, . . . would summon into his own presence, the Church in all its beauty, no stain, no wrinkle, no such disfigurement . . . holy . . . spotless' (Eph. 5, 26 f.), should be to admit with shame his personal contribution to the facts from which the question derives its relevance and its poignancy. And secondly, since voluntary adherence to a community means involvement in the moral record of that community, there is room too for a sense of shame which goes

beyond the direct personal contribution of any one of us. 'Woe
is me, because I have held my peace; because I am a man of
unclean lips, and I dwell in the midst of a people that hath
unclean lips, and I have seen with my eyes the King the Lord
of hosts.'[1] Whatever may be the sentiments of an uncommitted
individual, as he surveys the story of institutional religion and
echoes Lucretius' sombre comment: *tanta stat prae dita culpa*,
those of a believer and a member must be far more profoundly
engaged. And in particular, a Roman Catholic, looking back to
the origins and causes of the schism between East and West,
and again to the origins of the Reformation, cannot but admit
and grieve over the very large share of blame for the present
divisions of Christendom that must be assigned to men who
were, and in many cases remained, members of his own communion, and were often holders of high office in it. It was
Cardinal Pole, as papal legate, who addressed the Council of
Trent in these words:

> Before the tribunal of God's mercy we, the shepherds, should
> make ourselves responsible for all the evils now burdening the
> flock of Christ. The sins of all we should take upon ourselves, not
> in generosity but in justice; because the truth is that of these
> evils we are in great part the cause, and therefore we should
> implore the divine mercy through Jesus Christ.[2]

There is, however, more to be said. There must be more,
because, as the unbeliever would be quick to perceive, the argument, so far as it carries legitimate weight, is an argument not
simply against any one of, or all, the Christian communions; it
is an argument against Christianity itself: *Tantum relligio
potuit suadere malorum*. The 'pale Galilaean' has conquered,
and the world has been corrupted by 'his smile'.

Christian history records more than one attempt to 'leave the
accursed city' and to build some refuge for the true members
of Christ, to 'enclose' a 'garden' where nothing should be seen
except the fair fruits of the Spirit. They have failed, one and all.
They were doomed to failure because—as far as adults are concerned—it is the fact that, though God in his mercy redeemed

---

[1] Is. 6, 5 (Douay); Knox renders: 'Alas, said I, that I must keep silence; my
lips, and all my neighbours' lips, are polluted with sin; and yet these eyes are
looking upon their King, the Lord of hosts.'
[2] Quoted by Henry St John, *Essays in Christian Unity*, p. 12.

us 'without ourselves', it has not been his good pleasure to sanctify us except with our co-operation. Sanctification is the fruit of divine-human friendship, and to compel friendship is a metaphysical impossibility. And since baptism, while it removes the guilt of past sin, does not at once entirely heal the wounds that sin has left, it was always statistically to be expected that there would be Christians who were sinners. That the expectation has been deplorably justified by the facts we must all admit and lament. We have, moreover, to acknowledge that human sinfulness has not stopped short of using the very means of sanctification in ways which contravened the will of God. Each of us, however, must remind himself that the qualification for 'casting the first stone' is that one should oneself be 'free from sin'.

There is no contracting out of our human predicament. If we are believers, there is no contracting out of our Christian predicament. And it must be a soured heart which would wish to do so. For who, that has lived and laboured and loved in any of the Christian communions, but must acknowledge with humble gratitude that, whatever the 'scandals' and 'tares' which afford so easy an argument to those who object against the gospel its 'martyrdom of man', there is wealth of human goodness and of holiness which the outsider may often fail to notice, but which is derived from, and dependent upon, God's gift of his Word to man and the 'incarnation' of that Word in historical institutions?

Often enough, a long and painful investigation of some 'disputed question' ends only in undeniable failure to attain a satisfying answer. That, in my opinion, is not what has to be recorded of the attempt to answer the question: What sort of a thing is the Church which Christ established? There is a definite answer to that question, and there is no other answer that can maintain its 'right', on Christian terms and with Christian premises, against the right of the answer that has been given. But it is a common human experience that, when an answer to a question has been found, the weary and worried head and heart recoil from the categoric mode in which the answer is expressed. There are, so often, loose ends; there is the possibility, at least, that something has been overlooked; this fact, or that, which has been used to build up the presuppositions of the answer—could it not be interpreted in a different, and perhaps a contrary sense? And when the question asked, and the answer given, carry with them such enormous practical consequences, do we dare, or are we bound, to pass on from understanding to affirming the answer? After all, *must* one write 'Q.E.D.' at the bottom of an argument that has involved so many issues, and of which so many good people still fail to see the force?

To say 'I believe . . . one holy catholic Church' is an act of *faith*. The Church is one mystery within the total mystery of God's redeeming Act. We cannot expect, and are indeed obliged not to demand, the type of 'proof' which is necessary in geometry. 'Except ye see signs and wonders, you will not believe.' There was no mathematical demonstration on which the first disciples of Jesus could base their recognition of him as the 'one that should come'. They were required, and enabled, to go beyond, though not against, reason. This does not mean that, after all, Christianity is a 'great perhaps'. Those eyewitnesses, seeing what others saw and hearing what others heard, found themselves presented with an inescapable moral necessity of choice and decision: 'Would you, too, go away?' (Jn. 6, 69). Not to accept Jesus at his own self-assessment would be to reject him and the divine origin of his message. They had no 'demonstrative proof' of his claims such as would pass muster in mathematics. God had put them in an actual situation in which they had to decide—for or against—on what the world calls 'probabilities'. The important thing to note is that rejection, equally with acceptance, would be a decision based on 'probabilities'; and one thing they did know, that (whereas the world would always say that the Act of God in history is immeasurably improbable) in fact the 'probabilities' in favour of acceptance outweighed the 'probabilities' in favour of rejection. That being so, and a choice being inevitable, they did the reasonable thing: they accepted. And this acceptance, based, as the world would say, on 'insufficient' evidence, was in fact based on the truthworthiness of God himself, who will never allow our conscience to be so placed that there is no right decision that we can take. And if it is thought presumptuous in the Church to equate man's situation in face of her claim with the situation of the first disciples face to face with Jesus, she, for her part, remembers the words in her inspired archives: 'He that receiveth you, receiveth me: and he that receiveth me, receiveth him that sent me'; 'Behold I am with you all through the days that are coming, until the consummation of the world'.[3]

[3] Mt. 10, 40 (Rheims); 28, 20.

INDEX OF NAMES